P9-BIY-019

AN ANCIENT QUARREL CONTINUED

The Troubled Marriage of Philosophy and Literature

Louis Mackey

WITHDRAWN
UTSA LIBRARIES

University Press of America,® Inc.
Lanham · New York · Oxford

Copyright © 2002 by
University Press of America,® Inc.
4720 Boston Way
Lanham, Maryland 20706
UPA Acquisitions Department (301) 459-3366

12 Hid's Copse Rd.
Cumnor Hill, Oxford OX2 9JJ

All rights reserved
Printed in the United States of America
British Library Cataloging in Publication Information Available

Library of Congress Cataloging-in-Publication Data

Mackey, Louis.
An ancient quarrel continued : the troubled marriage
of philosophy and literature / Louis Mackey.
p.   cm
Includes bibliographical references and index.
1. Literature—Philosophy. I. Title.

PN49 .M373 2002
801—dc21   2002019972 CIP

ISBN 0-7618-2267-4 (paperback : alk. ppr.)

⊖™ The paper used in this publication meets the minimum
requirements of American National Standard for Information
Sciences—Permanence of Paper for Printed Library Materials,
ANSI Z39.48—1984

Library
University of Texas
at San Antonio

Contents

Preface

My objective in this book is to state and defend a view of the relationship between philosophy and the literary arts. Both the view itself and the considerations offered in its support are somewhat out of the ordinary. The novelty of the view is the source of whatever originality this work may have, and the soundness of its defense the measure of the work's achievement.

Philosophers have usually assumed that literary language, like the language of philosophy, is a means by which writers express an intelligible content and communicate it to their readers. Both literature and philosophy claim to give us truth: important truth about ourselves and the world we live in. The difference is in the way they do it. Philosophy gives us truth in the conceptual, logical, and argumentative mode, whereas literature offers us truth in a figural, narrative, dramatic, or lyrical form. It is implied if not expressly stated that the philosophical is the normative and the literary a deviant and inferior way to tell the truth. With some notable exceptions and with more than a few misgivings, the champions of imaginative writing have concurred with the philosophers. But they have almost always added one important qualification: the priorities are reversed, so that poetic truth is superior and discursive prose the deviation from poetry's norm. This difference aside, the common objective of philosophy and literature is to provide us with humanly enriching insights into ourselves and the world coupled with sage advice on how to live and what to do.

Dissenting from this view, which underwrites most college courses on "Philosophy in Literature" and is the unstated premise of many highly regarded books on the subject, I argue that philosophy and literature are neither simply the same nor simply different, nor are they two species of a single genus or the same content in different forms. Neither is the norm from which the other, to its detriment, defects. And whatever the case with philosophy, it is not the aim of literary art to tell the truth. As against the common opinion, I suggest that philosophy and literature are diverging modes of textuality, the relation between them compounded of dialectical interdependence and duplicitous distinction. In a word, their relationship is the deconstruction of their difference. This proposition, here painfully compressed, will be expounded at length and in many ways in the chapters to come. But it may be provisionally clarified as follows.

In archaic Greece the pre-philosophical vessels for the transmission of culture were the Hesiodic myths and the Homeric epics. Philosophy, Greek in origin, created itself by substituting naturalistic and conceptual explanations of reality for the traditional narrative accounts. In creating itself, philosophy created poetry, not inspired vatic utterance, but rather, by contrast with the truthful discourse of philosophy, lying fables. Of course the truth disclosed by the language of philosophy and dissembled by poetry was a truth defined, in the dialectical mode peculiar to philosophy, by philosophy itself in opposition to the epistemological unreliability of myth from the standpoint of philosophical logic. Philosophy and "literature" thus have a common origin in bad faith. Each is dependent upon the negated other for its own identity. From that common origin came the ancient quarrel between philosophy and poetry, a quarrel that persists to this day and that it is the purpose of this study to clarify. Not to resolve. That is not possible and perhaps not even desirable. But to explain their historical divergence and their necessary interdependence should serve at least *ad bellum purificandum*.

The defense of this position, so far as it is not adumbrated in its statement, is also unusual. It is not an argument in the philosophical sense; that is, a linear series of premises leading to and validating a final conclusion. Nor is it an argument in the literary sense, as for example the argument of Milton's *Paradise Lost*, which is little more than a synopsis of the plot. My strategy is to approach the question of philosophy and literature from several different angles. The first three chapters deal in a general way with the nature of philosophy and its relation to literary art. Chapters 4 through 7 discuss problems in literary theory, including (in Chapter 6) the problem of the relation between theory and practice. Chapter 7 is an essay on the philosophy of music, suggesting that philosophers often misinterpret music in the way they misread literature, as a (tonal) language expressing and communicating emotions. Part III contains readings of particular literary texts, sponsored by and tending to confirm the theoretical positions, both philosophical and literary, staked out in parts I and II. The remaining two chapters return to the larger question of philosophy and textuality. Together with the chapters that precede them, they converge upon a proof of the thesis stated above. I say "converge upon a proof," I do not say "prove." Chapters 13 and 14 are terminal but not conclusive. On the contrary, they resist finality and summation. It is an essential constituent of my view that the very notion of a total and culminating truth about the matters discussed in this book is not just unlikely but incoherent, the hope that someone may someday find it (though it spring eternal) vain, and the claim to possess it pure presumption.

The philosophic and the literary modes of textuality need each other as much as they strive to resist each other. The practice of poetry and criticism demands a theoretical exposition that only philosophy and critical theory are positioned to provide. Conversely, the philosophical understanding comes to the poetic imagination desiring the exhilaration of changes, and is rewarded with that proliferation of metaphor that is, for mere humans, their best approach to truth and reality. "Beauty is truth, truth beauty...." Well, maybe. But that is, in any case, all we know on earth, and if there is more we need to know it will have to wait.

Parts of this book have already appeared in public, and are reprinted here with permission of the following:

Chapter 1 is reprinted from "The Philosophy of Genre and the Genre of Philosophy" by Louis H. Mackey in *Dialectic and Narrative* by Thomas R. Flynn and Dalia Judovitz (Eds.), by permission of the State University of New York Press. © 1993 State University of New York. All rights reserved.

Chapter 3 is reprinted from Leonard Schulze and Walter Wetzels, eds., *Literature and History*, Lanham, MD: University Press of America, 1983, by permission of the publishers.

Chapter 4 is reprinted from "Anatomical Curiosities: Northrop Frye's Theory of Criticism," *Texas Studies in Literature and Language* 23:3, pp. 442-69. Copyright © 1981 by the University of Texas Press. All rights reserved. By permission of the publishers.

Chapter 6 is reprinted from *Rhetoric Society Quarterly*, v. 27, n.2, Spring 1997, pp. 51-68, by permission of the editors.

Chapter 8 is reprinted from K. M. Higgins and R. C. Solomon, eds., *The Philosophy of (Erotic) Love*, University Press of Kansas, 1991, by permission of the publishers.

Chapter 9 is reprinted from "Robert Coover's Dirty Stories: Allegories of Reading in 'Seven Exemplary Fictions'," *The Iowa Review*, v. 17, n. 2, 1987, by permission of the editors.

Chapter 10a is reprinted from "Meritorious Price: *Gravity's Rainbow* and the Economy of Preterition," in M. Vella *et al.*, eds., *William Pynchon's*

The Meritorious Price of Our Redemption, Peter Lang Publishing, Inc., 1992, by permission of the publishers.

Chapter 10b is reprinted from "Paranoia, Pynchon, and Preterition," *SubStance*, 30, © 1981, by permission of the University of Wisconsin Press.

Chapter 10c is reprinted from *Pynchon Notes*, 14, 1984, by permission of the editor.

Chapter 11 is reprinted from "The Name of the Book," *SubStance*, 47, Vol. 14, No.2, © 1985, by permission of the University of Wisconsin Press.

Everything in this book, previously published or not, began as an oral performance of one sort or another: invited papers and lectures, class presentations, seminars, and the like. Chapter 2 was read at the annual meeting of the Modern Language Association in 1995. Chapter 5 was read at a meeting of the Søren Kierkegaard Society held in conjunction with the annual meeting of the Eastern Division of the American Philosophical Association in 1994. Chapter 7 was read at a symposium on "Aesthetics and Psychology" held at The University of Tulsa, Tulsa, Oklahoma in 1983. Chapter 12 was read at the annual meeting of the American Comparative Literature Association in 1987. Many versions of chapter 13 were given as invited lectures in many places. The version here offered expands upon a keynote lecture given at a graduate student philosophy conference at Emory University in 1995. Chapter 14 was the keynote lecture for a graduate student philosophy conference at the University of Texas at Austin in 1998.

I am grateful to the many students and colleagues, here and elsewhere, who provided the occasions that elicited these ruminations. Special thanks to Leslie Crooks and Molly Collins of the Department of Philosophy at the University of Texas at Austin, who helped prepare this manuscript for publication, to Janet Cooper, who produced the camera-ready copy, and to Karen Mottola, who made the index.

In view of the fact that all of these essays originate in the spoken word, it may seem that the argument winding its way through all of them ungraciously aggrandizes textuality at the expense of orality. But while it does attempt to expose the illusion of the "living voice," it confesses at the same time its invincible dependence on the illusion it discredits. What is offered here is not a solution but an intensified experience of the problem. And that I take to be an authentic (*sit venia verbo*) effect of deconstruction. All of life's solutions are temporary. In endless closure, the problem remains and the ancient quarrel continues.

I

1

The Philosophy of Genre
and The Genre of Philosophy

One of C.S. Lewis's characters describes Aristotle's *Metaphysics* as a long and difficult book without meter.[1] That the book is long and difficult no one doubts, and anyone who has tried to read it has wished that it were both shorter and simpler. That it is without meter is also obvious. But has anyone ever suggested that it should have been written in, say, dactylic hexameters? If there have been complaints of this sort, I have not heard them.

In Book XII of that long, difficult, and prosaic work Aristotle is discussing the nature of the celestial substances. In the course of this discussion he makes the following observation *aparté*:

> Our forefathers in the most remote ages have handed down to us their posterity a tradition, in the form of a myth, that these substances are gods and that the divine encloses the whole of nature. The rest of the tradition has been added later in mythical form with a view to the persuasion of the multitude and to its legal and utilitarian expediency; they say these gods are in the form of men or like some of the other animals, and they say other things consequent on and similar to these which we have mentioned. But if we were to separate the first point from these additions and take it alone—that they thought the first substances to be gods—we must regard this as an inspired utterance, and reflect that, while probably each art and science has often been developed as far as possible and has again perished, these opinions have been preserved like relics until the present. Only thus far, then, is the opinion of our ancestors and our earliest predecessors clear to us.[2]

Aristotle refers in this passage to the mythical cosmogonies produced by the canonical poets of ancient Greece. These poetic accounts of the cosmos (more ancient no doubt than those who wrote them down) transmit an important truth: that the celestial substances are divine. The narrative form of these accounts—their *mythos*—Aristotle regards as sugar-coating added for purposes of social control, and therefore dispensable without detriment to the truth it makes palatable to the masses.

I am fairly sure the ancients were not such cynical social engineers as Aristotle supposes. But that is not what concerns me. What concerns me is, first, the clear implication that the truth communicated by the cosmogonic myths may be distinguished *simpliciter* from their poetic and narrative form. And, second, the implication, less clear but there nevertheless, that now, in Aristotle's notoriously unmythical and unmetrical essays in first philosophy, that truth is finally communicated in an adequate and appropriate form.

There is a truth about the world. In poetry and narrative this truth is expressed in an improper form, a form alien to itself. But in philosophy this same truth is expressed in proper form: truth's own form, the mode of expression demanded by its nature as truth. Content (the content of truth) and form (the mode of expression) are distinguishable, separable, and subject to a certain amount of mixing and matching. One and the same content of truth can be mixed with an improper form, as in narrative, or matched with its proper form, as in philosophical argumentation.

(There is a duplicity here—a double gesture—the first of several I shall note in this essay. On the one hand form and content are distinguishable and separable, so that a given content of truth may be expressed in a form inappropriate to itself. On the other hand certain contents demand certain forms. There is a proper form of expression dictated by the essential nature of truth—the form of philosophical discourse—so that philosophy can claim to be the voice of truth itself. Duplicities of this sort will be my recurring preoccupation in the remainder of this discussion.)

But back, for a moment, to Aristotle. In the *Poetics*, also composed without meter, Aristotle explains that poetry is "more philosophical" than history, since poetry tells us not just what did happen but what might have happened or what ideally should have happened.[3] If history is merely true stories and philosophy pure argumentation, then poetry is more philosophical than history because poetry gives us narrative structured by the dialectic of possibility, necessity, and ideality. Poetry approaches truth as it edges away from history (narrative) and snuggles up to philosophy (dialectic).

What we have in these Aristotelean observations is the seed that finally flowers (if that's the word) and perhaps even bears fruit (and here I stop the figure before it runs out of control) in Hegel's *Phenomenology of Spirit.* (Another duplicity, by the way, since for Hegel truth *achieves* its proper dialectical form—*das absolute Wissen* delivered by philosophy—only at the end of a long and tortuous historical narrative.) But of course what Pater said of Plato applies even more aptly to Aristotle. Though he looks primitive to us, he was already quite belated. Ancient in his own time. Not ancient in the sense of primordial or prehistoric, but ancient in the sense of *already very old.*[4] Long before Aristotle the pre-Socratics who, so far as the historical record may be trusted, originated philosophy, accomplished their intellectual breakthrough by distinguishing their own approach to the world from that of the poets. Some of them, like Xenophanes, were content to call attention to the epistemological errors and moral excesses of the poets. And that, as we know, became the standard philosophical critique of poetry, recited with something like ritual monotony down through the ages: poets tell lies and encourage indecent behavior. More of this later. But the major development in pre-Socratic thought is represented by people like the Milesian physicists. Whether they think all things are water (Thales), air (Anaximenes), or the "unlimited" (Anaximander), they are offering in place of a narrative account of the origin of the world what they take to be a rational explanation of the constitution of nature. Instead of genealogies of the gods they propose a theory of dialectical transformations by which the multitude of things is alternately separated out from and reabsorbed into a single underlying substance. Heracleitus, for all his obvious and not insignificant differences from the Milesians, does much the same thing, except that on his view the underlying unity imagined by the Milesians as a substance of sorts is identified with the dialectical exchange of opposites. What is symbolized for Heracleitus by fire is apparently the truth that the only stability is the all-pervasiveness of change. Parmenides goes to extremes in the opposite direction. The way of truth proclaimed by the goddess—"Is is and Is-not is not"—proscribes change and narrative development in a way that threatens to deconstruct the poetic vehicle by which it is communicated. The atomistic revision of Eleatic monism explains the cosmos in terms strictly naturalistic and neatly rational—matter and motion—an explanation that still appeals to many students of ancient cosmology.

Northrop Frye's *Anatomy of Criticism,* which for many years shaped the minds, methods, and curricula of students of literature, supposes that myth is the primordial form of human discourse. That supposition is by no means unexceptionable, as we now know. The originality of myth may be only the myth of originality thrown up by our intolerable belatedness.

Nevertheless it is historically (or prehistorically) the case that myth does precede philosophy and that philosophy (historically) begins with a response to myth. Myth is of course narrative rather than discursive, and what we have come to think of as philosophy is originally a dialectical critique of myth. Introductory texts in the history of philosophy often tell us that the Greeks discovered reason. Whether they discovered it (as Sutter discovered gold) or invented it (as Alexander Graham Bell invented the telephone) shall remain a disputed question. What is certain is that they invented philosophy. And what they produced (for what other reason do we call them philosophers and begin our histories with an account of their views?) was rational explanations designed to replace mythic narratives. For a long while the narrative form of myth subsists alongside its dialectical counterpart. Plato's dialogues, for example, interweave myth and argument. The logical form of medieval philosophy is qualified by its submission to the canonical narrative of the Scriptures. Theology defines the context within which philosophy unfolds in the middle ages, but theology in turn is just the restatement of Biblical narrative in conceptual—that is, philosophical— form. And so on. But the tendency has been to replace myth altogether with logic, and narrative with discursive modes of exposition. That is the founding gesture of philosophy, and the history of philosophy in the West has been, constitutively, the progressive demythologizing of the human consciousness. Contemporary philosophy is pure dialectic and its literary form strictly discursive. At least that is the consummation it devoutly wishes and the norm from which it rarely and reluctantly departs.

Philosophy is, foundationally and constitutively, the substitution of dialectical for mythic modes of thought and (equivalently) the substitution of discursive for narrative means of expression.

Now of course the philosophical critique of myth is undertaken—any philosopher will tell you this—in the interest of truth. But what (to coin a phrase) is truth? The philosopher replaces myth with dialectic and narrative with discourse in order to get at the truth about the world and (same thing) in order to express that truth in the form demanded by truth itself. Which implies that truth is a system of concepts and judgments that cohere with each other in obedience to the canons of logic and correspond to the structure of reality according to the norms of representational adequation. If philosophy is the dialectical critique of myth for the sake of truth, truth itself is defined in and by the terms of that critique. The philosopher serves a truth that he himself has produced.

The mythographer tells a story. The philosopher (spontaneously generating himself thereby) asks: but is it true? In mythic narrative the question of truth does not arise, because the distinction of true and false is first opened up by the dialectical critique of myth and expressible only in discursive form. By the time of Aristotle it was already proverbial that "bards tell many a lie."[5] But that proverb is itself sponsored by the philosophically originated conception of truth as the discursive presentation of conceptual formulations achieved through dialectical reflection. In a word: from the beginning truth has meant, in and for philosophy, the prosecution of a dialectical/discursive mode of thought and inscription. What the philosopher declares to the world is: to know the truth you must think as I do, and to tell the truth you must speak as I do. Having thus given birth to truth out of his own innards (like Zeus extruding Athena from his Olympian wetware), it is no wonder the philosopher also proclaims himself her guardian.

(Parenthetically, the Scriptures describe the devil as the father of lies. The serpent insinuates into the innocent mind of Eve the suspicion that the word of God is not to be taken at face value and without question. So doing he opens the breach between true and false and in that way begets mendacity. What this does to the self-concept of the philosopher I shall not try to imagine. Suffice it to say that it is consistent with other New Testament references to philosophy.[6]

Close parenthesis.) The philosopher having constituted himself the parent and guardian of truth, myth and narrative are consequently remanded to literature, a discourse in which (philosophers have always supposed) truth is systematically dissimulated. For every action there is an equal and opposite reaction. Proclaiming itself the native land of truth, philosophy thereby creates "literature": the anarchic domain where ignorance and error run riot. The pseudography of fiction as opposed to the orthography of philosophy: the necessary other than philosophy by creating which philosophy creates itself. And this cleavage between philosophy and literature (opened up by the founding and constituting movement of philosophical reflection) has had two historical consequences that are certainly problematic and quite possibly lamentable.

(1) Though exiled from philosophy into literature, myth persists in even the most austere dialectic, as a fossil at least, and oftener than not as a structure displaced from the narrative into the discursive mode and defining covertly the shape of the argument. For instance, the evolutionary philosophers of the late nineteenth and early twentieth centuries were responding to the mythic demand for origins as much as they were generalizing from public and observable data, replacing the discredited myth of Genesis with a respectable myth of science. Or again, the Hegelian-Marxist

view of history, recommended as the finest and final achievement of dialectical *Wissenschaft*, displaces and takes the place of the Hebraic-Christian myth of redemption. And that, I should suppose, is the source of the power of Marxist rhetoric: it offers an alternative soteriology to a world that desperately feels itself in need of salvation but can no longer invest in the Scripturally sponsored economy of redemption. This list could continue indefinitely. What is important, however, is not the persistent intrusion of myth into the structures of dialectic, but the fact that philosophy, by defining itself as the dialectical/discursive pursuit of truth (a truth it has itself defined), and by excluding myth and narrative in principle from its precincts, has also systematically obscured from itself the way its logic continues to be nourished by myth and its discourse governed by the demands of narrative form. This self-incurred oblivion to its own roots and resources amounts to a kind of perennial bad faith that troubles the conscience or at least clouds the consciousness of Western philosophy throughout its history.

(2) This bad faith of philosophy is matched by a corresponding contamination of self-awareness on the part of the poets. Philosophers have always complained that poets are epistemologically unreliable: they tell tales with no regard for their truth or falsity and retail lying fables at least as enthusiastically and infectiously as they tell true stories. To this charge the poets have replied with their own double gesture. First, they say, you philosophers do not understand the nature of poetry. We are not trying to tell the truth. That's your job. We are only imagining. Everything we say is hypothetical, and therefore our fictions are not subject to judgment by your criteria of truth and falsity. Stories are neither true nor false. They are well written or badly written, that is all. And then they add—here's the second gesture—: anyway, we communicate a higher and deeper truth than any your pedestrian minds can even conceive. We, not you, are the true, albeit unacknowledged, legislators of the world.[7] With this double gesture the poets first attempt to elude the judgment of philosophy and its norms and then re-submit themselves to an escalated interpretation of these same norms. Thus the poets buy back into—or offer to buy back into—the very enterprise of philosophy from which they were in principle excluded.

So the filiation of philosophy from literature persists unacknowledged by the philosophers, and so the poets attempt to recover the patrimony which the philosophers have alienated.

In the remainder of this discussion I intend to examine these same phenomena from another angle and eventually come to what will have to pass, for the time being, as a conclusion. But first let me insert a bit of intermissionary diversion: a kind of entr'acte which may be regarded either as philosophical narrative or as a piece of narrative philosophy.

It has been necessary over the years for me to participate in departmental discussions of the logic requirement imposed on all philosophy graduate students at my university.[8] Our department actually makes very few specific demands of its graduate students. There are certain area requirements to be met. But these requirements are vaguely stated and may be satisfied by selecting from a variety of course offerings. The only course which as such is required of all graduate students is a course in advanced formal logic— and a particular course at that. This requirement is the bane of many graduate students, and from time to time someone proposes to eliminate it or at least to relax it a bit. Such proposals always meet with adamant resistance from the logicians, and the requirement is still in place. Historically of course the logic requirement is the last colony of the long-since-dismantled empire of the logical positivists. The logic requirement is for logicians what India was for the British Empire, and as yet philosophy has produced no Gandhis. But the logic requirement is always defended with an argument that goes somewhat like this. If there is one thing all philosophers have to do, it is to argue. Therefore all would-be philosophers must be obliged to master the techniques of sound argumentation, whatever else they may choose to learn. It might be objected that what a student learns in a course in formal logic has virtually nothing to do with most of the actual arguments she is likely to examine or to propose, formal logic being no longer an *ars disserendi* but an autonomous and autotelic visual art with (for those who like that sort of thing) its own interest and appeal. Or one might object that there is no such thing as plain vanilla logic, only multiple logics intricately interdependent with the world-views they organize and the texts they sustain. But such objections would plainly be given no quarter. So I have often reasoned in this way: arguing is one of the things philosophers have to do but not the only one. They must also, for example, read and interpret texts, produce texts of their own, give lectures and take part in discussions. Therefore they should also be required to take (in addition to logic) courses in literary criticism, expository writing, and rhetoric. At this point the question is called and the matter decided by an up-or-down vote. With what results you already know.

Take this story as a parable. And take the rest of what I have to say as its explication.

My title suggests, if it does not actually promise, that I will say something about the philosophy of genre and the genre of philosophy. So far I have ignored the one and utterly neglected the other. It's time to make amends.

The status, the legitimacy, and the utility of genre distinctions is a topic of continuing debate among literary theorists. I'm not qualified to intervene in that debate, and I don't want to. In this connection I wish to make just one observation. This one: it was a philosopher who first formulated a *theory* of literary genres. He didn't create them, since they were recognized in the literature long before his *Poetics*, but it was Aristotle in his philosophy of poetry who defined the differences among tragedy, comedy, epic, and the dithyramb. It was also Aristotle who, in the same work, distinguished the super-genus of poetry from the super-genera of history and philosophy, proclaiming poetry more philosophical than history and (presumably) less philosophical than philosophy.

If the philosopher is in a position to define and differentiate the kinds of literary discourse, then philosophy itself must be a superior discourse: a discourse of mastery qualified to judge the claims and achievements of other inferior kinds of discourse, *exempli gratia* the discourse of poetry. The legislator-judge is not above the law, but he is the authorized interpreter of the law and by virtue of the authority thus vested in him—in which he has thus vested himself—he assesses the legality of subjects and behaviors that fall within his domain. (But of course the fact that he is the author and interpreter of the law implies that he is above it after all. Another duplicity. Be that as it may.) Philosophy, the science of sciences or the super-science, judges all the (other) arts and sciences by reference to the law of which it is the source and privileged arbiter. One thing traditional philosophers have agreed on—almost the only thing they have agreed on—is that philosophy is the custodian of the norms of truth, keeper of the master representations of being by which all (purportedly) lesser representations of reality (e.g., poetry) are to be evaluated. I suspect most philosophers still believe that, though nowadays they tend to whisper it apologetically among themselves rather than proclaim it with authority at interdisciplinary congresses. Once Queen of the Sciences, philosophy is scarcely even a lady any more, and discretion is the better part of a monarch in exile. It has certainly always been clear to the philosopher that philosophy is not poetry, but the guardian of the norms of verity. A kind of universal ontological bureau of standards and a court of epistemological last resort. Philosophy sits upon the rock of truth, on which rock all other representations of reality, truth-telling or fictive, are either founded or foundering. In Aristotle's generous verdict, poetry comes off rather well. Better, certainly, than it did in the sterner court of Plato's *Republic*.

This view of philosophy, the philosopher's own view which I have here only slightly caricatured, one might be inclined to indulge if not actually endorse—were it not for a couple of disconcerting facts.

One of them is this. Aristotle presumes not only to define poetry and distinguish its kinds. He also distinguishes poetry as a whole from other modes of representation: history and philosophy. We might even allow him the prerogative of comparing poetry and history. But when he orders history, poetry, and philosophy in a climactic progression that culminates in philosophy, we begin to be a bit suspicious. The judge who passes sentence, however benign, on history and poetry and the kinds of poetry makes a large claim. But the judge who is vindicated before his own tribunal claims at once too much and too little, and his claim is *ipso facto* questionable. Is philosophy the maker and keeper of the law? Then it cannot fall under the law of which it is the legislature and executor. The norms of representation are not themselves representations to be measured against these norms. As Augustine said of eternal and immutable truth, *non de illa sed secundum illam judicamus.*[9] Is philosophy just another system of representations, to be ranked in comparison with things like poetry and history? Then it is not, as such, the repository of the *norms* of representation. The philosopher who presumes (as custodian of the norms) to judge philosophy (as subject to those norms) betrays a duplicitous self-consciousness at least and bad faith at the worst. A philosophy of genre cannot be one of the genres of which it is the philosophy.

(I know: *de me fabula narratur.* But I shall deal with self-reference later on. I can only do one thing at a time. I have to cook my crow before I can eat it.)

But of course philosophy *is* both a genre and the philosophy of genre, and this is the second disconcerting fact. Not only does Aristotle's ranking of history, poetry, and philosophy confess it. The fact is evident also from the circumstance that philosophy itself has a history. Not that philosophy is thereby reduced to a historical phenomenon, so that it is subject to judgment by the generic norms of history—though it may well be that. More pointedly: if philosophy has a historical point of origin and undergoes a course of historical development, then it forfeits the transcendence required to sustain its authority as the definer of genres and the assessor of generic performances. But philosophy does have an origin. It originates as the dialectical critique of poetry. Does it therewith become a phenomenon or an epiphenomenon of poetry? As an actuality among other actualities, philosophy is subjected to the indicative logic of history. As an event in the devolution of poetry, its preoccupation with necessary truth might seem to be a modally constricted form of the subjunctive or optative logic of poetry, which ranges over all possibilities from the actual to the necessary. In any event, philosophy does originate, and it does have a history, at the end of which (we have been told ever since St. Paul)[10] we now stand. However we may presume to untangle these generic snarls, it is clear that the presumptive position of philosophy, as master of the genres, is hopelessly compromised. The philosophy of genre becomes the genre of philosophy. And this is a difficult identity to preserve intact.

By distinguishing its own dialectically ordered discourse from the language of myth, philosophy brought itself into being as the genre of philosophy. At the same time it created the genre of poetry, conceived as fictional fabulation in distinction from the more primitive conception of poetry as vatic utterance and canonical scripture. There is nothing exceptional or exceptionable in this. New genres, or what are presumed to be new genres, come into being all the time, and by so coming into being alter the whole existing framework of generic conventions. What is exceptional—and perhaps exceptionable—in the case of philosophy is the claim implicit in its founding and constituting gesture and explicitly advocated in the later conception of philosophy as Queen of the Sciences. The claim, namely, that this new genre is not just a genre but the genre of genres: the definer and delimiter of all genres and the arbiter of all merely generic claims and performances. That particular *Selbstbehauptung* on the part of philosophy may well appear an unprecedented and wholly unjustified piece of arrogance.

Of course one might protest that all this is nothing but gratuitous indignation. In the down to earth and often refreshing spirit of positivism it might be alleged that the appearance of philosophy in the West, along with all the extravagant claims made on its behalf by its representatives—claims we now all acknowledge to be (at least) overstated—is just a matter of historical fact, not a matter of principle or program, and therefore quite innocent and devoid of ominous implications.

This allegation would be plausible if there were such things as mere facts, historical eventualities, empirical coincidences, and the like. But we know there aren't. History is not so guileless as all that. History—which is always the representation of history—is filtered through philosophical presuppositions, not to mention poetic and narrative conventions. The allegation itself is not innocent. And so, while there may not be an eternal and immutable system of generic norms—not for our consciousness, at any rate—it is also the case that there are no mere happenings or historical coincidences either. The constitution of philosophy as a genre and the elevation of that genre by the same act to the status Master of the Genres was no accident. It was done on purpose.

On purpose. The deepest desire of philosophy—a desire that comes to full self-consciousness in the philosophy of German idealism—has always been the desire to ground itself, to constitute its own objects and objectives, and to enact its own canons and criteria. Only as self-grounded and self-sustaining—as the self-originating discourse of being—can philosophy legitimate its presumptive eminence as master science and master of the sciences. Philosophy is, historically and in its own self-understanding, the discourse of the desire to lay the foundations of truth in a truth it alone possesses by methods it alone authenticates.

It is this desire to ground itself that finds expression in Kant's critical rejection of all previous philosophy as parasitic on a truth and a reality merely given it to think and not constituted by it. It is this same desire that motivates Hegel's dialectical *Aufhebung* of Kant's doctrine of the *Ding-an-sich* and the irreducible givenness of intuition. Or Husserl's determination to locate a presuppositionless starting-point for philosophical reflection, and the abyssing of this determination in *Sein und Zeit*. And so on for pages of examples.

Now of course philosophy does, as I have insisted, found itself and constitute itself by breaking away from poetry, which it defines in the same act by which it defines itself. But the coup by which philosophy thus brings itself into being is a gesture of renunciation directed against that which it thereby excludes as its other and on the negative presence of which it thereby confesses itself to depend for its own identity. That philosophy is always only the discourse of the *desire* for self-sufficiency testifies that it is never yet the fulfillment of this desire. And this duplicity—whereby philosophy achieves originality and totality by leaving out that which left out belies its totality and left in betrays its originality—this duplicity, though historical, is no mere historical occurrence but the self-deconstructing moment in the definition of that which by definition is self-defining. The desire of philosophy—perhaps like all desire in this respect—is the desire for that the failure to possess which is the frustration that constitutes its life and the possession of which is the death implicit in its fulfillment.

To illustrate this ambiguous situation of philosophy, and as a relief from these heady abstractions, it may help to recall a phenomenon with which (I am sure) every critic and (I suppose) every philosopher is familiar: the typical course on "philosophy in literature"—or at least the course that used to be (typically) offered under this rubric. Classically conceived as a conjunction of the *dulce* and the *utile*, literature is taken to provide both entertainment and instruction. With regard to the latter philosophers have thought of literature as (at its best) a kind of popular or popularized philosophy. Though it lacks the self-sustaining truth and the rigorous self-discipline of the real thing (and therefore stands in need of philosophical supervision), literature nonetheless expresses philosophical ideas and discusses philosophical problems. Albeit in a non-philosophical (say lyric or narrative or dramatic) form. Literature presents a philosophical content (a content of truth) in an improper form (the form of fiction). The literary form is the *dulce* which both recommends and misrepresents the philosophical content—the *utile* which, insinuated and dissimulated by the *dulce*, can be rescued by the philosopher and reinstalled in its proper form. Thus the syllabus of your typical—or once typical—course in "philosophy *in* literature" (the name says it all) will contain literary works chosen because they express philosophical ideas or discuss philosophical problems that the teacher takes to be important. Russian, German, and French existentialist novels— philosophically garrulous as a rule—are ideal for this purpose. Having read these works, the class under the guidance of its mentor will abstract from them their philosophical content and consider that in abstraction from their literary form. Eat the raisin, as it were, and discard the cookie that made it palatable.

However effective such techniques may be in swelling the enrollment of philosophy courses with non-majors, this is rather obviously an inefficient way to do philosophy and a perverse way to study literature. Literature is not illustrated philosophy, candy-coated philosophy, painless philosophy, or any other kind of philosophy. A novel is not an inferior instance of the philosophic genre. Literature is philosophically interesting, but what is philosophically interesting about literature is not that it contains treatments of philosophical problems or traces of philosophical ideas. What is philosophically interesting about fiction is that it exists.

The circumstance that there *is* fiction (especially if one recalls that philosophy gave birth to fiction in giving birth to itself) makes philosophical theories about the *relationship between* truth and fiction irredeemably problematic. Suppose, as philosophers have classically thought, that there are norms of truth and that philosophy is charged with administering them. Given its norms of truth, philosophy can (not without difficulty, to be sure) handle simple falsehood: unwitting error or deliberate lie. He who utters a falsehood is either deceived or deceiving. All that sort of thing falls within the province philosophy has marked out as its own. But the person who produces fiction is not deceived—she knows her statements are not true—nor does she will to deceive—the novelist is not trying to fool you. Do fictions then elude the distinction of true and false, as Sidney thought? That view gives rise to the standard philosophical problem of fictional discourse.[11] Or does the existence of fiction deconstruct the opposition of true and false? If so, that's another problem. Or maybe the same problem in another form.

Take the following two propositions. (a) Fictional discourse is hypothetical discourse—discourse in the mode of "what if"—and therefore neither true nor false. But (b) true and false are contradictories, between which *tertium* (as they say) *non datur*. If the latter proposition is taken to be true (*sic*), then there are no fictions, only falsehoods. But if we take our stand on the former, then the distinction between true and false will not hold firm. Neither of these conclusions is acceptable. No one can seriously deny the existence of fiction as distinct from falsehood. And no one can consistently relinquish or relativize the distinction between true and false.

The second proposition, which excludes a middle between true and false, is the premise of philosophy. The former, which asserts that fiction is the middle so excluded, is the defense of poetry. And the difference between them is one way to characterize the difference between philosophy and literature. But, given the invincible philosophicity of fiction and the equally invincible ficticity of philosophy, that difference itself will not stay where we put it. It is (perhaps) the metastability of this difference that explains (though it could hardly justify) the double gestures by which philosophy and literature struggle to define themselves, each against the other, and the suspicion of bad faith that doggedly pursues them as they work out the historical destinies implied by these self-definitions.

A philosophy is a system of representations that takes itself to be true, a representation (perhaps) of the norms of representation and truth, truthful representation, and representational truth. A fiction is a system of representations that knows itself to be false and is therefore neither deceived nor deceiving—that is to say, not false. But the professional humility of fiction dissembles its commitment (after all) to norms of truth, just as the pretensions of philosophy dissimulate the ambiguity of its own representations vis-à-vis those same norms. The relation between them is the deconstruction of their difference.

Any representation necessitates reflection on the question: how much of the representation is a re-presentation of the represented? And how much of the represented is an effect of representation? St. Anselm was convinced that the formula *id quo maius cogitari non potest* (which he felt he had received as a revelation) was a form of words (a representation) perfectly transparent to its referent (a representation wholly determined by the represented).[12] His critics have consistently complained that Anselm's "God" is no more than a figment of language. Does the ontological argument give us reality represented in the language of philosophy or the language of philosophy represented as reality? When you look into a mirror—the mirror that art (or is it philosophy?) holds up to nature—do you see *yourself reflected* in the mirror or a *reflection of yourself* in the mirror? Such questions are both decisive and undecidable.

It is no accident that philosophy in the twentieth century has become more and more a meta-philosophical reflection on the means of representation. By and large Anglo-American philosophy of language has been a concerted effort to retain at all costs the founding and constituting assumptions of philosophy concerning meaning and reference, whereas recent continental philosophy has systematically mistrusted those very assumptions. That, I think, may be the tap root of the misunderstanding that still divides them.

This is no accident. Philosophy was destined, sooner or later, to be brought up against those presuppositions by which from the first it has founded and sustained itself. Nor is it an accident that philosophy, so fried in its own fat, finds itself approaching the condition of that literature which it defined in defining itself and from which it has always distinguished itself. The repressed has returned as it always does, and the problem (or the predicament) of both philosophy and literature has become the problem of language. The medium has displaced, if it has not actually become, the message. The genre of philosophy, constituted as such by philosophy as master of the genres, is a commitment to a particular way of writing (take a position and defend it with arguments) and a particular way of reading (extract the arguments from the text and examine them with a view to accepting or rejecting the position they support). The commitment of philosophy is a commitment to logic as opposed to narrative, which commitment enshrines a whole system of assumptions about truth and reality—e.g., that they are non-temporal and therefore always distorted or lost in narrative representation. But that commitment, with its attendant assumptions, is now seen to be duplicitous, and the genre of philosophy— which also presumes to be the philosophy of genre—can no longer disclaim its inextricable entanglement with and its inevitable contamination by the other it had to exclude in order to become itself.

I hope it is clear that my intention is not to inculpate philosophy nor to compassionate its victim. There are no villains and no victims here. My intention is rather, and more constructively, to harp on the essential complicity of philosophy and literature—the complicity in their duplicity—and their complex commitment to all the possibilities, powers, problems, perils, and paradoxes of language. The complicity (not quite a unity) underlying the difference (which is really a duplicity) of philosophy and literature is not an external but an internal (dis)relationship, rooted both historically and essentially in that decisive clinamen by which both philosophy and literature have entered upon and acted out their historical essentiality.

By now my goose—or my crow—is pretty thoroughly cooked, and I shall have to eat it. I have spent so much time roasting and basting it that I shall be obliged to gobble it down in great haste. Probably that was no accident either. But before I take that first nibble, let me add just one thing more. Everything I have (however inadequately) done in this essay would have to be done again (and done better) from the side of literature and criticism if we wanted to get the whole picture. Philosophy is not the only suspicious character in this affair. If I have maliciously picked on philosophy, it is perhaps because I am a philosopher of sorts, and it is always more gracious to pick the beam out of your own eye than to rail at the mote in your neighbor's. In any case I know philosophy better—more inwardly— than literature, and my benign neglect of the latter may only betray my lack of that familiarity which inevitably breeds contempt.

So much for justice. I hope (also) that no one will take me to have suggested that philosophy *is* literature and that literature *is* philosophy, and that if we just recognize this all our problems will be solved. For one thing, the equations won't wash. Any librarian knows the difference between *Gravity's Rainbow* and *The Critique of Pure Reason*. And any philosopher (ditto any critic) knows that the difference is deeper than Dewey decimal. The thing is to recognize our common duplicity: the difference in our identity and the identity in our difference. Not only are there philosophical narratives (*The Brothers Karamazov* and *Madame Bovary*) and narrative philosophies (Augustine's *Confessions* and Hegel's *Phenomenology*). Philosophical dialectic and literary narrative attract and repel each other in every literary and philosophical text. But to recognize this is not to have solved a problem. It is only to have faced it. That is step one. Whether we then march forward toward a solution or just continue to mark time is something time (perhaps) will tell. In any event there is no stepping outside or above or beyond the problem. For the philosopher that means no moving to another department and no ascent to the meta-level from which an impartial view of philosophy, a decisive critique of its follies, and a wholesome reformation of its character might be achieved. True to its destiny, philosophy reappropriates the discourse that would delimit it, and every critique of philosophy is another piece of the problem. Philosophy is a lot like malcontent: you can't complain about it without committing it.

And what about that crow sitting there on the table getting colder and less appetizing the longer I put off eating it? Have I put myself in the position of the philosopher I excoriated earlier, who presumes to lay down the law, to preside over its enforcement, and finally to vindicate himself in his own court? Of course I have. Everything a novelist writes redefines the novel, however minimally. And every act of the philosopher, however perverse, repeats with variations the founding and constituting gesture of philosophy. There is no solution to the problem that does not reconstitute the problem at another level, which of course means that the problem is not a problem but a predicament. I will therefore not be surprised, though I may not be pleased either, when it is pointed out to me that it is also my predicament nor am I out of it. The founding and constituting gesture of philosophy is, as I have tried (by repeating it) to point out, a double gesture. I cannot escape the duplicity, I can only acknowledge my complicity in it. To which end, and by way of ending, I appropriate the words of a novelist, Ursula LeGuin, reflecting philosophically on her own fictions: "Distrust everything I say. I am telling the truth."[13]

2

Kant, Vaihinger, and the Fiction of Philosophy

Toward the beginning of the *Critique of Pure Reason*, a work not often cited as an example of stylistic elegance, we encounter this rather remarkable passage: [1]

> The rainbow in a sunny shower may be called a mere appearance, and the rain the thing in itself. This is correct, if the latter concept be taken in a merely physical sense. Rain will then be viewed only as that which, in all experience and in all its various positions relative to the senses, is determined thus, and not otherwise, in our intuition. But if we take this empirical object in its general character, and ask... whether it represents an object in itself..., the question as to the relation of the representation to the object at once becomes transcendental. We then realize that not only are the drops of rain mere appearances, but that even their round shape, nay even the space in which they fall, are nothing in themselves, but merely modifications or fundamental forms of our sensible intuition, and that the transcendental object remains unknown to us. (CPR 84-85, KrV A45/B63-A46/B63)

Or, as Kant says a few lines earlier, we believe that we know things in themselves, but "however deeply we enquire into...objects, we have to do with nothing but appearances." (CPR 84, KrV A45/B62)

In the Preface to the second edition of the *Critique* (CPR 22, KrV Bxvi), Kant claims that he has brought about a revolution in metaphysics comparable to Copernicus' revolution in astronomy. The essence of this revolution— we might in these latter days call it a paradigm shift— has nothing to do with whether objects revolve around subjects or vice versa, but rather with Kant's fundamental contention that all we ever know or experience are appearances (*Erscheinungen, phenomena*) or, as he also calls them, representations (*Vorstellungen*). External objects situated in space and time are only representations, as are the occasions of our inner experience situated in time alone. Even the self that has the experience, together with all the formal structures that make up the Kantian *a priori*, is not the *res cogitans* of Descartes, but only the representation "I think" that can accompany all our other representations. And unify them: the unity of experience (that is, of representations) is the representation of the unity of representations as their unification in/by the consciousness of an ego that is itself only a representation of unity—the transcendental function of the *cogito*, not its metaphysical reality. Of the thing-in-itself, and of those perennial grails of the metaphysical quest—soul, world, and God—we have not even representations, or only barren representations, mere thoughts that cannot, like the raindrop or the rainbow, be so much as perceived.

The radical nature of Kant's revolution—his undermining of the foundations of metaphysics and morals—was not lost on his contemporaries and successors. Though he insisted that he had only denied knowledge in order to make room for faith, his repudiation of rationalist metaphysics seemed to many of his readers the veritable abyss. It is sometimes said that Heinrich Kleist was propelled toward suicide by his reading of the first *Critique*. Be that as it may, most of Kant's philosophical successors, the greatest of whom is Hegel, set to work on a program of philosophical renewal designed to rebuild the metaphysical structure Kant had demolished. We are no longer made suicidal by Kant, nor do we mourn the death of traditional metaphysics. Most of us are born skeptics, and those who aren't are quickly made such by their education. Yet it does not follow that we have earned our insouciance, and if we haven't it may be that we have not yet fully understood Kant. A propos of which, it is not insignificant that Anglo-American readers of Kant in the twentieth century have treated him, by and large, as an epistemologist. Disregarding or suppressing his own expressed intention to revolutionize metaphysics, they have reduced him to an episode in the Cartesian tradition that continues to define their philosophical preoccupations just as if (*sic*) Kant had never existed.

One reader who did get the point was Hans Vaihinger. From Kant's doctrine that all we know are representations, from his insistence that the categories of the understanding and the forms of sensibility are neither ontic facts nor ontological structures but only conditions of the possibility of experience, and from his demotion of God, world, and soul from metaphysical ultimates to heuristic guidelines for the regulation of the understanding, Vaihinger concluded not unreasonably that all of our important scientific and philosophical concepts are fictions.[2] What Kant said of the ideas of reason—though they may not be veridical we must treat them as if they were—Vaihinger extended to all ideas. The result was his *Philosophie des 'Als Ob,'* published in German in 1911 and in 1924 in English as *The Philosophy of 'As If.'*[3]

Early in his argument Vaihinger tells us that sensations "alone are ultimately given." (67, cf. 76) And later: "sensations [are] the sole reality." (151) To say this is not to say that "elementary sensations are copies of reality" (16)—that is, that sensations mimic the physical objects which realism naively supposes give rise to them. What is real about sensations is the fact that I have them and they have the characters—red, hard, cold, smooth, etc.—they seem to have (105), since their reality *is* their seeming.

To say that sensations are given is Kantian enough, though (as the history of post-Kantian philosophy shows and as we shall soon have occasion to remark) neither the meaning nor the truth of this statement is immediately evident. But to say that *only* sensations are real is not even Kantian. For Kant phenomenal reality is not sensation alone but a synthesis of sensory content and intellectual form. This initial clinamen turns Vaihinger out of the Kantian line in the direction of a sensationalism that importantly qualifies his understanding of fiction. But I want to stay with Vaihinger's argument for a while before subjecting it to critical analysis.

Sensation then (the fact and form thereof) is rock-bottom, the real and unshakable foundation of the edifice of thought. But to what purpose is the construction of this edifice? At the opposite extreme from sensation, the purpose of thinking is to aid and abet action, in particular ethical conduct and in general social intercourse among men. Kantian in this as in other things, Vaihinger says that not theory, but practice, is the destination of thought. (65, 66, 101-102, 170) And so, one might say, Vaihinger is initially sensationalist and terminally pragmatist.

What comes between this beginning and this end? "What lies between [sensation and action] are mere points of transit." (102) Vaihinger's name for these points of transit is *fictions.* The primary fiction is the distinction between subject and object conceived as things in themselves. From this root grow all the other fictions that carry us from our origin in perception to our goal in action.

> The actual purpose of thought is not thought itself and its products, but behavior, and ultimately ethical behavior. The means thereto is the objective world in the form of a world of ideas. (65)

In the beginning are sensations, in the end actions, and connecting them a world of ideas, one and all fictions. The name of this doctrine—Vaihinger's doctrine and "the only fictionless doctrine in the world"—is "Critical Positivism." (77)

What, more precisely, is a fiction? Fictions should not be confused with hypotheses. A hypothesis, Vaihinger says, is aimed at reality. It is an ideational construct that hopes to be verified. That is, it hopes to coincide with some perception(s) in the future. The evolutionary hypothesis, for example, would be verified by a system of perceptions (fossil remains and the like) that would enable us to trace the development of complex forms of life from their simplest unicellular ancestors.

A fiction, by contrast, cannot be verified. It is an imaginary ideational construct, false in itself, and known to be so, which is nevertheless justified by its utility. With the help of fictions we are enabled not only to formulate and verify scientific hypotheses, as Goethe's archetypal animal prepared the way for Darwin's hypothesis, but more generally to advance understanding and ultimately to power action. "Without the imaginary factor, neither science nor life in their highest form are possible." (44)

Fictions are not merely false, they are necessarily false. Inspired by and expanding upon the Kantian dialectic, Vaihinger insists that every fiction incorporates a contradiction (53) and is therefore proven to be false (147). But since they are nonetheless useful for the advancement of knowledge and the improvement of human life—"fruitful errors," Vaihinger calls them (147, 169)—we use their mendacity in order to access their utility. Long before it became a central text in the post-structuralist canon, Vaihinger had read Nietzsche's *Über Wahrheit und Lüge im aussermoralischen Sinne*, from which, along with other Nietzschean texts, he concluded that "what we…call truth…is *merely the most expedient error*." (84, 108) All the concepts by which we organize our perceptions (to the end of ordering our lives) are subjective. But what is merely subjective is fictional, what is fictional is false, and falsehood is error. The entire world of ideas, together with the notion that this world of ideas corresponds to the world of fact, is nothing but illusion and deception if taken to be true. Known to be false and yet treated *as if* true, it is an indispensable aid to action. Even the words "as if" signify contrary to fact, so that every instance of the *als ob*—every fiction—is a case of "*conscious, practical…, fruitful error*." (91-94)

There are a number of moderately disconcerting particulars in Vaihinger's account of fictions. For example, he says that fictions are subjective constructs (108), but he also says that subject and object themselves are the primary fictions. (77) All fictions are fictions of objectivity: fictions objectively regarded and therefore objectively false. Are they also fictions of a fiction? I think he might disallow this kind of superfetation. Again: the fact that he attributes to Kant the view that concepts such as space and causality are subjective only allies him with a certain (I think mistaken) interpretation of Kant, as does his claim that only sensation is real. When he says that sensations alone are given, he seems closer to Kant's expressed views. And yet it is possible to wonder why he did not suspect that even sensations are not simply and immediately given, but constituted in part by the preconceptions brought (*a priori*) by the mind to perception.[4] In which case nothing is given but givenness itself, and even this forfeits its immediacy the moment it enters into experience. Taken to the end of the line, suspicions of this sort might lead to the conclusion that everything we call real is (shall I say "in reality?") nothing but a tissue of fictions. Vaihinger occasionally flirts with this possibility:

> To understand is to reduce to known ideational constructs.... These apperceptive constructs are fictions.... Thus the immense work of modern science reduces all existence, which in the last analysis is absolutely incomprehensible, to an entirely subjective and purely fictional standard. (52-53)

That's radical enough. Too radical for Vaihinger, who maintains in spite of such flirtations that his own fictionalism (Critical Positivism) is the one and only fictionless doctrine.

Which brings me to the point toward which all these reservations tend. Vaihinger thinks all fictions are imaginary, by which he means unreal. (44) Every fiction in the strict sense is logically false, since it includes a contradiction. But for all that, it is a useful and even necessary falsehood. We can only understand our sensations, which alone are real, by analogy with conceptual structures of our own making (for example, Kant's categories), which are imaginary and therefore false. All knowledge is symbolic. It gives us an image of reality but not reality itself. The very notion of a direct and adequate knowledge of reality (for example, by intellectual intuition) is itself a fiction. (29-30) And in any case, knowledge is not an end in itself, but a means to action. The passage from reality (sensation) to action ("the intercourse of sentient beings" (67)) is made possible by the necessary and useful falsehoods Vaihinger calls fictions.

It is impossible not to suspect that Vaihinger is talking out of both sides of his mouth. On the one hand he claims that all knowledge as well as all practice is mediated by fictions and that we never know the real itself but only symbols of it. On the other hand, he insists that fictions are demonstrably false, that only sensations are real, and that his own philosophy is fictionless. (77) He can't have it both ways. If some things are known to be real, and if "Critical Positivism" is known to be true, then not all our contact with reality is fictional. But if all our contact with reality *is* fictional, then the reality of sensations is an effect of the imagination, there is no fictionless doctrine, and it makes no sense to say that fictions are falsehoods.

Suppose it *is* the distinguishing mark of fictions that they are self-contradictory and therefore self-evidently false. If that were the case, then to make such necessary falsehoods the basis of all theory and practice would require of us *either* an abysmal ignorance of our basic concepts *or* an almost superhuman capacity for self-deception. It is hard to see how such a fiction could be a "fruitful error" (45, 46), since any falsehood known to be such is at once rejected. It can only be useful on the condition that it is not known to be erroneous, or on the even less likely supposition that we are willing and able to believe what we know to be incredible.

Vaihinger says that fictions are the work of imagination. (44) But the imagination doesn't deceive. It imagines. And the products of its imagining are not lies but hypothetical constructs situated outside the distinction between real and unreal and the parallel distinction between true and false. The phrase *als ob* (=*wie wenn*) does not, as Vaihinger thinks, express a condition contrary to fact (91-93), but only (and this is more in keeping with Kant's usage) a state of uncertainty: an indecision epistemically undetermined and provisionally available for imaginative supposition.

Nabokov's Lolita, albeit a real fiction, neither does nor does not exist, and that precisely because she is (really) a fiction. A fictional narrative like *Pride and Prejudice* is neither true nor false, because it is (truly) a novelistic fiction. The reality of fiction is that it eludes the difference between real and unreal, and the truth of fiction is that it is not subject to the jurisdiction of a simple two-valued logic.

Our intellectual and imaginative lives—and our active lives as well—are not built on contradictions. It may be, as Kant argued, that we are forced into contradiction at the extreme limits of our thought, and that by the nature of reason itself. But it may also be the case, as his doctrine of imagination suggests, that our thinking is built on an imaginative synthesis located beyond and before the logic that governs our convictions of truth and reality. And if fiction exceeds and antecedes contradiction, then true and false, real and unreal, and the differences between them rest on a foundation fundamentally neither. The real (that which demands to be dealt with) and the true (that which commands our belief) are subsets of the fictive (that which can be imagined). If this can be believed (or at least imagined), then Vaihinger's fictionalism may also be fiction: the fiction of philosophy underlying the philosophy of fiction. It might then be supposed not the fictionless truth but, in the words of a later connoisseur of the "as if," the supreme fiction which, knowing it to be a fiction, we nonetheless believe. *That* kind of fictionalism, the cautious *credo* of modernism, is what remains of the Romantic faith in the imagination after its battering by the terrors of twentieth-century reality.

Midway through his argument Vaihinger says:

> [T]his conceptual world is…*our world,* in which we live and feel. Only we must not put any philosophical system in the place of reality…. (161)

To which he adds a few lines further on: "we must be neither dogmatic nor skeptical, but critical." (162) Good advice. But instead of heeding his own wisdom and recognizing, with Salomon Maimon, that "'discursive thought…is a fiction'" (156), Vaihinger goes on to identify criticism with (of all things) logical positivism. (163) That has got to be the anticlimax of this book, as it was the anticlimax of the history of philosophy from Kant to the *Wienerkreis.* Conflating "critical" with "positivism" and identifying the conjunct as fictionless truth, Vaihinger falls back into the very dogmatism from which Kant labored to redeem metaphysics. Even Vaihinger was not prepared to embrace the implications of a thoroughgoing fictionalism. Especially its self-referential implications. Very much the Herr Professor, he prefaces his book with a personal account of the genesis of his philosophical system, and, having thus mounted the professional cathedra, he is bound to represent the issue of this long gestation as The Truth at Last and not just another instantiation of its own revolutionary insights.

Fiction then is final. Such is the ultimacy of fiction that even the philosophy of fiction can only stammer, over and over, this once and future last word. Perhaps. But what does it mean to say that fiction is final? Is that a truth or a falsehood or a fiction? My critical remarks may have been far too hard on Vaihinger and far too easy on myself. Vaihinger was after all familiar with Nietzsche, and he may be using "falsehood" and "error" the way Nietzsche uses "lie." If so, then Vaihinger's "falsehood," like Nietzsche's "lie," means something like catachresis. Catachresis is not strictly true, since it names things improperly, but neither is it strictly false, since the things it names improperly have no proper names. Nietzsche's "lie" and Vaihinger's "falsehood" would then mean "fiction" in the sense of "imaginary constructs that are neither true nor false." This is the sort of thing poets and defenders of poetry have often said on behalf of their art. But they have typically taken back with one hand what they have given with the other, so that poetic fictions, which are not subject to judgment by philosophical or scientific norms of truth, are nonetheless the chosen vessels of a superior kind of truth. The temptations of truth, deceitful though they be, are not so easily resisted.

Vaihinger doesn't resist them, nor does he line up behind Nietzsche and the poets. This is clear from his contention that fictions are necessarily false insofar as they entail contradictions. What is important here is not the soundness of his analysis, but what it symptomizes. Namely: one cannot so handily dismiss the logical law of excluded middle (every proposition is either true or false: T v F) in favor of the poetic law of epistemic neutrality (some propositions are neither true nor false: -T. -F). And the converse: the possibility of fiction (-T. -F) cannot simply concede to the demands of logic (T v F) any more than the laws of logic can be relativized in order to liberate the imagination. Neither the claims of the understanding nor those of the imagination may be forfeit, though it is not possible to define (who would define them?) the terms of their cohabitation. The law of excluded middle is the rock on which philosophy takes its stand. The middle so excluded is the free space needed for the exercise of imagination and the possibility of fiction. No rational being can conscientiously give up the law of excluded middle and the distinctions it sponsors. But neither can any sensitive being fail to perceive that fiction plays around and outside this law and its distinctions. And no one who is at once sensitive and rational can either deny the reality of fiction or renounce the authority of logic. Fictions are both (logically) false and (as fictions) neither true nor false. In this sense fiction does not escape the jurisdiction of the law of excluded middle. It is, rather, the self-deconstructing moment in the logic of truth. But it can never destroy that logic, since it is necessarily parasitic upon it, just as the logic of truth can never disavow the existence of that fiction by which its sovereignty is forever and fundamentally threatened.

Jacobi, quoted by Vaihinger, says that

> *without* the presupposition of objects as Things-in-themselves, and of ideational faculties upon which they work, it is not possible to enter the Kantian system, though *with* them it is quite impossible to remain in it. (151)

Take the Thing-in-itself as a necessary fiction and the Kantian system as an expression of the will to truth. Jacobi's statement, so understood, epitomizes the dialectic of the fictive and the cognitive that I am trying to insinuate. Recalling that the logic of truth is both the creation and the constitution of philosophy, and that the fictive, as distinct from the logic of distinction, is the space both created and claimed by literary art, it is clear that the philosophical and the literary are neither simply identical nor simply different. Their common fictionality and the truth about both is the dialectic of identity and difference—or: construction and deconstruction—in which they endlessly attract and repel each other. As the partisan of "as if" and the prophet of the supreme fiction put it, "the nicer knowledge of/Belief" is "that what it believes in is not true."[5]

Though his account may be, as I have suggested, lopsided and even skewed with respect to its own founding intuitions, still Vaihinger's recognition that all our concepts are fictions—imaginative creations—wholesomely disturbs both the complacency of the philosopher who thinks it possible to match language to reality and distinguish fact from fiction, and the confidence of Romantic artists, from Blake on down, that the imagination is able to create a new reality outside the jurisdiction of truth. Both philosophy and fiction are fictitious. But the fictitiousness of philosophy, like the fictitiousness of fiction, is not that it escapes from the distinction of truth and falsity into a prelapsarian neither/nor. On the contrary, philosophy and fiction alike both deconstruct and are sustained by that distinction. Whatever defenders of poetry have claimed, not even the propositions of poets can bypass the bar of truth. And in spite of the almost unanimous insistence of philosophers, their own figurations are never securely corraled within what Charles Peirce called the sheep-and-goat pens of a two-valued logic.[6] To speak of the fiction of philosophy in this connection is in part to call attention to the fictions by which every philosophical text is not merely decorated and enlivened but constituted. Every philosophical system is a fictional construction. But it is also a reminder, aided and abetted by Vaihinger's strong (or at least forced) misreading of Kant, that philosophy itself as traditionally understood is a fiction. It is a fiction of philosophers that there is such a thing as philosophy. And this statement of mine, *pace* Vaihinger, is not the first proposition of a meta-discourse by which the fiction of fiction and the fiction of truth are contained and mastered, but merely my own reflexive contribution to the general debacle. It goes without saying—it better, since it cannot be said—that if what I have already said is true, that everything we say is self-polluting, then anything else we might say will be no less contaminated. Not merely the rainbow of fiction and the raindrops of truth, but even the space, here and now, in which they fall, the space of this discourse, only iterate the dialectic of representation and prolong the critical revolution.

3

Poetry, History, Truth, and Redemption

> I love to tell the story,
> Because I know 'tis true;
> It satisfies my longing
> As nothing else can do.
> > Gospel Hymn

> You can go home again…, so long as you
> understand that home is a place where you
> have never been.
> > Ursula Le Guin,
> > *The Dispossessed*

In 1957 an English solicitor named Owen Barfield published a book entitled *Saving the Appearances: A Study in Idolatry*. In his introduction he describes the book "as a sort of outline sketch…for a history of human [mainly Western] consciousness."[1] In the body of the work he traces the evolution of consciousness from an edenic state of union with itself and nature (which he calls Original Participation), through a state of diremption and fragmentation (which he calls Idolatry), toward a state of eventual reunification (which he calls Final Participation). The book, which narrates the history of consciousness as a redemptive history, is itself a myth of redemption in which the redemptive agent, the power that saves the appearances, is the iconoclastic imagination.

A lot of theologians and literary people have found the book interesting. I know a few philosophers and one political scientist who have studied it. Whether historians have ever taken it seriously I do not know. Perhaps they should. For thereby hangs a tale.

Once upon a time, everyone knows, Aristotle declared poetry more philosophical than history. Everyone also knows, though not everyone agrees about, why he thought so. What Aristotle says on this head is said in the *Poetics*, early in his discussion of the tragic plot, that *mythos* which, as *mimesis praxeos*, is the *arche* and as it were the *psyche* of the tragedy. (Exceptionally rich cluster of words in this region of the text):

> [I]t will be seen that the poet's function is to describe, not the thing that has happened, but a kind of thing that might happen, i.e. what is possible as being probable or necessary. The distinction between historian and poet is not in the one writing prose and the other verse...; it consists really in this, that the one describes the thing that might be. Hence poetry is something more philosophic and of graver import than history, since its statements are of the nature rather of universals, whereas those of history are singulars.[2]

Philosophy is concerned to discover and state general truths: truths about genera and species, about the kind of things of which, fundamentally, the universe consists. For in spite of his opposition to the Platonic *chorismos*, Aristotle like his master is inclined to ascribe more reality to kinds than to the singulars that instantiate them. At least these are the subjects of knowledge and the topics of demonstration.

The historian relates particular events, the things done by or to particular people. Matters of fact. But the poet tells of things in general: what persons of a certain sort might do, could do, would do, should do, or would be bound to do in circumstances of a certain sort. And for this reason, that his subject-matter is universal rather than particular, the poet's work is more philosophical and therefore of more gravity than that of the historian. He gets closer to the structures of being and the sources of cognition, while the historian only skims the surface of truth and reality.

I have made it sound as if (and most of Aristotle's commentators have made it sound as if) the difference between history and poetry were a difference between their respective subject-matters: the one deals with singulars, the other with universals. That certainly makes the distinction clear. It also makes the superior philosophicity of poetry easy to understand. Aristotle's language, however, suggests another reading. It may be that the difference between history and poetry is a difference between the modalities of their discourses. History is written in the indicative mode, the mode of assertion and matter of fact. But poetry, at its most philosophical, is in the mode of necessity, and, at its least philosophical, in the mode of probability and possibility. When its discourse is not necessitarian (at which point it almost merges with philosophical science), the language of poetry is subjunctive or optative. On this view of the matter one might regard both philosophy, ideally a system of necessary truths, and history, never more than a relation of facts, as modally constricted forms of poetry, which has all of possibility, including the actual and the necessary, as its domain.

But it is unlikely that Aristotle, stalwart champion of poetry though he was, would agree to this privileging of poetry over both history and philosophy. He was after all a philosopher defending poetry, and it is clear where authority hangs its hat.

Here's another way to think of it. History tells (merely) true stories. Poetry tells likely stories. (I intend the full ambiguity of the English idiom: bards do tell many a lie.) But philosophy trumps them both: it offers essential truth, a vision of the structures of being as such. If we plot the hierarchy this way (and overlook the wobbling of "likelihood"), then poetry is more philosophical than history only on the condition that possibility (fiction in the "what if" sense of imaginative hypothesis: likelihood poised in stable equilibrium between probability and dissemblance) is closer to necessity than actuality is. Not all, maybe not many, philosophers would go for that. Appropriately, poetry has got short shrift from the philosophy department, while history has been accorded at least the lip service due a semi-science. Aristotle, however, might subscribe to the notion that possibility is higher than actuality and closer to necessity. He knew a bit about the modality of modalities. And he did regard poetry as more philosophical than (read: superior to) history.

Of course not many historians have been willing to accept Aristotle's description of their activity. Historians have not been content merely to tell true stories, in the mode of indication, about matters of particular fact. That, as any historian knows, is only chronicle, not yet elevated to the level of authentic history. Historians—a lot of them since the nineteenth century— have insisted that history is or ought to be or soon will be a science that enunciates the necessary laws of the development of the human race (sometimes spirit) through time. That view too has had its philosophers (often the historian and his philosopher are conveniently the same person), who have offered to formulate for the historian his method of inquiry, the nature of historical explanation, the arguments by which historians may legitimately defend their claims and even the mode of that necessary historical truth to which the historian may aspire.

One might go on in this vein, unprofitably enough, for a long time. But one thing is clear even from this timid shuffling of the counters. And that is:

however poetry and history may decide to arrange themselves at the foot of the table, philosophy is not about to be displaced as master of the revels. One thing traditional philosophers have always agreed on (almost the only thing they have agreed on) is that philosophy is the custodian of the norms of truth, keeper of the master representations by which all (purported) lesser representations of reality (e.g., poetry and history) are to be judged. I think most philosophers still believe that, though nowadays they tend to whisper it apologetically among themselves rather than proclaim it with authority at interdisciplinary congresses. Once queen of the sciences, philosophy is scarcely even a lady any more. Discretion is the better part of a monarch in exile.

Meanwhile, down at the foot of the table. In recent years Hayden White, to the consternation of orthodox historians but to the delight of the heterodox in many departments, has suggested (I do not say argued, but I will say that his suggestion is massively documented, rigorously sustained, and convincing) that history is more poetical than scientific. More poetical even than anything previously conceived as historical.[3] Historians tell tales. They dispose their information along familiar lines of emplotment, valorize their fictions by means of standard tropologies, and narrate them in obedience to conventions of traditional rhetoric. With the help of categories drawn from the works of critics like Northrop Frye and Kenneth Burke, White has persuasively shown that, for all their commitment to fact and truth, historians, just like novelists, epic poets, and tragedians, *shape* their narratives. And the shapes they give their stories are neither facts nor necessary implicates of fact nor scientific strategies of explanation demanded by the facts. But rather: formative principles of a different order derived from an altogether different source.

To what order do these principles belong? From what source do they derive? Rather than try to answer these questions directly, I recur to the observation made earlier, that philosophers, with few exceptions, have always thought philosophy the inventor and guardian of truth. Whether from the edicts of pure reason or the deliverances of brute experience or some combination of these, the philosopher garners a basket of basic truths (an exhaustive list of the predicaments of being *qua* being, a principled system of the categories of any possible experience, etc.) and protects them against assault with all the weapons in his arsenal of invincible logic. Or something like that. It has always been clear to the philosopher that philosophy is neither poetry nor history, but the keeper of the norms of verity. A kind of universal ontological bureau of standards and a court of epistemological last resort.

Philosophy sits upon the rock of Truth Itself, on which all other discourses, truth-telling or fictive, are either founded or foundering. Or something like that.

What interests me, however, is not these extravagant ironies, but another altogether. This: the history of philosophical theories, including theories of truth, plots a curve that coincides with the cycle of fictional modes proposed by Northrop Frye in his *Anatomy of Criticism*.[4] The same circuit that Hayden White has traced in the modes of nineteenth-century historiography. That is, philosophy's purported custody of truth *sub specie aeternitatis* is interrupted by the intrusion into its own discourse of the (purportedly secondary and derivative) discourses of the poet and the historian. Philosophy is *written*, and it has a *history*: it is inscribed in history, just as history is inscribed in the forms of fiction.

This poltergeist of deconstruction inhabiting the structure of philosophy recommends an irony over the philosophical enterprise as such. An irony not unlike that recursiveness which, in the texts of Kenneth Burke, appears to be the trope of ultimacy.[5] An irony more extravagant even than Hayden White's ironies over historiography: more extragavant because the radical of self-distrust undermines the foundations of a discourse that has always already had to regard itself as fundamental. An extravagant irony, more ironical yet its extravagance.[6]

According to Frye the principle of all narrative is myth. Both genetically and structurally, myth is the primordial mode of discourse. Prior to the distinction between truth and falsity, the language of myth is an undisplaced metaphoric identification of opposites: Jupiter *is* the thunder, in Christ the divine *is* the human. But chiefly the identification of the radicals of representation: the myth, both the telling and the ritual enactment, *is* reality.

Every other (i.e., subsequent) mode of discourse is a displacement of myth: a distribution of the unities of myth into the distinctions prescribed by increasingly strict demands for plausibility, verisimilitude, rationality, and moral responsibility. Romance, at one remove from myth, changes metaphoric identity into the concrete universal or the Coleridgean symbol. The romantic narrative itself is synecdoche of the structure of reality. Another step down the ladder of displacements, high mimesis (the home of tragic heroes) rewrites metaphor as an analogy of proportionality. The high mimetic work (e.g., *Oedipos Tyrannos*) is an analogy of fate or a proportional representation of the rational order of nature. At the next remove, low mimesis (the scene of comedy) reduces metaphor to simile: disparate terms linked with each other and with the world they describe by external relations of similarity. The characters and events of the naturalistic novel are (we say, in low mimetic admiration) *just like* real life. At the bottom of the scale, in the mode of irony, the metaphoric bonds that hold the mythic narrative together and confuse it with reality are completely relaxed. The terms of ironic discourse are juxtaposed (to each other and to the things they seem to represent) without commitment to, or even allegation of, any determinate mode of relationship. Irony is, as we say, detached. Ironic poems don't *mean*. They just *be* (and not much of that) in hermetic purity.

Mythic narrative celebrates the exploits of gods and heroes. Ironic discourse, by contrast, victimizes both its characters and its themes. The sequence of the modes becomes a self-iterating cycle by virtue of the fact that ironic discourse, taken to the end of the line, reconverts to myth. If the victimization of the anti-hero is sufficiently brutal, he ceases to be merely ridiculous and becomes (at first) pathetic and (eventually) a divine scapegoat who suffers for our sins. It is not far from the church of *The Hippopotamus* to the Church of *The Rock*. And when Hume says that the Christian faith was not only attended at the first by miracles but to this day cannot be believed by any reasonable person without one, it is not clear whether he is mocking or genuflecting; just as Kierkegaard presented Christianity with such sublime indirection that his readers (and occasionally himself) could not tell if he was friend or foe.[7]

Thus irony, pursuing its own reductive purposes and faithful to its own diremptive logic, returns to myth. Or perhaps we should call it—in view of the sophistication picked up in the first go-round—mythopoeia. Naiveté forever behind it, the cycle repeats itself sentimentally (if not farcically) the second time around.

In order to protect the autonomy of literature (imaginative writing) and criticism (the systematic study of literature) Frye classifies philosophy as assertive discourse. This suggests that philosophy, centrifugally opened on the world rather than centripetally withdrawn into itself, escapes the categories of literature and exempts itself from the canons of criticism. But Frye knows better and on occasion will permit himself a remark *aparté* that gives it all away. For example, this one:

> All verbal structures with meaning are verbal imitations of that elusive psychological and physiological process known as thought.... Anyone who imagines that philosophy is not a verbal imitation of this process, but the process itself, clearly has not done much thinking.[8]

Encouraged by this and by many other such *obiter dicta* systematically disseminated throughout the *Anatomy*, I can imagine how a philosophical notion might trace its path along the sequence of Frye's historical modes. I take, not quite at random, the notion of truth.

The notion of truth most favored by philosophers—almost the only notion of truth that is even discussed by recent Anglo-American philosophers—is the notion that truth is the correspondence of symbols (mental or verbal) with reality (matters of fact or states of affairs). Whatever its intrinsic merits, it is fairly clear that the correspondence theory of truth reflects a commitment to low mimetic conventions of writing. Truth means the representation of things just as they are, where "things as they are" means nature and society as directly given to our awareness.

The second most popular theory of truth (in the West, at least) is the coherence theory. On this view truth is the coherence of all propositions in a systematic totality, and a true proposition is one that coheres within such a totality. The coherence theory is often adopted because of an apparently insuperable difficulty in the correspondence view. The trouble with correspondence is that we can never distinguish things themselves from our ways of symbolizing them, since we only have access to things as already symbolized. There is no meaningful sense in which indistinguishables can be said to correspond. Reality cannot be distinguished from knowledge; therefore, truth is not the correlation of symbols with unsymbolized reality, but simply the coherence of all symbols (=realities) in a totality.

Since, on this view, reality itself is taken to be an ideal structure, the coherence theory of truth reflects a commitment to the conventions of the high mimetic mode. Truth is the conformity of thought and language, not to the facts of quotidian experience, but to a higher and (of course) more rational order of things. As the correspondence theory is commonly held by empiricists, so the coherence view is almost universally favored by idealists.

These are only the most widely held and generally debated theories of truth in recent Western philosophy. There are other theories of truth adapted to other conventions of representation. For example, all classical theologians will affirm the proposition, "God is truth." Theologians of different times and persuasions qualify this statement in different ways. But at bottom the "is" of "God is truth" is the "is" of identity, and "God is truth" is a proposition in the mythic mode.

Opposite the metaphoric identification of God and truth is the skeptical doctrine that truth is unattainable or the nihilistic doctrine that there is no such thing as truth. Views of this sort are patently ironic. As is also Nietzsche's

suggestion that truth is a woman who will not allow herself to be possessed—
or violated—by dogmatic philosophers; or his other suggestion that truth is
no more than the system of conventional lies (he calls them metaphors)
honored by a society and necessary to its survival.[9] Romantic theories of
truth are a bit harder to track down, lurking as they do in the crannies of the
tradition. There is an element of romance in any philosophy (usually it's a
form of idealism) in which truth is offered as the term of a heroic intellectual
quest. For example, in Hegel's *Phenomenology*, where truth *an und für
sich* is achieved only at the cost of the struggles, the sufferings, and the
eventual triumph of the Absolute Spirit. In the more high-minded kinds of
pragmatism, where truth is the goal of inquiry, and in the more pragmatic
forms of idealism—e.g., the philosophy of Josiah Royce, in which the
ultimate value is "loyalty to loyalty"—truth is conceived in accord with the
conventions of romance.[10] (Ordinary forms of pragmatism, or the low-
minded part of any pragmatism, tend to rewrite the coherence theory in
terms of low-mimetic conventions—and to insist that it is really a version
of correspondence. Pragmatism after all is just idealism naturalized and
brought down to earth: transcendentalism for the preterite.)

Kierkegaard's proclamation that "subjectivity is truth" is romantic in
one of its meanings but ironic in others.[11] Likewise romantic is the exhortation
to seek truth not in the conformity of one's propositions to fact but in the
fidelity of one's life to the sources and powers of one's own being, or to
some paradigm of humanity. Truth in the sense of authenticity is perhaps
the most recent attempt to rehabilitate romance, a reconstruction already
under attack by the forces of deconstruction.

One could rewrite the history of philosophy from this perspective by
incongruity. But even this all-too-brief review indicates that one can find,
several times over in the course of Western thought, theories of truth
answering to all the modes of fiction. And (though I have not tried to show
this, I think it could be shown) they arrange themselves in historical
sequences, with a historicity at least as precise as Frye's. This should not be
surprising, in view of the fact that the philosophical presentation of truth
and the literary production of narrative are both ways of representing reality.
In the case of literature, Frye says that life and thought are only the content
of the work, whereas its form is wholly a product of the conventions of
representation. But surely the same is true (whatever that means) of
philosophy, insofar as "Nothing built out of words can transcend the nature
and conditions of words, and…the nature and conditions of *ratio*, so far as
ratio is verbal, are contained by *oratio*."[12] Philosophical and literary

techniques of mimesis are alike verbal and therefore alike subjected to the modalities of representation and the law of their sequentiality.

In the formula of St. Hilary of Poitiers, quoted throughout the Middle Ages, truth is "declarative being."[13] For all philosophers, including the skeptic, truth as the manifestation of reality is something to be acknowledged, lived by, and revered. That is almost a definition of philosophy. And for that reason the primordial designation of truth would be the mythic identity, "God is truth." Or, since identity converts *simpliciter*, "truth is God." All other accounts of truth—romantic, high mimetic, low mimetic, and ironic—would be, Fryewise, displacements of this original metaphor in the interest of greater credibility, rationality, and responsibility. It is also worth noting that just as irony among the literary modes turns back into myth , bending the sequence into a circle, so there is a cycle in theories of truth. Skepticism has flourished during at least two periods in the history of Western Philosophy: once at the end of the ancient world, and once again at the end of the Middle Ages. In both cases the victimization of truth by skepticism was associated with a reassertion (more or less ironic in tone) of the rights of religious faith. In Fathers like Tertullian and Augustine, and in philosophers like Hume and Kierkegaard. Even in Nietzsche, though the myth that is resurrected out of Nietzsche's vision of nihilism is no more pure Christian than it is pure Dionysian.

The appearance in this list of a belated thinker like Nietzsche betrays the fact (which I could scarcely conceal) that skepticism has visited Western philosophy a third time: at the end of the modern world, among those upon whom (as we so often feel) the ends of the world itself are come. This third advent of skepticism—represented perhaps by this discussion—seems to argue for another and more devastating kind of irony. An irony that may not be the unwitting agent of the cunning of myth. An irony more Burkean than Northropian, because it is an irony over the whole project of philosophy.

What am I doing in this text if not standing back in ironic detachment from the whole history of philosophy (to which I am at the same time a miniscule amendment) and suggesting (ironically indeed, in view of the passion for truth by which philosophers have always been driven) that we regard the story of the philosophical search for truth as a merry-go-round of the modes of intellectual mimesis? A merry-go-round, perhaps, without a brass ring. A Burkean dialogue in which everyone gets to speak his piece, but in which no one has the last word. In which there is no last word, just more words. The final and apparently unredeemable irony would be to detach the question of the philosophy of truth from the question of the truth of philosophy.

Of course it might be argued (I am again following a clue from Frye) that my view of philosophy is guilty of a fatal perspectival fault. I may be taken to have suggested that philosophy is nothing but a kind of poetry. But that, it will be objected, is absolutely the wrong slant on this thing. Frye points out that every literary work in whatever mode projects a metaphysic appropriate to that mode.[14] For example, myth projects a theological world view as its *mise en scéne*, high mimesis projects a form of Platonic idealism, low mimesis naturalism, romance a world of fantasy, and irony something like existentialism. But these are only functions of particular literary forms. If you're writing a low mimetic novel, you need to locate the action in a naturalistic world, whereas tragedy requires something like the rational order of nature for its setting. And so on. It would be a fallacy—Frye calls it the fallacy of existential projection—to infer from this that every poet himself is taken in by it. The world view of the poet is part of his formal achievement, not a philosophical content recommended for our belief.

Frye's argument is easily converted. Every philosophy (it might be said) discovers a literary form appropriate to its statement. Plato wrote dialogues for the same reason that Descartes wrote meditations, Hume essays, and Nietzsche aphorisms. The form matched the content and served the purpose. But it would be a *non sequitur* to conclude from this that philosophy is poetry. Perhaps we should call this the fallacy of hypothetical retrojection or aesthetic subjection. A whole clutch of mouth-filling neologisms rise in the throat.

However, it is not my intention to argue that philosophy is only (or really) poetry, any more than I suppose poetry to be philosophy. On the contrary, what I mean to do is blur all such distinctions, compromise all such discriminations, and thereby evacuate all facile identifications. My point is to suggest that categories like "philosophy" and "poetry" are essentially metastable, just as Hayden White has shown that the category "history" is pretty shifty. More to the point, I think that "philosophy" (as the custodian of necessary truth) and "poetry" (as the superintendent of possibility and/or the purveyor of lying fables) are not baskets into which all verbal objects may be dropped, but the terms of an uncertain and restless dialectic. A dialectic which we have reason to think constitutes the nature of language itself. If language is the house of being, it is also a house of mirrors.

Be that as it may (to quote one of my favorite disclaimers), it might still be protested that my ironizing over philosophy is superfluously pretentious or at least belatedly valedictorian. For as we all know, nobody—not even the philosophers themselves—any longer thinks of philosophy as the bastion of truth.

That may be the case. I doubt it, but it may be the case anyway. But if it is the case, it is not so for the reason that is usually alleged. Namely, that truth has passed from the keeping of Dame Philosophy, who was far too casual and compromised a guardian, into the hands of her more responsible children, the sciences. The natural sciences, first of all, but also those behavioral sciences which with diligence, hard work, good behavior, and a bit of luck may some day become natural. The hard sciences, and those that are doing their best to stiffen up.

This, I think, will not do. Because, to cite only one reason, too many remnants of myth are already at work forming those theories in which the sciences presume to enshrine the truth. The truth of science itself is shaped around a fiction or two, including the fiction of its own truthfulness.

A single gross instance will suggest the sort of thing I have in mind. Evolutionary theory, though it may be supported by factual evidence, is motivated by the need for a myth of origins. At its first emergence and beyond, the theory of evolution, like the speculative cosmologies occasionally perpetrated by theoretical physicists, told a tale of beginnings designed (more or less consciously) to replace the discredited story in *Genesis*. (It is true that the theory of evolution helped to discredit the creation myth, but it is also the case that the theory of evolution was attractive because a lot of people no longer wanted to believe the Bible. More of this duplicity later.) Theological opponents of evolution argued that the facts adduced by evolutionists as evidence for their theory—all those bones and fossils and strange survivors—had been planted by the devil to expose unbelievers and trap the unwary. The theologians' claim was mocked by the advocates of natural selection. But their raillery was not justified by any fault in the fundamentalists' logic. The theologians' reasoning, given their premises, was flawless. The target of the evolutionists' attack was the whole theological *story* about man and the world, a story that had become ridiculously implausible to right-thinking (i.e., scientifically minded) people long before evolution provided them with an alternate account of the *arche*. The theory of evolution did not simply replace a theological fiction with a scientific truth. It substituted for the relatively pure religious myth of beginnings a low-mimetically displaced form of that same narrative. The question of the "truth" of evolution vs. the "truth" of *Genesis* can be raised, if at all, only in the context of a consciousness of their common mythic motive. (I almost said "their common mythic origin.")

The point of all this is not to badmouth any scientific theory nor to resuscitate fundamentalism, but only to suggest that if philosophy is no longer the guardian of truth, it is not because her care and feeding have been taken over by the sciences, who know how to treat her right. For the sciences themselves are entangled in the same dialectic of displacements—the same uneasy cohabitation of truth and fiction—as philosophy, poetry, and history. And if neither philosophy nor science any longer has secure dominion over truth, it is not because these disciplines have forfeited their right to such dominion by philandering with myth and fable. If the parents and guardians are corrupt, it may be a corruption owed to the delinquency of their child and ward.

It is useful to ask ourselves what we mean by truth. More exactly, what is the significance of our desire for truth? What is it we want when we want truth? St. Anselm of Canterbury, in one of the most spectacular *tours de force* in Western philosophy, his *Dialogus de Veritate*, begins with the correspondence theory of truth, which all of us accept as a rule of thumb in daily life, and tries to translate it by a series of equipollent substitutions into the proposition Christians hold by faith, "God is truth."[15] In this way he both finds necessary reasons for an article of faith (his theological program) and returns a low mimetic displacement to metaphoric identity with its mythic Origin. The nerve of his argument is the contention that truth, even in the low mimetic sense of correspondence, has gerundive force. A proposition, whether or not it conforms to fact, is still a proposition: a genuine predication, hence a real proposition, truly a proposition, and in that sense a true proposition. But in fact we call a proposition true in the fullest sense only if it represents things as they are. "Elephants are a species of fish," though truly a proposition, is not what we would call a true proposition.

Propositions, Anselm says, are under obligation to tell the truth in the sense of correspondence. Truth is to be told. It is, in the pale vocable of modern logic, a "value." Verbal symbols are bound by their nature to faithful representation. To use symbols so as not to tell the truth is an abuse of discourse. Frustrating the purpose for which speech was created, failure of correspondence is a moral fault and an offense against God.

The interesting and perhaps unique feature of Anselm's dialogue is that it raises and tries to resolve a question not even imagined by most of those who profess a passion for truth. The question, namely, Why do we care about truth? Anselm defines truth as the rectitude of the mind (it is the intellectual counterpart of justice, the rectitude of the will) and implies that what we seek when we seek truth is an uprightness in our relationship to God. In a word: righteousness.

However one judges Anselm's claim, it is a fact that philosophers have always had an almost religious horror of skepticism. St. Augustine, whose capacity for religious horror was boundless, confronted the skeptic with the following *reductio*. If the proposition "there is no truth" is true, then there *is* truth. That one at least. So there. If you say you have discovered that truth cannot be discovered, then you are saying you have discovered a *truth*[16]. Similar discomforts attend other notions of truth. The coherence theory, which drops the question of reality altogether or sublates it without remainder into the web of belief, has always seemed a bit like cheating. And the pragmatist who never ceases to tell us, Wait just a little longer, appears to be temporizing in matters that demand decision.

The passion for truth, like the passion for mimesis, is a passion for reality. All definitions of truth, as Aquinas observes, invoke the name of correspondence.[17] Every truth is an allegory of *adaequatio*. But our concern to make words correspond to reality is, I believe, a soteriological impulse. The passion for correspondence is, more or less displaced, a passion for salvation. That is: a desire for the reunion of verbal signs with that being of which their being is the alienation.

Perhaps we should call this desire to reappropriate the alienated a rhetorical passion, since rhetoric, according to Burke, is the attempt to achieve in language the consubstantialization of terms (radically language and being) which are originally, in and by language, transsubstantiated.[18] But whatever we call it, the passion for truth is plainly a paradoxical passion. For (this too in the name of Burke) at the same time that it desires a reunion of signs with reality, it presupposes a distinction between being and the signs by which we purport to represent it. The sign can be sign only as and by virtue of its difference from reality. Perhaps I should have written "differance." For it is also the case that reality is not the reality desired by the desire for truth unless it is a reality not already alienated in the sign. The passion for truth— this is the source of its intensity and its poignancy—at once presumes the diremption of word and thing and longs to repair it. Therefore, the acquisition of truth (in the sense of correspondence) would frustrate the desire for truth (for the reunion of sign and reality) in the very act of gratifying it: the truth of correspondence iterates the difference that the passion for union craves to obliterate. And conversely, the achievement (*sit venia verbo*) of a real union of sign and being would efface the difference between them that motivates the search for truth and makes it possible in the first place: the solution would destroy the problem. The original differance (the silent "a" is now a necessity) of sign and signified both generates the passion for recuperation and indefinitely defers its satisfaction.

Therefore skepticism, which tries to quell the desire for truth rather than gratify it, only outrages the passion and prompts refutations of the sort

Augustine offered: an epistemological return of the repressed, in which the reality of truth returns as the truth of the assertion that there is no truth. The achievement of truth in the sense of coherence, which abrogates any distinction of sign and reality, also annuls (this is why coherence has always seemed too facile to be true) the difference of (self) consciousness by which the notion of truth is constituted and truth itself made desirable. Truth as the object of a romantic quest postpones gratification so perfectly that it never comes at all. Pragmatism, whatever its other virtues, doesn't work.

It is the paradoxical essence of the passion for truth itself, not the historical fact of the supercession of philosophy by the sciences, that calls into question the claim of philosophy (or any other discipline) to be the inventor and purveyor of truth. Truth, it appears, does not subsist, but only stands—or rather: perpetually recedes—as the term of a desire that can never be satisfied and never quenched. The impasse, we have been led to believe, lies in the nature of the linguistic sign and its relation to extra-linguistic reality. Unless the sign in some way participates the reality it signifies, it cannot do its job, which is to mediate cognition of the thing signified. But sign and thing signified cannot be identical, for in that case there would be no sign distinct from the thing signified and so, once again, no cognition of the thing mediated by the sign. In order to do what it is supposed to do the sign must be both the same as and different from the thing it stands for. The signified is both implicated in the sign (to be a sign is to signify the signified) and ontically-epistemically distinct from it (so that no sign is sufficiently motivated by its signified). These are the conditions which must, impossibly, be met in order for truth to occur.

Therefore, when we *are* offered truth, we are asked to accept either a symbolic representation of reality so fragile and precarious that it does not quiet our desire (the contingent truths fostered by low mimetic correspondence) or an identity of symbol and reality so faultless that it severs the root of our desire (the necessary truths enunciated by high mimetic coherence) or an indefinite postponement of the advent of truth that sets us on pins and needles forever (the romance of pragmatism) or a divorce of symbol and reality so final that it bids us to be satisfied with frustration as a matter of principle (the ironic renunciations and jejune abstentions of skepticism). What we really want is the metaphoric confusion of identity and difference: God, who is Truth Itself because his intellect and his essence, rationally distinct, are ontologically one (*differunt ratione, subjecto idem*). But that, it appears, *is* a myth.

I have suggested that the many theories of truth advocated by philosophers may be conceived as displacements, in Frye's sense, of an original mythic identity of sign and signified. But of course myth—and its equivalent opposite, irony—are never actually given in their putative purity. The most primitive and unitive kind of discourse is no longer myth, and the most sophisticated and fragmented specimen of language is not yet irony. All actual discourse converges toward romance, high mimesis, and low mimesis, in all of which the distinction of symbol and reality is preserved, and in all of which truth is sought as a relation of the two. How we conceive of truth and truthful discourse depends on how we imagine the human condition. But in any estimate of our situation the distinction of symbol and reality is presumed. That is the condition of estimation. And imagination. For pure myth (identity without difference) and pure irony (difference without identity) would be wordless, and therefore beyond the distinction of truth and falsity. Mysticism and a world perfectly deconstructed would, equivalently and equivocally, solve the problem of truth by eliminating it. They would be, if they were possible at all, not solutions but dissolutions.

Implicit in the passion for truth in all its forms is the nostalgia for a mythical Eden in which symbol and reality were not yet disconnected, a prelapsarian state in which the symbol-using animal had not yet fallen out of harmony with being and with itself, but was still one and at one with all that is. Every religion postulates such a paradise lost and nurtures the expectation of paradise regained. Religion itself, which is close to the (alleged) mythic sources of human thought and feeling, is the soteriological trajectory from paradise lost to paradise regained along some revealed axis of redemption. Our closest approximation to the purity of myth itself, religion is, mythopoetically and mythomorphically, the myth of myth.

That is why I propose that we regard the passion for truth as a displacement of the soteriological impulse natural to religion and originating in myth. Truth is salvation removed from the quasi-mythic categories of religion into the alienated categories of historical humanity. As the quest for salvation is an attempt to recover original righteousness, so the search for truth (in Burke's sense of the word, a rhetorical project) is an attempt to recover being, to reinstate reality in our alienated symbols. A projection from myth to myth, nostalgia protended as apocalypse, philosophy, which originates (historically) as a critique of myth (the religion promulgated by the old Greek poets), is a strategy of salvation: a displaced redemption myth.

But not philosophy only. Any discourse that aims at the discovery of truth, or for that matter any discourse that disavows this purpose, falls under the same judgment. It may be appropriate here to return to Aristotle's distinction of philosophy, poetry, and history. From what has been said we might extrapolate that philosophy, poetry, and history are the conceptual, imaginative, and narrative forms, respectively, of a single myth of redemption. Philosophy essays the recuperation of being conceptually and in the mode of necessity. Poetry, always the most disillusioned of these enchantments, endeavors to redeem the symbol imaginatively and in the mode of possibility. (Poetry is "most disillusioned" because it is always conscious of and so never convinced by its own fabrications.) And history, speaking narratively in the mode of actuality, has always contended (in one way or another) that the story of the world is the justification of the world. Otherwise, why write it? Derrida has observed, laconically but astutely, that history "has always been conceived as the movement of a resumption of history, a diversion between two presences."[19] Or even more pointedly, apropos of my argument here, "history and knowledge, *istoria* and *episteme* have always been determined...as detours *for the purpose of* the reappropriation of presence."[20] Western historiography, from *The City of God* down to Hegel and beyond, has always been the most direct transcription of the prototypical Western redemption myth. Every version of Western history is a revisionary displacement of the story told in the Old and New Testaments: the original, total, and final story of the world, from its beginning at the creation, through its redemption in the fullness of time, to its ultimate restoration in the last day.

Unfortunately, there's a catch to all this. When I say that the desire for truth is a displaced soteriological passion and the definition of truth a transportation of the metaphor of redemption into the categories of diremption, I iterate the displacement in reverse. Having drawn the signifieds of philosophy, poetry, and history into the play of signifiers, I reinvest these (my "own") signifiers with the authority of a transcendental signified. I valorize my "own" miniscule amendment. That is, I have (once more with feeling) posited myth itself as the transcendent origin and the inner substance of both truth and (my "own" contribution) the truth about truth. I might now try to displace *that* move. But what would be—what has always already been—the source of the displacement? Either it comes from within the myth that is proposed as the undisplaced origin, or it comes from a source outside of myth. If it comes from within, then myth itself is always already fractured, tending to diaspora, and not the seamless unity demanded by the use of "displacement" as a category of explanation. If it comes from without, then the supposed mythic unity is not the comprehensive origin it must be in order for the explanatory strategy of displacement to work. In either case, myth is (must be, in order for displacement to "occur" at all) aboriginally displaced from/within the cause of its own displacement.[21]

Is displacement something that happens to an original myth? Or is myth something that happens in and by reason of the original non-originality of displacement? Is myth itself a myth? Is the origin an origin, or is origin itself a retrojection from an always already prior "condition" of ab-originality? Is the center a fiction of the periphery? And is our nostalgia a sign of paradisal beginnings, or only a symptom of our always already alienation?

Philosophy is, historically, a dialectical critique of religion which proposes to restate the content of myth in the form of truth. But the "content of myth" is a piece of philosophical mythopoeia and the "form of truth" a philosophical mythomorph. The philosophical critique deconstructs its attempt to reconstruct a viable redemption myth. As the prophetic bard knows that his vatic insights are also lying fables, and as the historian, perpetually recasting *Heilsgeschichte* as *Weltgeschichte*, is also always profaning the shrines at which he worships, so the philosopher's fictions undermine the truth they sustain. Philosophers, poets, and historians are all language-users (or in the more accurate phrase of James Branch Cabell's Queen Freydis, "used by language"[22]), and for that reason they are and can only be their own worst enemies. That is part of what it means to be (one last Aristotelian tag) *zoon logon echon*. The unexamined life is not worth living...and barely viable.

A paragraph back I asked a lot of embarrassing questions. The point of this excursion is just to make these questions questionable. As Derrida observes in an essay from which I have already quoted, it is not possible—or even meaningful—to align oneself with either of the alternatives apparently opposed by such questions.[23] For the language in which we are destined to think these options also requires that we embrace, ambiguously, both of them.

At the beginning of this paper I have placed two mottoes. Both of them are, I think, necessarily true. Or if you will, matters of fact. At the very least, worth pretending. There is no question of a choice between them.

II

4

Anatomical Curiosities:
Northrop Frye's Theory of Criticism

Begin with the title: *Anatomy of Criticism.* "Anatomy" is a genre term. As Frye defines it, it identifies a

> form of prose fiction, traditionally known as the Menippean or Varronian satire and represented by Burton's *Anatomy of Melancholy*, characterized by a great variety of subject-matter and a strong interest in ideas. (365)[1]

Suppose the *Anatomy* to be an anatomy. In that case it will be a form of prose fiction, a kind of satire encompassing a vast and diverse subject-matter and much concerned with ideas.

There is no question about the subject-matter and the ideas. Frye's book is crammed with both. But it might be worthwhile to ask what it means to think of the *Anatomy* as a satirical fiction.

I

In his Polemical Introduction Frye remarks that

> just as there is nothing which the philosopher cannot consider philosophically, and nothing which the historian cannot consider historically, so the critic should be able to construct and dwell in a conceptual universe of his own. (12)

Leaving the historian to his own devices, I infer from this that I am free to consider the *Anatomy* a philosophical text and interpret it accordingly. And also that I may regard it as part of that conceptual universe which this book of criticism constructs. (Or begins to construct. Frye's claims for his own achievement are systematically modest, and this is a matter of no small importance.) The intersection of these two readings—philosophical and critical—is a locus of eventualities.

In the Fourth Essay—his theory of genres—Frye says that the anatomy is "fiction but not a novel." (308) For "Menippean satire deals less with people as such than with mental attitudes." People "are handled in terms of their occupational approach to life as distinct from their social behavior." The satire's characterization "is stylized rather than naturalistic, and presents people as mouthpieces of the ideas they represent." (Like most attempts at philosophical dialogue since Plato.) And most significantly, perhaps, this:

> The novelist sees evil and folly as social diseases, but the Menippean satirist sees them as diseases of the intellect, as a kind of maddened pedantry which the *philosophus gloriosus* at once symbolizes and defines. (309)

"At its most concentrated the Menippean satire presents us with a vision of the world in terms of a single intellectual pattern." Either " entirely fantastic or entirely moral" or some "combination of fantasy and morality," the anatomy locates its "dramatic interest…in a conflict of ideas rather than of character." (310)

In the first instance "anatomy" means "dissection" or "dismemberment for purposes of analysis." The verbal anatomist,

> dealing with intellectual themes and attitudes, shows his exuberance in intellectual ways, by piling up an enormous mass of erudition about his theme or in overwhelming his pedantic targets with an avalanche of their own jargon. (311)

Not surprisingly, in the light of these observations, it

> is the anatomy in particular that has baffled critics, and there is hardly any fiction writer [hardly any critic?] deeply influenced by it who has not been accused of disorderly conduct. (313)

By calling itself an anatomy Frye's book classifies itself with works like these. Paradigmatically, Burton's *Anatomy of Melancholy*. But also *Gulliver's Travels, Emile, Candide, The Way of All Flesh, Point Counter Point, Brave New World, Gargantua and Pantagruel, The Water-Babies, The Consolation of Philosophy*, and *Tristram Shandy*. As well as many, many others. Anyone who can perceive the generic identity of Boethius and Sterne should have no trouble classifying the *Anatomy* as an intellectual fiction packed with erudition and serving a satirical purpose. Strange that so many readers have taken it as a straightforward statement of a scientific theory of criticism.

The "intellectual" is obvious enough. What about the "fiction"? The book opens with a Polemical Introduction. The figure itself is mildly paradoxical, tending to oxymoron. The one thing you don't do in an *exordium*, if you've conned your *Rhetoric*, is pick a fight. Hardly a *captatio benevolentiae*, the language (and not only the language) that follows (and not only in the Introduction) is satirical. More than once it seems to comment ironically on itself.

Yet the purpose of the work, as propounded in the Introduction, is anything but satiric. Or so it appears. Frye expresses a desire to make criticism a science: the science of literature, as physics is the science of nature. That presumes a concern for truth. As physics is the conceptual structure which corresponds to nature, so criticism should be the conceptual correlate of literature. To aspire to the condition of science is to aspire to systematic verity.

But the explication of this project—to raise criticism to the dignity of cognition—requires of Frye a rather large assumption. He calls it a "hypothesis," but since it cannot be tested by the critical methodology it makes possible, it is not a hypothesis but a presupposition. The presupposition, namely that "just as there is an order of nature behind the natural sciences, so literature is not just a piled aggregate of 'works,' but an order of words." (17) That is most unusual and not at all self-evident. The demotion of "aggregate" in favor of "order" flies in the face of an almost universal supposition that literature, as opposed to the routine and law-governed operations of nature, flows unpredictably from the boundless spontaneity of the imagination...and is therefore unorderable by any principle. Frye himself allows that, while the physical sciences might exhaust their subject-matter, "the search for a limiting principle in literature in order to discourage [not the production of literature or the expansion of the imagination, but] the development of criticism is mistaken." (17)

What an order might be without a limiting principle I do not know. It is evident in any case that Frye's "hypothesis" is a fiction. The "order of words" postulated here is more or less identical with what is called, in the Second Essay, the literary "monad." (115-122) In the later setting it is even more clearly an imaginative rather than a cognitive necessity.

To demand that criticism become a science privileges the quest for truth. But that science and its truth are built on a fiction. Perhaps that is part of what it means to call this book an anatomy; i.e., an intellectual fiction.

Another duality comprehended in the notion of anatomy is the duality of fantasy and morality. Menippean satire is said to be sometimes purely moral, sometimes purely fantastic, sometimes an amalgam of both. *A propos*, two passages from the Introduction:

> There are no definite positions to be taken in chemistry or philology, and if there are any to be taken in criticism, criticism is not a field of genuine learning. For in any field of genuine learning, the only sensible response to the challenge "stand" is Falstaff's "so I do, against my will." One's "definite position" is one's weakness, the source of one's liability to error and prejudice, and to gain adherents to a definite position is only to multiply one's weakness like an infection. (19)

> ...[C]riticism has no business to react against things, but should show a steady advance toward undiscriminating catholicity. (25)

The tone of these passages is decidedly moral. But their intent is to exclude from criticism the value judgments impertinent to scientific inquiry. This is a notorious and often (if not often usefully) debated aspect of Frye's theory of criticism. But what is the valor of this value-laden prohibition of evaluations? What is the point, other than to raise the dust, of thus sweeping out the interpreter's parlor in the spirit of the law? (29)

The "catholicity" with which the last citation concludes is glossed by the words that follow:

> The dialectic axis of criticism, then, has as one pole the total acceptance of the data of literature, and as the other the total acceptance of the potential values of those data. This is the real level of culture and of liberal education, the fertilizing of life by learning, in which the systematic progress of scholarship flows into a systematic progress of taste and understanding. (25)

It is not far from here to the conclusion of *The Educated Imagination*, a reduction *pro populo* of the argument of the *Anatomy*:

> But now that we've discovered that the imaginative world and the world around us are different worlds, and that *the imaginative world is more important*, we have to take one more step. The society around us looks

like the real world, but we've just seen that there's a great deal of illusion in it, the kind of illusion that propaganda and slanted news and prejudice and a great deal of advertising appeal to. For one thing, as we've been saying, it changes very rapidly, and people who don't know of any other world can never understand what makes it change. If our society in 1962 is different from what it was in 1942, it can't be real society, but only a temporary appearance of real society. And just as it looks real, so *this ideal world that our imaginations develop inside us looks like a dream that came out of nowhere, and has no reality except what we put into it. But it isn't. It's the real world*, the real form of human society hidden behind the one we see.[2]

That (which comes from a chapter entitled *via* St. John Perse "The *Vocation of Eloquence*" (my emphasis)) suggests a union of morality and fantasy, not to mention a "vision of the world in terms of a single intellectual pattern." (310) It sounds like evangelical Romanticism or wishful Platonism. But all of these—the vision and the union, the affirmation of all the data and all their powers: undiscriminating catholicity—are, in another mode, attributes of anatomy.

If this is satire, who or what is it aimed at? Put otherwise, what is the status of all the dualities that surface in Frye's account of anatomy: science vs. fiction, morality vs. fantasy, the mass of real or professed erudition vs. the interest in ideas, the relentless analysis vs. the single intellectual pattern? Are these dichotomies? Contradictions? Or are they polarities to be dialectically resolved? In *A Study of English Romanticism* Frye writes:

Poetic thinking, being mythical, does not distinguish or create antitheses: it goes on and on, linking analogy to analogy, identity to identity, and containing, without trying to refute, all opposition and objection. This means, not that it is merely facile or liquid thinking without form, but that it is the dialectic of love: it treats whatever it encounters as another form of itself.[3]

Is the *Anatomy of Criticism* the dialectic of love? Or is it, as anatomy is often said to be, just "disorderly conduct?" (313) "It treats whatever it encounters as another form of itself." Is that love...or narcissism?

The radical question is the question of the relationship between truth and fiction. Wallace Stevens wrote: "In the long run the truth does not matter."[4] "Our own time," he declared, "is a time in which the search for the supreme truth has been a search in reality or through reality or even a search for some supremely acceptable fiction."[5] More emphatically:

We have been a little insane about the truth. We have had an obsession. In
its ultimate extension, the truth about which we have been insane will lead
us to look beyond the truth to something in which the imagination will be
the dominant complement.[6]

What would it be like to imagine truth in terms of fiction?

II

In the beginning Frye says that his work consists of essays (trials, incomplete
attempts) on the possibility of a synoptic view of criticism. He wants to
offer reasons for holding such a view and to provide a tentative version
sufficient to persuade his reader that such a synopsis is possible. But he
acknowledges (his detractors have often ignored the disclaimer) that his
work is full of gaps, and that what he has produced is "an interconnected
group of suggestions" rather than a system, the effect of the mind's free
play about a subject much discussed but little understood.

Having thus understated his accomplishment beforehand Frye defines
criticism as "the whole work of scholarship and taste concerned with
literature." So defined, criticism is an essential part of liberal education,
culture, or the study of the humanities. The subject of literary criticism is an
art, and criticism is "evidently something of an art too." (3) But there is a
difference. "Criticism can talk, and all the arts"—including the art of
literature—"are dumb." (4) It is an axiom of criticism that the poet, who
may know what he is talking about, "cannot talk about what he knows."
Literature is distinguished (in the Second Essay) from that kind of descriptive
or assertive writing which derives from the reason and the will and which is
primarily concerned to say something. But criticism is (descriptively and
assertively) "a structure of thought and knowledge existing in its own right,
with some measure of independence of" literature. (5) Criticism is based on
"what the whole of literature actually does." It deals with literature in terms
of a "specific conceptual framework." But the framework is not that of
literature, nor is it something outside literature. It is difficult to imagine
what is left after these negations. But they must be made, otherwise "the
autonomy of criticism would…disappear." (6)

Criticism, which is a kind of art, must also be a science. As such it
cannot be parasitic on literature nor reducible to some other discipline. Its
autonomy is the guarantee of its scientific character. And yet the conceptual
framework of criticism derives from "an inductive survey of the literary
field." (7)

The uncertain relationship between criticism and literature frames the question about the ratio of truth to fiction in the science/art of criticism as Frye conceives it. To be a science and to deliver the truth about its subject-matter, the structure of criticism must correspond to the structure of literature. But in order for criticism to enjoy the autonomy necessary to science, it must have its own structure, which is not that of literature: a fiction of its own.

A bit farther on Frye says that the first question for the student of literature to answer is, What follows from the fact that criticism is possible? (10) What follows is, in the first place, that there is no "direct learning of literature itself." (11) One may learn about literature from criticism. But one does not learn literature. All that can be directly taught and learned is criticism. Just as one studies not nature but physics, so one studies not literature but criticism. Not the thing itself, but its signs. For criticism "is to art what history is to action and philosophy to wisdom: a verbal imitation of a human productive power which in itself does not speak." (12)

But what is the relationship between the loquacious imitation and the speechless power? Immediately after the sentence on imitation Frye states his conviction that "the critic should be able to construct and dwell in a conceptual universe of his own." (12) That is: the relationship between literature and criticism is defined paradoxically. Criticism is about literature and derives inductively from it. Yet the critic builds and inhabits a universe all his own. And the only thing he can teach—the only thing we can learn—is not literature, but criticism.

I am not suggesting that there are contradictions in Frye's account. Hunting contradictions is a tiresome sport, finding them a cheap and hollow victory. My inkling is—and the effect of its confirmation might be to render Frye immune to a lot of facile charges, including the charge of contradiction—that the relation between criticism and literature is, on his own showing, ironic.

In criticism one is always saying what one does not say and never talking about what one is talking about, so that criticism is the signifier of a signified which is never the content of its own signification. The relation "criticism: literature" is an indeterminable juxtaposition of derivation and detachment. In Frye's own terms (123, 116), it is an ironic metaphor, in which criticism is, literally and without benefit of predication, both a part of and apart from the corpus of literature.

Citing Bacon, Frye observes that every modern science has had to emerge from its primitive state of naive induction by taking a "leap, occupying a new vantage ground from which it can see its former data as things to be explained." (15) He thinks "it is time for criticism to leap to a new ground from which it can discover what the organizing or containing forms of its conceptual framework are." The first postulate of this leap is "the assumption of total coherence" in the subject-matter of criticism. (16) The critic must assume that literature may be seen "not only as complicating itself in time, but as spread out in conceptual space from some kind of center that criticism could locate." In words already quoted, "literature is not a piled aggregate of 'works,' but an order of words." (17)

In order for criticism to be a coherent structure, literature itself must be a structure the coherence of which is assured by its organization about a center. Only on this assumption can criticism progress as a systematic discipline must, for "whatever dithers or vacillates or reacts is merely leisure-class gossip." (18) Criticism has, Frye says (we have heard these words before), a dialectical axis strung between two poles. One—the historical pole—is the total acceptance of the data of literature. The other—the ethical, social, or cultural pole—is the total acceptance of the potential values of these data. By moving along this axis criticism achieves "undiscriminating catholicity," and advances culture and liberal education, "the fertilizing of life by learning, in which the systematic progress of scholarship flows into a systematic progress of taste and understanding." (25)

Well and good. But the problem is to locate the center of the order of words (literature) and the center around which (Frye himself suggests this mixture of metaphors) criticism revolves on the dialectical axis reaching from fact to value. And the place (if there is one) where these centers meet.

Late in the Introduction Frye identifies the direct experience of literature as "central to criticism, yet forever excluded from it." Criticism is excluded from this center because criticism "can account for it (the experience of literature) only in critical terminology, and that terminology can never recapture or include the original experience…. However disciplined by taste and skill, the experience of literature is, like literature itself, unable to speak." (27)

Criticism is a second-order reflective activity, founded upon a leap. It is thereby in principle alienated from the first order of immediacy—the immediate presence of literature to itself and to its reader—and can never recuperate this immediacy. Literature and the experience of literature are and remain without a voice. Criticism has a voice—it is in a sense all voice— but it can never say what it "means."

Frye adds: "The presence of incommunicable experience in the center of criticism will always keep criticism an art, as long as the critic recognizes that criticism comes out of it but cannot be built on it." (27-28) Criticism is a self-contained structure: an autonomous conceptual framework. And therefore centered: centered in literature and the experience of literature. But it is not built on that center. The center is and is not the origin. This peculiarity of the center of criticism—that it both is and is not a center—destructures the structure of criticism…and keeps it an art. That is: makes it ironic in relation to its own sources and its own claims.

The center of criticism is the center of literature: literature itself in its immediacy. From this center criticism is excluded. It is therefore alienated from its subject-matter and from itself at the same time. Criticism is truthful (scientific) only insofar as it is fictive (artful). Its truth is its supreme fiction. And its supreme irony.

The realization that criticism is ambiguously situated in its own project prepares the final irony of this text. These are the words with which Frye concludes his Polemical Introduction:

> The strong emotional repugnance felt by many critics toward any form of schematization in poetics is again the result of a failure to distinguish criticism as a body of knowledge from the direct experience of literature, where every act is unique, and classification has no place. Whenever schematization appears in the following pages, no importance is attached to the schematic form itself, which may be only the result of my own lack of ingenuity. Much of it, I expect, and in fact hope, may be mere scaffolding, to be knocked away when the building is in better shape. The rest of it belongs to the systematic study of the formal causes of art. (29)

A Derridean neographism locates the irony in Frye's theory of criticism. Criticism is said to center in the direct experience of literature. But it does not originate from this center. It originates on the other side of an inductive leap by which it opens between itself and literature a distance sufficient to guarantee its own autonomy. The center of criticism is a *différance*: a distinction from its subject-matter which perpetually defers the understanding of that subject-matter. In order to explain literature criticism must postulate a difference from literature that postpones the explanation indefinitely.

By a similar strategy criticism may be called the *supplément* of literature. On the one hand criticism completes literature and literary experience, makes good their deficiency by giving them the voice they lack. But at the same time it replaces literature and the experience of literature with itself. In lieu of these mute immediacies—"the precious portents of our own powers"[7]—it gives us the infinitely garrulous but always disconnected stream of critical discourse.

How much of the schematization of critical theory is scaffolding to be knocked away when the building begins to shape up? How much is an abiding part of the systematic study of the formal causes of art? What is this edifice supposed to be under construction? On what ground, other than differance and supplementarity, will it stand?

The relation, within the *Anatomy*, of the erudition with which it is replete and the abstraction with which it is fascinated is just the question of the scientific status of criticism. The question is raised by the ambiguous *rapport* of criticism to its source in literature and literary experience. Scientific criticism as Frye imagines it keeps turning back into an art. And the relationship of the scheme of categories to the the concrete literary detail is more like the relationship of a work of art to its sources than it is like the relationship of an hypothesis to the facts that suggest it and confirm it. That criticism is proposed as a science is itself an artful gesture. For which reason the book that makes this proposal bears the name and the nature of a work of literary art.

Of a genre, in fact, which the work itself, ironically, defines. Words like "science" and "system" together with all their forms and cognates and associates function in the *Anatomy* as rhetorical operators. They do not describe states of affairs or define essences. They appeal rather to a desire, point to a lack, mark out an absence yearning to be filled. And in this way, ironically, they circumscribe that locus of ironies which is criticism.

A parable of Frye's doctrine is found in the work he identifies as the type of all anatomies, Burton's *Anatomy of Melancholy*.[8] In the prefatory declaration entitled "Democritus Jr. to the Reader" the author is explaining, in his typically expansive and evasive way, why he calls himself after the famous philosopher. For one thing, he confesses that he like Democritus Senior suffers from melancholy. And then:

> ...Hippocrates relates...how...he found Democritus in his garden at Abdera, in the suburbs, under a shady bower, with a book on his knees, busy at his study, sometimes writing, sometimes walking. The subject of his book was melancholy and madness; about him lay the carcasses of many several beasts, newly by him cut up and anatomized; not that he did contemn God's creatures, as he told Hippocrates, but to find out the seat of this *atra bilis*, or melancholy, whence it proceeds, and how it was engendered in men's bodies, to the intent he might better cure it in himself, and by his writings and observations teach others how to prevent and avoid it.[9]

Not an atomist only, but an an-atomist as well, Democritus is a paragon of the Anatomical critic.

Superficially the targets of Frye's satire are the partial critics and the wrong-headed critics: those self-proclaimed arbiters of taste and assessors of literary merit whom, throughout his book, he roundly and openly derides. Deeper down, criticism itself is satirized. What is understated by Frye's irony and undercut by his satire is the critical project itself, as he defines it. Like Democritus anatomizing in order to cure himself, Frye is the subject of his own discourse. His work is, quite literally, an anatomy not of critics but of criticism.

III

In the First Essay of the *Anatomy* Frye suggests that myth is the primordial mode of discourse. In post-mythic discourse the metaphoric identities of myth are loosened and fragmented. Romance, high mimesis, low mimesis, and irony are displacements of myth, representations of its substance in other forms. In any mode of discourse, the content is always the content of myth. What is added by the mode itself is just a displacement of this content in response to stricter demands for credibility and moral responsibility. (51-52, 136-137, 365)

The source of these demands is problematic. It might be thought that they issue from the *episteme*, the reigning philosophy and science of the age. But the history of the *episteme* displays the same structures of displacement as the history of fiction and poetry.[10]

It is not difficult to imagine philosophical theories of truth arrayed like Frye's fictional and thematic modes. There is a mythic doctrine of truth ("God is Truth"), a romantic theory (truth as authenticity, fidelity to one's deep self or to some paradigm of humanity), a high mimetic theory (truth as coherence), a low mimetic theory (correspondence), and an ironic disclaimer (skepticism). Their order is roughly historical, and their successive emergences exhibit the same *ricorso* that Frye discovers in the modes of narrative. Just as irony if pushed far enough reverts to myth, so theories of truth tend to circle. The victimization of truth in skepticism is often associated with a reassertion, more or less ironic in tone, of the rights of religious faith: in Hume, for example, and in Kierkegaard, in fathers like Tertullian and in philosophers like Nietzsche.

For all theories, including the skeptical, truth is the manifestation of reality: "declarative being," in an early medieval formulation.[11] Truth is to be honored in thought, word, and deed: acknowledged, confessed, lived by, and reverenced. In the pale vocable of modern logic, truth is a "value." But in what might be supposed its original epiphany, truth is divine. All subsequent formulations would then be displacements of this tautology in the interests of superior intelligibility.

But what defines the terms and limits of intelligibility and prescribes the displacement of mythic identity into ever more discursive approximations and remotions? It does no good to appeal to the *epistemé:* this *is* the *epistemé.* Historically (by a historicity as good as Frye's, if not better) the *episteme* itself is a displacement of the substance of myth. Philosophy, science, and even theology emerge at the origins of Western thought as dialectical critiques of myth and mythic poetry: transformations of insights bungled or obscured or dissembled by myth into the "truer" propositions educed by logical analysis and experimental scrutiny. If anything poetry is older than the *episteme.* In any case philosophy and fiction are alternate types of mimesis, different ways of representing reality, and displacement is at least equiprimordial with the *episteme.* Both philosophy (with all its associates and progeny) and fiction (in all its forms) seem to be entangled in some larger dialectic of displacement, which motivates the alembications of both.

If the *episteme* itself—which both defines truth and is defined by the passion for truth—originates as a displacement of myth, then displacement cannot originate from the *episteme.* There is no undisplaced myth at the origin, else displacement were inexplicable. Either displacement would have to come from within myth, in which case myth would be already metastable, tending to dissolution, and not the simple unity demanded by Frye's theory. Or displacement would supervene from a cause outside of myth, in which case the original mythic unity would not be all-inclusive but would have the source of its partition external to itself. Displacement cannot be something that happens to myth. Rather, myth is something that happens in and by reason of displacement. Displacement is original, and myth a projection from the condition of fragmentation: a nostalgia and a hope generated if not nurtured by the experience of alienation.

On Frye's account of metaphor (122-125) what is identified in myth is only loosely linked in other "more realistic" conventions by such devices as analogy, simile, association, and juxtaposition. In an essay entitled "Myth, Displacement, and Fiction," published four years after the *Anatomy,* Frye remarks that the free imagination of the writer is chiefly inhibited by "the need to produce a credible or plausible story, to come to terms with things as they are" rather than portray them as he would like them to be.[12] Things as one would like them to be are the burden of myth, and so the writer with an eye to his credibility rejects myth. And yet myth is the only principle of literary structure he has, since life itself provides him with none. Therefore, "the result of turning one's back on explicit myth can only be the reconstructing of the same mythical patterns in more ordinary words."[13]

> To this indirect mythologizing I have elsewhere given the name of displacement. By displacement I mean the techniques a writer uses to make his story credible, logically motivated, or morally acceptable—lifelike, in short. I call it displacement for many reasons, but one is that fidelity to the credible is a feature of literature that can affect only content. Life presents a continuum, and a selection from it can only be what is called a *tranche de vie*: plausibility is easy to sustain, but except for death life has little to suggest in the way of plausible conclusions. And even a plausible conclusion does not necessarily round out a shape. The realistic writer soon finds that the requirements of literary form and plausible content always fight against each other.... Literary shape cannot come from life; it comes only from literary tradition, and so ultimately from myth.[14]

Whence Frye concludes that "literature is a reconstructed (displaced) mythology, with its structural principles derived from those of myth."[15]

The mechanism of displacement is absolutely crucial for Frye's theory of criticism. Only by invoking it can he argue that myth is the informing principle of all literature from the most fantastic to the most naturalistic. Only if this "adaptation of myth and metaphor to canons of morality or plausibility" occurs can myth be the *leitmotif* of criticism. (365)

Geoffrey Hartman, however, has voiced the suspicion that

> Frye has not shown that myth is displaced but that it is historical. It is never found in that unaccomodated state he posits when he mentions "the pure myth of death and revival" or when he claims that literature is a reconstructed mythology. One can make such a claim only by reducing myths to archetypes in the strictly Platonic sense of simples rather than complexes. But anyone who has read the *Anatomy* will agree that there are no simples in it.... We do not find myth pure of religion or literature; it comes to us institutionalized from the beginning, and, though it may also be a body of structural principles, there is no point in underplaying the war in the members of that body.... What is true of the realist is true of any writer, as Frye's own theory of displacement has shown: reality is never more than the plausible artifice. But in that case the notion of displacement becomes unnecessary except to indicate the direction of human credibility— credibility defining that realm in which contraries are no longer felt.[16]

Myth is never pure. It is institutionalized from the beginning, and from the beginning torn by inner conflict. Reality is the putative other than myth, alleged to constrain its free expansion in literary space. But reality is never more than plausible artifice, and credibility simply the realm in which the war of the contraries is not perceived as such.

Pure myth cannot exist. For if it does, it can never get displaced. If myth is simply one and perfectly self-contained, then it cannot be invaded by demands for rationality, verissimilitude, or morality. If such urgencies do present themselves—be their source either within or without the circle of myth—then, whether myth succumbs to their importunities or not, it shows itself inherently vulnerable. And its liability to corruption belies its supposed purity. " Myth" functions as a god-term in Frye's text. Like every god-term it remembers the restless stirrings of the dialectic that threw it up.

There is displacement at the heart of myth. The "myth" of Frye's theory is itself a fragment of mythology: a mythomorphic consolation for the anxious and mythogenetic displacement-from-origin that is always already the human condition.[17] And the condition of poetry. It is significant that no actual discourse perfectly instantiates the mythic or the ironic modes of Frye's theory. All actual discourse converges toward the three imperfectly displaced modes of romance, high mimesis, and low mimesis. The impropriety of metaphor is original.[18] Its difference and its supplementarity are the spurs of mimesis: the motive for metaphor. All poiesis is mythopoietic.

As is criticism itself. Frye as critical theorist does exactly what he says all literature does: he goes in search of an absolute center and an absolute origin. We have already seen that the center is not originary: criticism emerges from its center by a leap that the center itself does not and cannot motivate. Now it appears that the center will not hold at all. It is only a fictive projection from a circuit of displacement that is always prior to its own beginning and more central than its own centrality. The irony of criticism, that its truth is always already a fiction, is itself ironically displaced into those structures of displacement of which it would have been the redemption.

IV

The five phases of symbolism discussed in Frye's Second Essay are modeled on the four levels of meaning recognized in medieval exegesis. The resemblance is close. But the differences are at least as important as the similarities.

Frye gets five out of four by dividing the *sensus litteralis* and considering *littera* and *sensus* as distinct kinds of symbols. For Frye the reference of word (*littera*) to thing (*sensus*) is not, as it was for the medievals, a matter of course. The modern sensibility cannot disallow the possibility that words will spin off from signification and ensconce themselves in the text as opaque motifs. Nevertheless, when Frye examines the literal and descriptive phases of symbolism, he has to examine them together. Each is defined in terms of the other, for while the ontic commitment of the letter may not be taken for granted, neither may its pretension to autonomy.

The hierarchy of levels of meaning culminates in anagogy. Frye's sequence of phases culminates not at all or only ambiguously. The largest unit actually available for critical inspection is the archetypal symbol. The literary monad, necessary *for* the integrity of criticism as a scientific discipline, is never more than a postulate *of* criticism. It is no accident that Frye is renowned as a "myth critic" and not as an "anagogic critic." The latter can never exist, although his existence is demanded by the project of criticism. The former is, given Frye's presuppositions, the best—and the most—we are likely to get.

All four levels of meaning are incarnationally fused in the *sensus allegoricus:* Christ is uniquely and hypostatically both *res* and *signum*. The corresponding phase in Frye's series, the formal phase, is not incarnational or only provisionally so. The image, which unites sign and motif, immediately requires the distinction between itself and its meaning. The allegory is not a substantial part of the image, but a conceptual gloss.

In brief: Frye's phases of symbolism enact a dialectic which has no origin (the difference between word and thing is always already opened, their identity always already past), no center (they do not perspective a moment of incarnational presence), and no closure (the union of symbol and reality is postponed to infinity).

Every text of whatever sort, Frye says, points its reader in two directions at once. It points him away from the words toward the things they mean, or more accurately toward his memories of the conventional associations of word and thing. But it also pulls him toward the words themselves and the patterns they make. The former direction Frye calls centrifugal, the latter centripetal. Verbal symbols centrifugally directed are said to be used descriptively and are called signs. Centripetally directed, they are said to be used literally and are called motifs.

All writing contains both signs and motifs and draws the reader outward and inward at once. In descriptive or assertive writing (philosophy, science, and the like) the final direction of meaning is outward. In literature the predominant direction is inward. Literary verbal structures, therefore, are neither true nor false nor merely tautological. Their relation to the real world is hypothetical ("what if...") or imaginative ("suppose that..."). In literature the question of truth is subordinated to the aim of producing an order of words valuable for the sake of its pleasure, beauty, or interest.

> Wherever we have an autonomous verbal structure of this kind, we have literature. Wherever this autonomous structure is lacking, we have language, words used instrumentally to help human consciousness do or understand something else. Literature is a specialized form of language, as language is of communication. (74)

Frye does not explain nor even note the paradox in these lines: that literature is at once opposed to language and a special form of language. If this is not a simple contradiction, what kind of relationship is it, and what are the conditions of its intelligibility? A rehearsal of Frye's dialectic suggests an answer.

Frye defines a literary work in the literal sense as an autonomous structure of motifs, and in the descriptive sense as a hypothetical structure of signs. Both literal and descriptive aspects are present in every verbal object. But there is a tension nevertheless between these two dimensions of literature. The opposition is "of course complementary, not antithetical," but in the third phase of symbolism Frye proposes "to try to resolve the antithesis." (82)

Literal and descriptive phases of symbolism are united in the verbal object conceived as form. On the one hand form implies unity of structure, the characteristic mark of literal meaning. But on the other it requires as its complement terms like content or matter, and thus sustains the relation to reality outside the work that distinguishes descriptive meaning. The symbol formally regarded is the image: that unit of the literary work which exhibits an analogy between the work and nature. Like form itself, the image contains a duality. It is both a replica of a natural object and a device for suggesting ideas. (84)[19]

Formal criticism consists of commentary on the imagery of the work. The commentary it produces is a conceptual analogue of the image, and the formal critic sees all literature as potential allegory. In the contrast between the image and the allegory it provokes we encounter once again and at a new level—in the relationship between the work and its critical interpretation—the tension of literal and descriptive, motif and sign, centripetal and centrifugal directions of meaning. This tension is resolved in the fourth or mythical phase of symbolism.

Images not only relate literary works analogically to nature. They also relate verbal objects to each other. There are typical or recurrent images, which Frye calls archetypes. By virtue of its archetypal structure literature becomes a social fact, a means of communication among men, and a part of that "total human imitation of nature that we call civilization." (105)

Archetypal criticism (or "myth criticism") studies literature in the context of civilization. But literature regarded as a system of archetypes has society outside itself. It is therefore subservient to society: useful for the advancement of culture. The dialectic takes another turn. In the relationship of literature to civilization the original tension of literal and descriptive is resumed. The resolution of this tension is effected in the fifth phase of symbolism, the anagogic.

The study of archetypes presumes that the archetypes themselves are parts of a larger whole. Anagogic criticism postulates this whole: the symbol as monad. That is, it postulates the totality of the order of words— the sum and system of all actual and possible literary artifice, the consummate self-centered and self-sufficient verbal structure of which all other verbal structures are parts. This is of course identical with the postulate by which the possibility of a science of criticism is originally assured.

The symbol as monad is also "the completion of the imaginative revolution begun when we passed from the descriptive to the formal phase of symbolism." (119) It is the culmination of the dialectic of centripetal and centrifugal forces in language. At this point of anagogic fulfillment all of reality—nature, life, and society—is enclosed within literature as a self-contained universe.

Yet the monad is a fiction. A necessary fiction, no doubt, created by that necessary angel, the imagination. But a fiction nonetheless: hypothetical, not existential. Therefore, even at the moment of final resolution the dialectic repeats itself. Outside the literary monad there is religion, the only thing "as infinite in its range" (125) as the monad itself. The Logos of criticism is not identical with the Logos of faith.

Religion and literature, Frye says, must remain distinct and independent, if each is to retain its identity. Religion as a social institution "cannot...*contain* an art of unlimited hypothesis." (127) And art cannot without betraying itself refrain from its imaginative critique of religion. For every assertion, even the largest assertions of theology, there will always be on the side of literature a contrary supposition. For every "this is..." of doctrine there will always be an opposing "but suppose *this* is..." of imagination. Between doctrine and imagination "there must always be some kind of tension, until the possible and the actual meet at infinity." (128)

Since at this juncture in his exposition Frye is dealing with literature as a whole, having driven his imaginative revolution to the end of the line, one is tempted to read this account of the monad as a definition of the imagination. The imagination is: the creator of contrasts, the power of contrariety. Perhaps: the expositor of alterity. In the same line, criticism would be the reality of this perennial and pervasive tension—the perpetually reinaugurated difference—between the actual and the possible.

The dialectic of the phases of symbolism begins with the identity and the difference of motif and sign. The ambivalence of the literal and the descriptive, the centripetal and the centrifugal, is (implicitly) and becomes (explicitly) the ironic distinction between literature and criticism and a mirror of criticism itself. At once bound to the service of literature and released to its own autonomy, criticism is—shiftily—both truth-telling science and fictive artifice. And this tension of possible and actual is always already there. It does not originate with literature or with criticism or with their difference. It is prior to the origin of both their identity and their difference.

The dialectic ends—or does not end—at infinity. "Between religion's 'this is' and poetry's 'but suppose *this* is,' there must always be some kind of tension, until the possible and the actual meet at infinity." (127-128) Which I take it means never.

The difference between literal and descriptive phases of symbolism never begins. As the dialectic of signifier and signified it is itself the unoriginated and unoriginating origin of all difference. And it never ends. The resolution of the antithesis (which is also a complementarity) of motif and sign is no more than a figure of speech. The meeting of parallels at infinity is the signifier of a signified unity that never is. Between the beginning that is not and the end that is not there is no center—no point of presence— only the incessant promptings and evasions of the dialectic.

Mythic metaphor (A=B) and ironic metaphor (A;B) are equivalent and equivalently unrealizable. The "=" of identity makes a difference, and the ";" of sheer juxtaposition provokes a relationship. Both are fictive. The brutality of juxtaposition draws attention to the gratuitousness of the identity, and the fragility of identity begs a motive for juxtaposition. Metaphor is always both two and one, "a relation between two symbols." (366) Between identity and juxtaposition are actualizable possibilities—the displacements. The concrete universal (A in B), analogy (A:C::B:D), and the simile (A is like B) are rationalizations of the essentially irrational, and therefore only provisional dissatisfactions of an impulse which could only be (impossibly) satisfied by myth and (impossibly) frustrated by perfect ironic fragmentation. Heaven and hell alike are always tantalizingly out of reach. Only reaching is.

Readers of Frye are tempted—irresistibly as a rule—to make diagrams of his architectonic.[20] But the spatializing suggested by his categorial schemata and sponsored by the postulate of scientific criticism (17) is illusory. The categories will not be still, and the phases of symbolism are not so much "contexts or relationships" (73) as they are the ever-changing aspects of a satellite that will not stand (even against its will) but continues to trace its dubious orbit.

The moon is language. Language is a system of signs. And every sign contains a contradiction. The signified is analytically contained in the concept of the signifier: to be a signifier is to signify the signified. But just as the signified is ontically distinct from the signifier, so the signifier is distinct from the signified. Unless signifier and signified are both the same and different, signification is impossible. The sign is a mediation. Were signifier and signified either simply the same or simply different, mediation could not occur. How chaste is Diana?

The tendency of assertive writing (e.g., philosophy) is to insist (in language and by means of language) on the revelation of the signified in and by means of every use of the signifier: by means of a mediation it wills to cancel mediacy and enjoy the immediate presence of the signified. Literature, by contrast, tends to insist (in and by means of language) on the ontic independence of the signifier in all its uses. These tendencies are just Frye's centrifugal and centripetal directions of meaning, each asserted at the expense of the other. In this light one can see how (cf. p. 74) literature is both opposed to language (to its paradoxical duality) and a special case of language (the case that privileges the autonomy of the signifier over its complicity with the signified).

Criticism is the conceptual experience and the verbal performance of the dialectic of the assertive and the literary forcings of language. That is what Frye's text, at once fictive and scientific in uneasy equilibrium, irresistibly suggests. Necessarily, because the dialectic tracks the structure of the linguistic sign, it cannot be resolved. Not even imaginatively: the supreme fiction would still be—is designed to be—an object of belief. Possibility and actuality, signifier and signified, never meet. The only conceivable resolution of the dialectic would be a transformation of the world so radical ("at infinity") that it would destroy the solution along with the problem.

V

In his Second Essay Frye remarks that while some people have regarded theology and metaphysics as centripetal, the critic must treat them as assertive "because they are outside literature" and create a "centrifugal movement in it." (75) It is almost possible to detect *petitio* in this. How is centripetality recognized? The *Anatomy* is too sophisticated to commit intentional or affective fallacies. A concern for the inherent value of the verbal object, as opposed to a concern for truth and utility, must show itself on the object. Else the distinction between literary and assertive writing is suspect, and with it the possibility of criticism.

Or at least the range of criticism. In fact literariness (in Frye's sense) is not a legible property of some texts but not others. The distinction between centripetal and centrifugal does not classify artifacts. It divides every text irreparably against itself.

Late in the Fourth Essay Frye appends to his theory of genres an account of "the rhetoric of non-literary prose." (326-337) Such writing, like literature itself, stands between social action on one side and individual thought on the other. Like literature, it projects and presents itself to an audience. In the social arena it stresses emotion and evokes action via the ear. Addressed to the individual it emphasizes the intellect and prompts contemplation through visual metaphors. The attempt, in a purely associative rhetoric, to purify affect of all thought leads at its extreme to an incoherent emotional babble. The attempt, by means of a rhetoric of analysis and dissociation, to purify thought of all emotion leads at its extreme to conceptual jargon: things like officialese and gobbledygook.

Frye is led to this conclusion:

> We are not surprised to find that the further we depart from literature, or the use of language to express *the completely integrated state of emotional consciousness we call imagination*, the nearer we come to the use of language as the expression of reflex. Whether we go in the emotional or in the intellectual direction, we arrive at much the same point, a point antipodal to literature in which language is a running commentary on the unconscious, like a squirrel's chatter. (331; my emphasis)

And to this corollary:

...the direct union of grammar and logic, which we suggested...might be the characteristic of the non-literary verbal structure, does not, in the long run, exist. Anything which makes a functional use of words will always be involved in all the technical problems of words, including rhetorical problems. The only road from grammar to logic, then, runs through the intermediate territory of rhetoric. (331)

The centrality of rhetoric among the arts of language is far from trivial. The link between grammar and rhetoric—the rhetoric of grammar—is verbal association: the oral-aural aspect of language, the social rhetoric of emotion and action. The link between rhetoric and logic—the rhetoric of logic—is the doodle or the diagram: the visual aspect of language, the individual rhetoric of contemplative thought.

The last words of the Fourth Essay are:

The notion of a *conceptual* rhetoric raises new problems, as it suggests that nothing built out of words can transcend the nature and conditions of words, and that the nature and conditions of *ratio*, so far as *ratio* is verbal, are contained by *oratio*. (337)

Brief and supernumerary as it seems to be, this part of Frye's text is loaded with surprising implications. First, any piece of assertive writing— philosophy, for example, or even criticism so far as it is "scientific"—is beset by literary and in particular rhetorical problems. By expansion, all literary and critical problems are problems of language as such, and not merely of that subdivision of language called "literary." Imagination, once identified as the demon of contrariety, is now hailed as the "completely integrated state of...consciousness." In line with this, literature is the normative and perfected state of language, and all other uses of language— including the philosophical and (*qua* assertive) the critical—are inferior and lopsided, verging on decadence and the subversion of language itself.

The *Anatomy's* Polemical Introduction is balanced by an equally ironic-to-oxymoronic Tentative Conclusion, in which some of these implications are pursued. Frye begins by insisting on the centrality of archetypal criticism. Since myth is "the structural organizing principle of literary form," (341) a focus on myth gives criticism "an end in the structure of literature as a total form." (342) Archetypal criticism imposes an order on and sets a limit to the proliferation of commentary.

Historical criticism relates literary culture to the past; ethical criticism directs it toward the future. By identifying the mythic patterns that unify all literature, past, present, and future, archetypal criticism integrates literature into the totality of civilization and discovers (creates?) the universal shape of culture: the tradition of humanity.

However, archetypal criticism is transcended and fulfilled in anagogic criticism. Frye writes:

> But we then had to complete our argument by removing all external goals from literature, thus postulating a self-contained literary universe. Perhaps in doing so we merely restored the aesthetic view on a gigantic scale, substituting Poetry for a mass of poems, aesthetic mysticism for aesthetic empiricism. The argument of our last essay [the Fourth], however, led to the principle that all structures in words are partly rhetorical, and hence literary, and that the notion of a scientific or philosophical verbal structure free of rhetorical elements is an illusion. If so, then our literary universe has expanded into a verbal universe, and no aesthetic principle of self-containment will work. (350)

This leads into a comparison of literature with mathematics, both of which

> drive a wedge between the antithesis of being and non-being that is so important for discursive thought. The symbol neither is nor is not the reality which it manifests. (351)

Hamlet and Falstaff neither exist nor do not exist. If the poet never affirmeth, he never lieth either. And so on.

But there is more. Literature is like mathematics in yet another way:

> Mathematics is at first a form of understanding an objective world regarded as its content, but in the end it conceives of the content as being itself mathematical in form, and when the conception of a mathematical universe is reached, form and content become the same thing. Mathematics relates itself indirectly to the common field of experience, then, not to avoid it, but with the ultimate design of swallowing it. (352)

Like mathematics, literature ends by engulfing the world it began by imitating. Evidence for this conclusion is provided by the religious terminology which pervades speculative mathematics (the mysticism of Pythagoras and Jeans) and forces itself on literature and criticism when they reach the anagogic plane. Even the assertive verbal structures of

> psychology, anthropology, theology, history, law, and everything else built out of words have been informed or constructed by the same kind of myths

and metaphors that we find, in their original hypothetical form, in literature. (352)

This last is put in the form of a (rhetorical) question, and/but it introduces a caution. This is perhaps the tentative part of the tentative conclusion.

> ...[I]t would be silly to use a reductive rhetoric to try to prove that theology, metaphysics, law, the social sciences, or whichever one or group of these we happen to dislike, are based on "nothing but" metaphors or myths. Any such proof, if we are right, would have the same kind of basis itself. (353)

Theology and metaphysics (*inter alia*), formerly (75) ruled centrifugal, are now declared to be formally irreducible to the purely literary. The reduction, if essayed by the critic, would turn on itself. Given the hypothetical character of his own discipline, the critic is barred from philosophical assertions that contradict themselves as fictive by their factual commitment and subvert themselves as factual by their fictive form.

In what mode finally—possibility or actuality—does the tension between the actual and the possible subsist? In neither. It subsists in language and in the metastases of language, both/neither sign and/nor motif. Description is construction:

> poets and critics alike have always believed in some kind of *imaginative truth*, and perhaps the justification for the belief is in the containment by the language of what it can express. (354; my emphasis)

Language is at once and never both the expression of content and the containment of what is expressed: the perpetuation of the sameness and the difference of the presentation and the presence. And criticism itself, being a(the) condition of language, is never possible save as the most acute self-consciousness of the inner dialectic of its medium.

Theory of criticism becomes in the end the story of language, its truth an ever-rising ever-ruined triumph of the imagination. As Frye says, "the Tower of Babel recurs." (354)

VI

When the *Anatomy* first appeared, it seemed to many students of literature that Frye had organized their field, integrated their endeavors, and specified their method in a wholly unprecedented way. In spite of its title, in spite of Frye's disclaimers, and in spite of the book's many internal ironies, it became for numberless critics (and for their English departments) a theoretical and methodological canon.

Prior to the advent of the *Anatomy*, critical hegemony had pretty much belonged to the New Critics (*Understanding Poetry* achieved its third edition three years after the publication of Frye's work). A battle had been won against historicism, but the war went on. The co-existence of poetry with positivist science was a pact of mutual non-interference that did not promise to become a genuine peace. Its author, I. A. Richards, had long since all but defected to idealism.

Coming upon this scene, the *Anatomy* seemed to have brought off a decisive coup. For one thing, Frye appeared to have purified, enlightened, and perfected the formalism of the New Critics. He included *in* form everything they had excluded *from* form in what they took to be the interests *of* form. In place of the proscriptive and austere formalism of the New Critics (who looked as a rule only at single poems, usually short lyrics), Frye proposed a rich and inclusive formalism that took the whole of literature as its primary object. The First Essay of the *Anatomy* is an essay in historical criticism. The Second Essay begins with the controversy between historical scholarship and formalist criticism (an aspect of the sign/motif, descriptive/literal dichotomy) and builds its dialectical edifice on that foundation. In the end it arrives (or seems to arrive) at a conception of literary form that includes—in the hypothetical and imaginative mode—absolutely everything. In Frye's hands, form became not the narrowest and most restrictive but the broadest and most comprehensive of literary categories.

Moreover, rather than oppose poetry to science, Frye attempted to reconcile them. In part by analogizing literature to mathematics, but mostly by defining criticism as the science of poetry. Poetry was made amenable to scientific inquiry and not just tossed into the waste-water of physics.

These are the purposes which many early readers of the *Anatomy* took Frye to have accomplished. But if my readings of fragments of his work are only occasionally misguided, then these purposes are not quite achieved. Or better: they are under-achieved. Achieved ironically. Whether this was clear to Frye himself I do not know. But it is something of which his text is aware. The stichomythia between form and substance, between self-contained object and hypothetical structure, goes on even at the level of the (suppositional) literary monad. The symbiotic antithesis, within criticism, of science and fiction remains in principle unresolved. The text, as theory of criticism, is always already displaced from its center and its origin, so that Frye's book can never be a *Systematics of Criticism*, but always only an *Anatomy of Criticism*. It is the metaphor of its own differences, the concrete universal of the always reopened problem of the possibility of criticism.

Frye's critical theory, more than once hailed as the redemption of the project of criticism, looks nostalgically toward Aristotle (14-15) and apocalyptically toward the critical eschaton, the beatific merger of the actual and the possible in the infinite. These are his mythic identities, the innocence and the glory of literature and criticism alike. But the Fall is language, a fall for which there is, in language, no reparation. Its worm dieth not. All human problems are problems of language, and there is no human solution for any human problem. There is some comfort in that.

The *Anatomy of Criticism* is, of necessity, a failed redemption myth. But a necessary failure. A redemption myth is not redemption. The supremest fiction, object of the intensest belief, is still a fiction. Language is the difficulty, and a question is not an answer. The best we can hope for is an authentic experience of the problem. The *Anatomy* is the possibility of that experience.

5

The Preface of the Question:
An Entertainment

The preface is but one possible site for all that philosophy would have
liked to neutralize, expel, limit,sublate....

—Sylviane Agacinski, *Aparté*

The incommensurable, which in earlier times one set down in the preface
to a book, can now find its place in a preface that is not the preface
to any book.

—Nicolaus Notabene, *Prefaces*

One might have expected "the question of the preface." One might have
been mistaken, red-herringed by what has now become a virtual
tradition—at least an obligatory gesture—of preliminary self-erasure among
post-modern writers—assuming that post-modern writers can have either
traditions or obligations. After all, Derrida did it, and his translator did it
after him. In *Dissemination*, e.g., and in Gayatri's Preface to *De la
grammatologie anglais*. But this is not that. This will not have been (at
least not from now on and with exceptions here and there) a post-structuralist
stunt. I am taking my cue, if not my inspiration, from that very respectable
and pre-structuralist author and translator, Walter Lowrie. In the Preface as
well as the Introduction to his translation of what was then (by him and
felicitously) called *The Concept of Dread*, the Reverend Doctor Lowrie
takes note of the little book *Forord*, by Nicolaus Notabene, and assures us
twice over that "it will not likely be translated into English."[1] In his *Short
Life of Kierkegaard*, published the year before his translation of *Dread*,
Lowrie announces even more confidently, the mandatory tone of his edict
all but unruffled by its anomalous placement in a list of "Kierkegaard's
Works in English," that *Prefaces* "will never be translated."[2]

The credibility of Lowrie's solemn assurance is somewhat eroded by the circumstance that his own translation of the preface to *Prefaces* was published seven years later in a British review, *The Wind and the Rain*, Volume VI, number 1, Summer, 1949, pages 18-25. Lowrie confesses this peccadillo in the Preface to his translation of Kierkegaard's *On Authority and Revelation*, in a passage remarking the many prefaces (three or maybe four, Lowrie isn't sure) that Kierkegaard wrote for this never-published work. The translator's arithmetical indecision (three or four?) is itself undecidable. Is he referring to the fact that Kierkegaard wrote, in addition to three prefaces, an introduction to his "book on Adler?" Or (since he sometimes confuses himself with Kierkegaard) is he adding his own preface to Kierkegaard's three? He drops hints, but he does not say. For that matter, Lowrie is not sure how many prefaces there are in *Prefaces* itself. There are in fact eight prefaces plus a preface. But Lowrie seems to think there are eight in all, since he describes his own translation of the preface to *Prefaces* as a translation of the first preface and adds, less pontifical in 1954 than in 1942, humbled perhaps by his subsequent scratching of the seven-year itch, that *"seven* of them *need not* be translated." (My emphasis.) The widespread inconscience, even among Kierkegaardians, of Lowrie's clandestine translation may be laid flatly at his own feet. In acknowledging the fact of his translation, he puts it in the 1947 volume of *The Wind and the Rain*, a miscue which caused the present writer an unconscionable and unaccustomed quantity of scholarly grubbing. Maybe it was Lowrie's concern for his reputation as a man of his word that prompted him to confuse his readers with all these lapses of mathematical memory.[3] He had, one may suppose, taken cognizance of Johannes Climacus' observation that "only over-precipitate people...are quick to take an oath; because the fact is that they are unable to keep it...."[4] In a prefatory note to his excursion into *The Wind and the Rain* [bracketed and in very small print], Lowrie says that *Prefaces*, along with (Professor Crites will be pleased to know this) *The Crisis and A Crisis*, "has become antiquated" and that he translates the preface to the former only in order to "salvage something from this little book..., an instance of Kierkegaard's humour in which there is not a trace of instruction nor edification."[5] Which remark serves the double purpose of assuaging his conscience (it was *not* to be translated after all) and providing an instance of his own quite possibly inconscient humor.

I assume that all of this was overlooked or unheeded by William McDonald, who simply disregarded Lowrie's magisterial ban, his manifold backings and fillings, and produced the elegant translation of Notabene's uninstructive and unupbuilding text which now pleasures if it does not improve its anglophone readers.

But it is time to be serious. Nicolaus Notabene was serious, serious about his literary projects and serious about his existential commitments, even when they collided, as they did in the case of his marriage. Nicolaus, as you will recall, had long entertained the desire to write a book. But then he got married, and his bride made it clear to him that she regarded the generation of books as a species of infidelity—"the worst kind of infidelity"[6]—and demanded of her spouse a sacred vow that he would never father one. Which oath he solemnly swore. And kept. Nicolaus Notabene never wrote a book. However, he reasoned—rather Jesuitically for one we know to be an honest Lutheran, schooled in Balles' *Laerebog*—: I promised you I wouldn't write a book, I didn't say anything about prefaces. His wife accepted the gambit, supposing the preface to be impossible without the ensuing book. (P28) Whereupon Nicolaus proceeded to compose eight prefaces to as many *opera quae non supersunt*, later provided with a preface of their own and aggregated in this volume which we must assume for the sake of his husbandly honor is not a book.

It is worth noting, however, that although Nicolaus writes his prefaces with a good conscience, he does so furtively, away from home and without his wife's knowledge. (P28) Was this just a reasonable precaution, a strategic move to skirt the ontological abyss—is the being of the preface possible in the absence of the being of the book?—or was it a dead giveaway, a clear-sighted but patently dishonest anticipation that his wife would recognize the genus in the species, the writing in the preface-writing, and since her quarrel was not with the species but with the genus, conclude (rightly) that her husband had dishonored the marriage bond? Regine Olsen's fiancé proved *his* fidelity to the intended by marrying neither her nor anyone else, producing instead in the solitary silence of his room and bolt upright at his writing desk a brood of brawling brain children, and then assuring her in his last will and testament that it was just as if she had always been his wife an allegation that she understandably could not understand and that Fritz (we may surely allow him this) could not allow.

Regine, we know, read the books. Well, at least we know she got them. Did Fru Notabene ever read this which we most firmly believe is not a book? And would she take in good faith her husband's prefatory protestations of his fidelity? Let us bend the analogy back on its base and find out. Nicolaus Notabene reasons: writing a book (figuratively) ruptures my marriage vow, writing prefaces does not. Analogously, a serious long-term affair makes me (literally) faithless to my wife, but a series of one-night-stands and other brief encounters would not. This sort of reasoning might open the way to a resolution of the crisis in modern marriage. If, that is, Fru Notabene (and her modern descendants, who are legion) accepts her husband's logic as artlessly as she (apparently) accepted his vow—or vows.

One might, however, wonder. A friend and former student of mine, some time after Vatican II, took a position at a Roman Catholic college. She noticed that more than one of the priest-professors there resident seemed to associate freely with women (some of them nuns) in a (shall we say?) social setting. Once she felt secure enough in her own position to broach the issue, she asked one of them, Aren't you vowed to celibacy? To which he, Of course. And she, Doesn't it trouble you that you spend so much time in the society and (evidently) the affections of women, especially your constant companion Sr. N. N.—sorry, make that Jane Doe? Doesn't the apparent (I say no more than that) hypocrisy ever bother you? This was his carefully considered reply: The vow of celibacy has long been misunderstood. It does not demand that you refrain from consorting with women altogether. It requires only that you do not pledge yourself to the sole service of a single woman in the bonds of matrimony. And in this way it leaves you open for Christian and charitable liaisons with all and sundry.

My friend was not convinced. Maybe she reasoned like Fru Notabene. The latter believed (perhaps) that if you don't write a book you can't write a preface. Hence her willingness to permit her husband prefaces after he has forsworn books. (P 28) So the former (my friend) may have inferred that if you are forbidden to marry you are at least by implication also forbidden to indulge in casual flirtations and similar diversions from the straight and narrow. Whatever her logic, she was not convinced. If only, she thought, it were generally known that the vow of celibacy is really a vow of promiscuity, young men by the thousands would experience vocations and the Church would never lack for priests. But of course (she knew a bit of history) that was not what the vow of celibacy intended; it was nothing but the flimsiest pretext for self-titillation. *Mutandis* several times *mutatis*, it should be clear that Nicolaus Notabene did not really propose to honor his non-writing vow or for that matter his marriage vow, the former as his wife saw it entailed by the latter. He is, to both vows, faithless. Not ardently, passionately, devil-may-care faithless, but only frivolously, dilettantishly, behind-your-back faithless. If Fru Notabene had nourished her spirit on a diet of contemporary German literature, she might have preferred cuckolding (or whatever it is when it's done to a woman) by a Romantic rather than a back-door man. It is evident she did not enjoy *quod erat demonstrandum.*

You might say that Nicolaus honored the letter of his vow but not its spirit. He did not, save *per accidens*, write a *book*. But he did *write*. And that was exactly what his wife was trying to forestall. If you did say that— or something like it—you would have stumbled upon (or over) the subject of this unedifying discourse. Just about the same time I did.

I should break off these preliminary remarks for a moment in order to say something about the origins of this indiscretion. Everything (well, almost everything) up to this point was written during an otherwise pleasant visit to Boston College some years back. In the midst of that otherwise pleasant sojourn, the APA representative of the Søren Kierkegaard Society, possessed by I know not what malign power or powers, asked me if I would read a paper at the December meeting. I reminded her that I had solemnly promised myself and the cultured public never again to write or formally declaim about youknowwho. Discounting my obligation to myself and the profession, she urged me to think about her request anyway. I promised her I'd take it under advisement, making as I did so a mental reservation to say No as soon as I was back in Texas and beyond supernatural importuning. So I returned to my quarters. I should note that during my stay at Boston College I was domiciled at St. Mary's Hall, the residence of the Jesuit community. My room assignment identified me as Louis H. Mackey, S. J., and all the service personnel addressed me as "Father." What that has to do with my mental reservation, or how my honorary but temporary vocation to the order of St. Ignatius interacted with your representative's diabolic agency I cannot say. But as soon as I got back to my room I sat down and wrote compulsively, in a fit of frenzied dissemination, most of what you have already read. "Sounds like it," you say. So said I. I was reminded of that philandering priest I mentioned earlier, and I asked myself, "Is this nothing but my form of self-titillation? Have I, forsworn as I am to dilate formally on the subject of this Society's devotions, or any serious issue or issues pertaining thereunto, nonetheless permitted myself the dilatory pleasure of a casual and momentary liaison with the most frivolous of his pseudonyms?" For it was already evident from my spate of automatic writing that I intended (or someone for me) to take the *Prefaces* of Nicolaus Notabene as my subject. Seriously, formally, and with his usual perspicacity, the Reverend Doctor Lowrie remarks parenthetically that Nicolaus Notabene is "one of the few pseudonyms which has no obvious significance,"[7] completely overlooking the obvious and obviously significant fact that N. N. is Danish for "anyone" and therefore why not me?[8] Concerning *Prefaces* itself, Lowrie adds, in the very next breath, that it is rightly subtitled "light reading" and deals (only) "in a sarcastic but entertaining fashion with authors, publishers, and reviewers."[9] Mere signs of signs, as if there were anything else. So there you are. Or there I am, linked indissolubly to the faithless Notabene and my friend's errant cleric, continuing and attenuating the chain of their offenses.

For note well: in all that I have said so far I have spoken not of Notabene's *Prefaces* but only of the Preface to his *Prefaces*. If the Preface to the book is already compromised, how parlously contaminated is the preface to the Preface? And what hope can there be for one who, out of due time and lost in space, by way of opening the preface of/to the question, is good for nothing but to add the merest unscientific postscript or dangling participial appendage to the infamies of his elders and betters? Unlike Notabene, I am not married. But that does not exonerate my inscriptions. My writing is to his (perhaps—and ignoring my vocation) as fornication is to adultery, a different sin *formaliter* but the same thing *materialiter*. And if one thinks of my promise to myself and the trade, the whole performance is nothing but self-abuse, like Arthur Dimmesdale's election sermon—which was hardly evidence of his election.

What should be evident by now and will surely be evident before this is over is that vows may be taken but cannot be kept. For in the first of Notabene's prefaces (right after the Preface) we read: to have written the book (that should be The Book, capital T capital B) or in other words to have written The System of Absolute Knowledge would give an author enormous pleasure. Indeed an Absolute Pleasure, since the publication of such a (capital) Book would render superfluous the production of any further (lower case) book, and in that way be a service to public morals. At the very least it would remove from the already temptation-littered path of husbands one of the many occasions of sin. For that matter, even in the absolute absence of the Absolute Book, the practice of reviewers and the extraordinarily wide and deep influence of their reviews makes the existence of books altogether gratuitous. (P35) The Polish science-fiction writer Stanislaw Lem, in a book called *A Perfect Vacuum*, has reviewed sixteen non-existent books including his own. Lem's readers will agree: the books are quite unnecessary, sufficient unto the day are the notices thereof. But the services of book reviewers are even greater and the need for books reviewed even smaller when a reviewer like Professor Heiberg misunderstands the book for you and offers his pleasant and palatable "aesthetic scribblings" *in loco* the difficult "thought and idea" of the work itself (45), all done up as a tastefully designed holiday gift book to grace the coffee tables of the cultured public.

The contrast between the frivolous and the serious—aesthetic scribbling vs. thought and idea, the ceremonial preface that threatens to become a book vs. the lyrical preface that expresses only a passing mood (P 19)—is repeated throughout the *Prefaces* at every turn of the page. In the manifesto of the Temperance Society, it appears as the distinction between the insignificance of personal morality and the importance of founding an organization for the betterment of public morals. It surfaces in the contrast between the fragmentary and unsystematic edification offered to the individual by Bishop Mynster's sermons and the proposed philosophical-scientific edification of the whole literate community in the name of Heiberg and Martensen. Another preface explicitly opposes promise to performance, with extreme prejudice to the latter, especially in the case of the long-promised and doubtless soon-to-appear eleventh book that mediates and synthesizes everything said on the subject by the now (i.e., then) *aufgehoben* previous ten. The proposal offered in the last of the prefaces, to found a journal designed to provide other and wiser heads the opportunity to instruct the founder, an ignorant man, in philosophy, and then presumably (when his head is stuffed with the wisdom of the age) self-destruct, has obvious analogues in the practice of Socrates. But, as we know, the patron of Western philosophers was not serious. An ignorant man himself, he was convicted of irony by, *inter alios*, Magister Kierkegaard. The irony of Notabene's aesthetic scribblings is by no means unfamiliar to readers of the scribblings of his alter ego (all his alter egos), and like the irony of Socrates must not be taken lightly—something we surely do if we solemnly expound its serious purpose and its true purport. For the irony of Nicolaus Notabene (I say this in all seriousness) is, like the irony of Socrates and the irony of the pseudonym Søren Kierkegaard[10] and all *his* pseudonyms, designed with malice aforethought in such a way that its purpose and purport can never be located amid the play of signifiers—prefaces to prefaces, signifiers of signifiers—and for that reason and in all practical and theoretical respects do not exist. Promises that cannot be kept.

It is at least of passing interest that many of Nicolaus Notabene's prefaces are spin-offs from or otherwise adventitious to what his "author" identified as his "authorship"—rejected prefaces to real books, unpublished replies to Heiberg, and the like. Mere leavings and scrapings of thought and idea, the detritus inevitably deposited by the creation of a serious body of work. So I, having once seriously sworn never again to speak or write *ex professo* about the unnamed and unnameable subject of these musings, thereafter seduced from my hermitage by witchcraft and false alarm, can offer only these paltry offscourings of reflection in evidence of the persevering gravity of my resolve. I have said and in these pages written nothing that could by any twist of the perversest imagination be regarded as a contribution to the understanding of that one who did not wish to be understood (and designed his communication accordingly), to the understanding of whom the Kierkegaard industry is solemnly pledged. Like Notabene in his *Prefaces*, the pseudonym Louis Mackey (S.J.) in his preface to the question chatters in a sarcastic but entertaining way about authors, publishers, and reviewers. Like Notabene's wife in her domestic colloquies, he's only teasing. (P22-26)

This is not to be taken lightly. If one has written a book, then one must engage with the question of the preface. But

> if without this, one can also have the inclination to write a preface, it is easily seen that it must not deal with a subject, for otherwise the preface itself would become a book, and the question of preface and book would revert.[11] The preface as such, the emancipated preface, must then have no subject to discuss but must deal with nothing, and as far as it is thought to deal with something, this must be an appearance and a feigned movement. (P 19)

The question of the preface is: given the book, the preface, whether written first, last, or midways, is unnecessary at least and impossible at most. The preface of/in (the) question turns everything bass-ackwards, arsy-versy, and upsodoun, so that once you have the preface there is no point at all in having the book and maybe not even the remotest chance of a book. Provided, that is, your preface is really a preface, i.e., meaningless, a preface to nothing, for once it means something it has become a book. A preface is a text and, as we know, there is nothing outside of that. Nothing, e.g., that the text could be about.

Really a preface? Is a preface without a book still a preface in any sense, real or otherwise? As a piece of pure textuality, the bookless preface is an anomalous gesture, something you do for the sheer fun of it—a gratuitous *jouissance* which nonetheless "entitles one to a certain amount of attention." (P 19) This must not be taken lightly. Seriously now and in connection with Nicolaus Notabene's author's obsessive subject, the Wholly Other in all its indeterminate and indeterminable forms, that absolutely Unknown and Unknowable that we cannot know even as the Unknown and for which or for whom as the case may be the signifier "God" is only a convenient dummy letter like the algebraist's X—on that subject the book can never be written. Lacking by definition both sense and reference, prefaces are all we get. The most and the best.

Since "the preface and the book cannot get on well together, then let the one give the other bill of divorce." (P18) But who is going to divorce whom? Hegel could not write a preface without betraying the book. NN, the unknown for whom "Søren Kierkegaard" is only a dummy letter, cannot write a book without infidelity to its subject. Shall we say that this (*Prefaces*) which is not a book is therefore the best and fullest treatment of his (whose?) real subject, saying as it does nothing about it or him as the case may be and in this way (Aquinas would have understood this) expressing most perfectly and most fully everything we know about the "vital, arrogant, fatal, dominant X?"[12] It cannot be denied, nor would Notabene wish to deny it, that "by defining my limit negatively one still defines me in continuity with the Other." (P89)

Vigilius Haufniensis, author of *Begrebet Angest*, published on the same day as Nicolaus Notabene's *Forord* and pointing to the doctrine of original sin, with scholarly scrupulosity abstains from discussing his ulterior object and confines himself instead to delineating in maddening detail, with maximal obfuscation and academic pedantry, its prefatory psychic state. From which original experience of dizziness—or dread—sin originates by a leap, of which the leaper is conscious only after the fact, into a life and a history of sin that engulfs its psychic presupposition and entraps the psyche it creates. Is it possible that, as dread is to sin, so the preface is to the book, which has the dreadful habit of devouring and disappearing the preface that introduces it?

The end of the book is the beginning of writing. Fru Notabene seems not to have known this. Did her husband? If he did, then his writerly goal would have been to produce an entire *oeuvre* consisting of nothing but prefaces, abstemious discourses from which the *unum necessarium* (necessary, that is, to the book) has always already (and necessarily for the preface) vanished. A perpetual dancing at the brink of the abyss, courting the vertiginous possibilities but never succumbing to their fatal enticements. Is this the case with the "authorship" of the pseudonym Søren Kierkegaard and all of *his* pseudonymous aiders and abetters? If we suppose it so, then Notabene's *Prefaces* is no longer a pleasant but fortuitous excrescence on the Kierkegaardian corpus, but rather a paradigm for the entire authorship— an authorship without books and therefore with nothing to say. No wonder Lowrie didn't want it translated!

As for the present writer—X knows whose pseudonym he is!—if he has said anything about his announced subject, it is only to point out that it is not in fact a subject but just an announcement. Like Notabene himself. The *nota bene*, abbreviated n.b., is normally followed by a colon, which in turn is followed by a description or at least some indication of what it is the reader (it *is* an inscription, not a pronouncement) is to "note well." The n.b. itself is just an attention getter, a kind of self-effacing preface which tells us nothing except that what comes after it is important. Nicolaus Notabene hands us a sheaf of eight n.b.'s, each of them in its prefatory way advising us to be on the alert and ready for what comes next. And of course nothing does, except another n.b. Eight n.b.'s prefaced by a prefatory n.b.

Followed by? Nothing. The thing itself—the systematic expression of absolute truth in *videnskabelige* form, the eleventh book that sums it all up, the New Year's gift book, the self-deconstructing philosophical journal, etc.—is missing. As usual. In a text like *Prefaces*—in any text—it is of first importance to respect the difference between the letter and the spirit. That is, the distinction between what is *literally there* and what is *really not there*.

Lowrie was (as usual) right. This book was not translated. It doesn't even exist. The Authorized Version is already complete without it, McDonald was wasting his time, and Nicolaus' wife is assured of her spouse's fidelity—though, given his washout as a writer and presuming comparable powers as a husband, she might have preferred to go a few rounds with Johannes the Seducer.

As for myself, I have kept the letter but dishonored the spirit of my promise to your representative (my momentary vocation having shielded me momentarily from her wicked wiles) and at the same stroke I have broken the letter but honored the spirit of my vow of silence *in re* the occasion of this session. And what about this, not even a preface but the merest prolegomena to any future preface? Concerning this inexcusable excursus, you may take comfort in the knowledge—you have my word for it—that it will never be translated.

6

Theory and Practice in
the Rhetoric of I. A. Richards

The early works of I. A. Richards, while not committed to hard-line verificationism, nonetheless seem persuaded of the central tenet of logical positivism, that the only truth strictly so-called is the truth disclosed by the methods of empirical science. This minimal positivism, coupled with a non-physicalist form of behaviorism, is evident in books like *Science and Poetry* (1926) and *Principles of Literary Criticism* (1925). However, if Richards was a positivist, he was a positivist who wanted to save poetry from positivism. Primitive positivists like A. J. Ayer impenitently regarded poetic discourse as meaningless. Since they are neither analytic nor available for empirical testing, the "statements" found in poems are really pseudo-statements, expressions of feeling and no more. Richards, who loved poetry, feared that people would cease to read it or write it if they were convinced that it was nothing but emotional gush. And so, in his early books, he developed an affectivism in which poetry, by helping us order our conflicting impulses, acquires a value distinct from the value of science. On this view poetry is not a means of expressing and communicating propositional truth— only science does that—but a device for constructive behavior-modification by means of language.

Meanwhile, from the very beginning of his career, Richards had been a diligent student of Samuel Taylor Coleridge. He was convinced that the works of Coleridge contained many important insights into the nature and effects of poetry which, in order to be made generally accessible and secure wider appreciation, needed only to be disentangled from the metaphysics of Romantic idealism in which they were embedded. Quotations from

Coleridge appeared with great frequency in his own writing and teaching.
Kathleen Coburn predicted that sooner or later Richards would have to
write a book on Coleridge, and eventually her prophecy was fulfilled. Setting
out to rewrite Coleridge in the language of empiricism, Richard produced
Coleridge on Imagination (1934), which suggested to some of his readers
that Richards had not converted Coleridge to empiricism but that Coleridge
had made Richards an idealist, if not a metaphysical then at least a linguistic
idealist. It is the Richards thus baptized in the Alphean flood who speaks in
the lectures on *The Philosophy of Rhetoric* (1936) delivered two years after
the publication of the Coleridge book.[1]

From first to last, in all his writings and through all his changes of
mind, Richards insisted that he was a pragmatist. And indeed, in every project
he undertakes, from Basic English to literary theory, he is unfailingly
preoccupied with the practice of reading and the possibilities of
communication. If behaviorism and Romanticism are just the low-mimetic
(preterite) and high-mimetic (elite) forms of pragmatism, respectively, then
Richards' progress from the former to something resembling the latter is
not a dramatic *peripeteia* but more like (in a figure that might have
recommended itself to both Coleridge and Richards) the natural blossoming
of a seed that had been germinating for a long time.

It was in this way that I first read *The Philosophy of Rhetoric*, early in
the 1960's, twenty-five years after its publication. During those years, literary
study in America had been conducted under the auspices of the New
Criticism. In that milieu, it was natural to read Richards' *Rhetoric* as yet
another chapter in the modernist *prise de conscience* of Romanticism.
Revisiting the book in the late 1970s and early 1980s, after working through
the deconstructive writings of Jacques Derrida, I was surprised to learn how
many of Derrida's positions had been anticipated in Richards' work—for
example, the notion that the meaning of a text is undecidable, that meaning
itself is an absence rather than a presence, and that the recovery of totality
attempted by metaphor necessarily fails. At the same time, it was obvious
that Richards, while he might not be comfortably domiciled in the modernist
establishment, was not a poststructuralist either. He may talk like a
deconstructionist, but he reads like a New Critic.

How this seeming marriage of incompatibles is possible is the question
this essay tries to answer. The following pages propose a reading of *The
Philosophy of Rhetoric* that first shows how much Richards and Derrida
have in common and finally tries to explain what distinguishes Richards'
rhetoric from the deconstructive rhetoric of Derrida. The root of this

difference is to be sought, I believe, in the diverse positionings of Richards and Derrida with respect to the relation of theory and practice. The peculiar mark of Richards' rhetoric, I shall argue, is its conjunction of a resolute recognition of the deconstructive forces of textuality and an equally resolute commitment to the pragmatics of interpretation and communication.

Toward the beginning of his first lecture Richards, reacting to Berkeley, argues that ideas do not exist independently of the words that are said to signify them. At least, they cannot be identified when stripped of the language that clothes them. Therefore, in order to further the practical aims of rhetoric—to remedy misunderstanding and promote good communication—we need to consider "closely how words *work* in discourse."[2] The realist tradition of which Aristotle is the founder maintains that we can always in principle and as a rule in fact distinguish ideas (passions of the soul), which are natural and common, from their verbal signs (utterances and inscriptions), which are conventional and culturally variant. Richards' divergence from this tradition, however guarded its statement, moves him in the direction of an idealism of language not distinct in every way from behaviorism and commits him to a hermeneutic that verges pragmatically on semiotics.

It is an error, Richards says, to suppose that each word simply has, among its other attributes, a meaning, and that the grammatical aggregation of such words-with-meanings produces the meaning of sentences and larger units of discourse in the same way that the proper aggregation of bricks produces a house. Meaning is not a constant property of words, whether natural or conventional (meanings are neither primary nor secondary qualities), which the words retain unchanged when combined with other words. Bricks stay the same no matter where you put them. Words change their meanings as they move from context to context. The meaning of any word is therefore a function of the context in which it occurs. Which suggests (without actually saying so) that semantics is swallowed up in syntax and reference reduced to a singular species of allusion.

Be that as it may, the view Richards opposes, which holds that meanings are attributes of words fixed by convention, he calls the "Proper Meaning Superstition." As against this "superstition" Richards insists that any piece of discourse "in the last resort, *does* what it *does*" only because "the other parts of the surrounding, uttered or unuttered discourse and *its conditions* are what they are" (10, my emphasis). The meaning of any word is contextually determined, and the way any bit of language works is "in the last resort" a function of its total context, uttered or unexpressed, both linguistic and non-linguistic. Richards immediately adds that "mercifully" the last resort "is a long way off and very deep down" (10). Mercifully, that is, for the practicing critic. The theorist, however, may wonder just how far is a long way and how deep is very. Where, if anywhere, does context close off and bottom out?

In practice, which is constantly engaged with the proximate and never required to brave the ultimacies of theory, we are shielded from the threat of universal indeterminacy and undecidability by the redundancies of usage. Richards observes that "the stability of the meaning of a word comes from the constancy of the contexts that give it its meaning. Stability in a word's meaning is not something to be assumed, but always something to be explained" (11).

What we usually call the "proper" or "literal" meaning of a word is simply the meaning it takes from the contexts that recur most frequently in our discursive practice. "Proper meanings" are not properties, they are the relatively stable functions of the relatively stable purposes and preoccupations of ordinary life.

The relation of words and meanings is not aptly conceived on the analogy of form and matter or its near equivalent form and content. As Richards says, "We shall do better to think of a meaning as though it were a plant that has grown..." (12). The plant metaphor, derived from Coleridge and one of Richards' many figurative links with romanticism, suggests that meanings are produced organically, by our adaptation of past experience to the needs of present life. Behavioral in origin and pragmatic in its effects, meaning does not so much record our theoretical apprehension of things as it does our practical dealings with them. The "meaning" things have for us is just this organically generated and continually accruing fund of experience. Governing our present responses and shaping the future, this reservoir of meanings extends farther than memory into the preconscious past.

Whence Richards concludes, first, that there are no sensations, that is, no mere data; and second, that all perception is (therefore) sorting. As to the first, to deny that we have any sensations "sounds drastic but is almost certainly true if rightly understood. A sensation would be something that just was *so*, on its own, a datum; as such we have none. Instead we have perceptions, responses whose character comes to them from the past as well as the present occasion" (30).

At the end of a discussion following his paper, "Structure, Sign, and Play in the Discourse of the Human Sciences," read at John Hopkins in 1966, Jacques Derrida said, "I don't believe that anything like perception exists." His reasons for saying this—he says it twice—are almost identical with Richards' reasons for denying the reality of sensation: perception "is precisely a concept... of a given originating from the thing itself, present itself in its meaning, independently from language, from the system of reference."[3] From considerations such as these Richards draws his second conclusion: "A perception is never just of an *it*; perception takes whatever it perceives as a thing of a certain sort. All thinking from the lowest to the highest—whatever else it may be—is sorting" (30). We do not begin with particulars or sense data and arrive at generalities by applying some version of the laws of association. On the contrary, we start with generalities, specify them, and eventually arrive at the congeries of universals that we call singulars. In Richards' words,

> we begin with the general abstract anything, split it, as the world makes us, into sorts and then arrive at concrete particulars by the overlapping or common membership of these sorts. This bit of paper here now in my hands is a concrete particular to us so far as we think of it as paperish, hereish, nowish and in my hand; it is the more concrete as we take it as of more sorts; and the more specific as the sorts are narrower and more exclusive. (31)

What we think of as perception is actually classification. But in order to classify, you need a set of rules that tell you how to "split" the "general abstract anything" and a corresponding system of categories ("sorts") to receive your precisions. Philosophers have been tempted to draw up a menu of absolute categories—transcendent (Plato) or transcendental (Kant) forms—the application of which to the given will guarantee faultless classification and therewith insure veridical perception. In other words, that we will see things as they are and as they must be. Richards, however, believes that our principles of classification and so our ways of perceiving are more or less *ad hoc*, determined by our practical interests and adapted to our life situation: "as the world makes us." Since both our interests and our situation change, so also our categories have to change. Ideally they should become ever more comprehensive and ever more subtle, enabling us to negotiate a wider range of experiences with greater delicacy and greater effectiveness. But in no case may we suppose that we have or that we are approaching a vision of things as they are in their essential truth and reality.

Except for its behaviorist roots and its pragmatic objectives (and maybe these are not really exceptions), Richards' view of perception—he calls it "a theorem about meanings" (26)—makes common cause with idealist doctrine. Its implications are clear. If perception is a process of sorting that begins with the abstract general and terminates at the concrete particular, then concrescence is a conjugation of abstractions. "Things…are instances of laws," and "out of these laws…, in our minds and in the world…the fabric of our meanings, *which is the world*, is composed" (36, my emphasis). And a little further on, "the world… is… a fabric of conventions" (41). To say that the world is a fabric of meanings knit together by organic—i.e., internal—relations is to adopt a characteristic idealist point of view. Albeit a pragmatic-linguistic idealism, as the facile substitution of "conventions" for "meanings" seems to suggest.

A further dimension of Richards' "theorem about meanings" is opened by two sentences from his second lecture:

> If we sum up thus far by saying that meaning is *delegated efficacy*, that description applies above all to the meaning of words, whose virtue is to be substitutes exerting the powers of what is not there. (32)

> It is enough for our purposes to say that what a word means is the missing parts of the contexts from which it draws its delegated efficacy. (35)

By way of explaining these statements, Richards offers this definition of "context:"

> Now for the sense of 'context.' Most generally it is a name for a whole cluster of events that recur together—including the required conditions as well as whatever we may pick out as cause or effect. But the modes of causal recurrence on which meaning depends are peculiar through that delegated efficacy I have been talking about. In these contexts one item— typically a word—takes over the duties of parts which can then be omitted from the recurrence. There is thus an abridgement of the context only shown in the behavior of living things, and most extensively and drastically shown by man. When this abridgement happens, what the sign or word— the item with these delegated powers—means is the missing parts of the context.(34)

In the texts here cited, the *topos* of absence is insinuated by the expressions "the powers of what is not there," "omitted," and (twice) "the missing parts of the context." The meaning of a word is the "delegated efficacy" of its context. Otherwise: what a word means is *not there*. Its meaning is omitted, the word itself a proxy exercizing the powers of the absent. There is nothing exotic about this. The word "cow" is vested with all the powers of the cow (even) in the absence of the cow herself. It calls up cow-associations, elicits (at least) symbolic cow-responses, and may trigger cow-relevant behavior. But the commonplace character of this phenomenon should not blind us to its implications for our ordinary view of language. If Richards is right, words do not stand for but stand in for the things they mean. Plenipotentiaries of the absent, they substitute for—in the technical sense, supplement—a deficiency of presence. Replacements rather than references, they do not mirror an existing world but construct a world of their own. To the extent that they represent things, they do so not as (we think) pictures represent things, but as a congressman represents his constituents. As your congressman takes your place in the legislative assembly and acts in your stead, so words represent their absent referents in the fabric of meanings that compose the world. If we ask what has become of the "real" world, the thing itself that is the "source of our meanings," we are reminded that "our beliefs are a veil and an artificial veil between ourselves and something that otherwise than through a veil we cannot know"(42). The "missing parts of the context" that constitute the meaning of signs are not remote presences—presences left behind or set aside. On the contrary, since the world is a fabric of meanings, they themselves are (or were: *Wesen ist was gewesen ist*) constituted in their being (as meanings) by a process of delegation receding through a chain of absences without end. They are, absolutely and aboriginally, "the powers of what is not there." To say this is not to say that there is no thing-in-itself, no "indecipherable cause"[4] of phenomena, only that it shall remain undeciphered. To the same effect, Derrida writes that "representation does not...encroach upon presence; it inhabits it as the very condition of its experience...."[5] The mother of all that was and is and is to come is never unveiled, the less so as speaking creatures, themselves creatures of language, attempt with words to undress her.

Of the number and variety of veilings, however, there is no end. Since all words, save the most exotic coinages, function in a great many interlocking and overlapping contexts, all discourse is polysemous. Perplexingly so, since the fact that any word has or may have multiple meanings makes for maximum ambiguity. But ambiguity, according to Richards, is not a fault to be regretted and if possible corrected. Equivocation is natural and original. Univocal meaning is a late development, either a fortuitous and misleading byproduct of the fact that certain contexts and so certain meanings recur far more often than others, or a stipulation designed to serve limited technical or scientific purposes. But neither frequency nor fiat can finally eliminate ambiguity, which is a normal feature of language to be understood and exploited.

Discussing the "interinanimation of words," Richards attacks what he calls the "Usage Doctrine." This is the view that there is a "good" and "correct" use for each word and that finding it is the key to linguistic success. As the Proper Meaning Superstition holds that words possess their meanings as fixed attributes, so the Usage Doctrine decrees that every word has, as an inalienable property, its right use. But words interact with their neighbors, and it is this contextual interaction that gives rise to their meanings. Richards prefers to "interaction" the term "interinanimate," on loan from Donne's "The Exstasie," which implies that words in their actual uses breathe life into each other. The Usage Doctrine obscures this interinanimating process.

> Its evil is that it takes the senses of an author's words to be things we know before we read him, fixed factors with which he has to build up the meaning of his sentences as a mosaic is put together of discrete independent tesserae. Instead, they are resultants which we arrive at only through the interplay of the interpretative possibilities of the whole utterance. (55)

But even the "whole utterance" does not sufficiently determine its own interpretative possibilities and the meanings of its component words. Every word uttered or written gets its meaning and effect from its interrelations with all other words whether uttered or written or only tacit. Richards is aware that he is making trouble for himself:

> I may seem in danger of making the force of a word, the feeling that no other word could possibly do so well or take its place, a matter whose explanation will drag in the whole of the rest of the language. (63-64)

Trouble notwithstanding, Richards does not think

> that we need be shy of something very like this as a conclusion. A really masterly use of a language...goes a long way towards using the language as a whole. (64)

If this is the case, then every use of every word, masterly or not, may be supposed to bear the delegated efficacies of the entire language; or conversely, the entire language is focused and all its powers concentrated at each use of each of its words. If we also keep in mind that the total context of any word is not just the surrounding discourse, expressed or unexpressed, but also "its (non-linguistic) conditions," then we may have come at last to that "last resort" of which Richards says early on that it is "a long way off and very deep down" (10). Though in quotidian practice we are ("mercifully") arrested far short of the deep end, theory and a theoretically conscientious hermeneutic must face the facts. A command of the language as a whole, along with the totality of its conditions, is strictly requisite to the interpretation of any piece of language. Particular meanings come fully and clearly into view only in light of a synoptic vision of the whole: a single comprehensive grasp of all the interactive contexts—the context of all contexts—in which any word might conceivably be used.

That would be a breathtaking vision, as it is (for the Platonist in us) an exhilarating and intimidating prospect. But it may also be the occasion of an insoluble problem. It is fairly clear that no actual human being enjoys the requisite holistic vision. For that matter it is not thinkable that any finite being or assembly of finite beings *could* constitute themselves a hermeneutic court of the "last resort." This is not just unlikely in fact, it is in principle impossible. The context of the whole would itself have no context, and since all meaning is contextually imparted, the context of the whole would necessarily be meaningless. By a version of what Kenneth Burke calls the "paradox of purity,"[6] it would be unintelligible in terms of the logic that posits it. In the strictest Richardsian sense of the word, "context of the whole" is a nonsensical idea.

A Platonist might deal with the problem by postulating a unique mode of cognition (*noesis* as opposed to dialectic) that enables us to comprehend the otherwise incomprehensible context-of-contexts. Once again, Richards will not make the Platonic move. He turns instead, in the last two chapters of his *Rhetoric*, to metaphor as a way of coping with the problems generated by the contextualist theorem of meaning.

In his critical writings, Coleridge demeans metaphor, in its traditional sense the nominal substitution of one thing for another it happens to resemble. No more than "a fragment of an allegory," metaphor would seem to be the work of fancy.[7] By contrast, and by way of illustrating the activity of the imagination, Coleridge offers a definition of symbol. It is, he says,

> characterized by a translucence of the special in the individual, or of the general in the special, or of the universal in the general; above all by the translucence of the eternal in and through the temporal. It always partakes of the reality which it renders intelligible; and while it enunciates the whole, abides itself as a living part in that unity of which it is the representative.[8]

Richards tacitly appropriates what Coleridge says about symbol to his own understanding of metaphor (109). So conceived, metaphor is not just an exemplary case of the way meaning is produced: it is the "omnipresent principle" of language (90). An instance that enunciates the whole of which it is an instance, metaphor becomes microcosm, in idealist language the concrete universal. It focuses—makes real and perspicuous—all the contexts which, absent, exert their powers in and through its present being. If meaning is produced by the interinanimation of words, then metaphor is the sacrament of meaning and the incarnation of the interinanimated word. It offers that fabric of universals which is the world a local habitation and a name.

In a passage that cites Coleridge's "Dejection," Richard writes:

> Our world is a projected world, shot though with the characters lent to it from our own life. "We receive but what we give." The processes of metaphor in language, the exchanges between the meanings of words which we study in explicit verbal metaphor, are superimposed upon a perceived world which is itself a product of earlier or unwitting metaphor, and we shall not deal with them justly if we forget that this is so. (108-109)

It is impossible not to detect, in the distinction between "explicit verbal metaphors" and "earlier...unwitting metaphor," an oblique allusion to Coleridge's distinction between primary and secondary imagination and behind that to Kant's distinction between the imagination that synthesizes phenomena and the imagination that creates aesthetical ideas. As a project of the imagination, the world itself is metaphor, explicit or unwitting, through and through. And the "command of metaphor" of which Aristotle speaks is the "greatest thing of all" because it is "a command of life" (95).

Necessarily, metaphor will occupy a central position in rhetoric as it does in life. In lieu of a logos, metaphor provides the requisite norm of interpretation. We cannot get the sense of our words by fitting them into the big picture. We can only do it by attending closely to those paradigmatic instances of significance in which the principle of signification is revealed. For it is the nature of metaphor at once to enunciate the whole and to participate in the reality it represents.

In all perception, all thought, and all discourse, Richards says, we move from the general through the specific toward the unique singular. Not simple, discrete, and vacuous particulars—there are none of these in a world made of meanings—but fully determinate congregations of universals. Richards also believes that perception, thought, and discourse are creative. Not only language, therefore, but also thought and *a fortiori* perception are metaphoric. They generate the meanings that constitute our reality. The production of metaphor is the activity by which singular meanings are generated, and metaphors themselves are the singular realities that compose the world. This is the finality of metaphor. What cannot be given in principle metaphor gives us in fact: a closure of meaning in practice compensating for the impossibility of closure in theory. In Richards' doctrine of metaphor we see once more, and never more clearly, the intersection of the idealist and pragmatist vectors of his thought. Idealist, insofar as metaphor creates the world; pragmatist, insofar as metaphor is the reality and intelligibility of the world it creates.

A closer look at a few excerpts from Richards' discussion of metaphor will expand and qualify the above remarks. First the following:

> In philosophy, above all, we can take no step safely without an unrelaxing awareness of the metaphors we, and our audience, may be employing; and though we may pretend to eschew them, we can attempt to do so only by detecting them. And this is the more true, the more severe and abstract the philosophy is. As it grows more abstract we think increasingly by means of metaphors that we profess not to be relying on. The metaphors we are avoiding steer our thought as much as those we accept. So it must be with any utterance for which it is less easy to know what we are saying than what we are not saying. And in philosophy, of which this is almost a definition, I would hold with Bradley that our pretence to do without metaphor is never more than a bluff waiting to be called.(92)

For Richards and in opposition to the classical tradition, metaphor is not a stylistic feature peculiar to *belles lettres* nor a device by which poets give their productions reader appeal. It is at work in all discourse save the most narrowly technical, and even there it works unacknowledged after it has been banished. As the above passage indicates, it is especially important in philosophy. Philosophy (along with all its kindred discourses of science and theory) and literature are not related as literal and figurative. They are modes, possibly distinct modes, of metaphor. Literal language of the sort found in the vocabularies of the exact sciences is possible only (and only imperfectly possible) as a repression by stipulation of the natural and original metaphoricity of all discourse. The literal is a reduction of the metaphorical. But the metaphoricity of language is irreducible, and what we call "literal" is not really so.

Richards speaks of meaning as "the delegated efficacy of signs by which they bring together into new unities the abstracts, or aspects, which are the missing parts of their various contexts," so that "a word is normally a substitute for (or means) not one discrete past impression but a combination of general aspects." To which he adds, "that is a summary account of the principle of metaphor" (93). The significance of the signifier is a function of the absence of the signified—all the signifieds—for which it is the lieutenant. Add to this the fact that "there is no whole to any analogy" and "no…limits to the relations of tenor and vehicle" (133)—i.e., no constraints on metaphor—and it is possible to appreciate the full force of Richards' conviction that our reality is a tissue of meanings created by metaphor and that both reality and meaning are therefore fictions (91). "Here the total artifice reveals itself/As the total reality."[9]

In spite of the hierarchic ordering implied by their names, tenor and vehicle—Richards admits that it is often difficult to know which is which—interact in a limitless variety of ways, even to the extent of exchanging or confounding their roles. Metaphors do not work by recalling sense-perceptions or suggesting images (98). The metaphors we do not regard as such, writing them off as "dead" and therefore as good as "literal," are in fact "the most regular sustaining metaphors of all speech" (101). And the power of a metaphor derives not only from the similarities of tenor and vehicle, but just as much from their differences (127). In short, "a metaphor may work admirably without our being able with any confidence to say how it works…" (117). Metaphors—or for that matter words, since all words are metaphoric—work whether nor not we know how they do it. Our understanding or lack of it is irrelevant to their effective functioning. It should be no mystery that metaphor, as an omnipresent and originary principle of language, remains something of a mystery. As the founding agency of language, it cannot be comprehended and mastered by the language it constitutes. And that, in a handful of words, is the burden of Derrida's "White Mythology," the definitive deconstructivist discussion of metaphor and its aboriginal place in philosophy.[10]

Richards' view of metaphor is the Romantic inversion of Aristotle's doctrine. "Literal" and "metaphoric" change places as the original (proper) and derivative (improper) forms of language respectively. The mimetic function of words is replaced by a world-making poesis. But in this upending of the Classical hierarchy, the hierarchy itself is disturbed, and there is a consequent loss of presence and intelligibility. Reality itself becomes a fiction created by a power of language which we wield and from which we benefit but which we do not understand. This is the deconstructive moment in Richards' doctrine of metaphor. But in Richards the theoretical objectives common to Aristotle and Derrida give way to purposes predominantly pragmatic: finding remedies for misunderstanding and ways to improve communication. For the Classical tradition words express and communicate our knowledge of a world that is what it is prior to and independent of us and our language. For the Romantic, the only world we know is the one we make. For the deconstructivist we and the world are both effects of the disseminative energies of language. For Richards the world we make, exploiting but not comprehending these agencies, is the one we need in order to attain whatever objectives we deem, for whatever reason, necessary or desirable. From thinking God's thoughts after him, from continuing or rivaling his creation, we descend to the humbler but humanly indispensible task of cultivating our garden.

In the preceding survey of Richards' rhetoric, I have called attention to three of its distinguishing features. One is the way Richards' account of meaning and interpretation seems to entail deconstructivist doctrines of dissemination and undecidability. Another is the romantic-idealist (mainly Coleridgean) roots of his views, especially his view of metaphor and his belief that language is poetic rather than mimetic. And last is the pragmatist adaptation of idealism by which he counters and/or copes with the twin perils of misunderstanding (undecidability) and failed communication (dissemination). In the remainder of this essay I shall discuss the problem posed and the solution proposed by these elements of Richards' doctrine. I shall also suggest what I take to be the implications of Richards' position, both problem and solution, for contemporary critical practice, especially the practice of deconstruction.

For Richards, the meaning of any word is generated contextually by that process of interinanimation of which the constitutive instance is metaphor. What we ordinarily regard as the literal meaning of a word is the result of ignoring or suppressing the metaphoricity and plurisignificance of all words. However, since all words occur in an indeterminate number and variety of contexts, all words are overdetermined. The full and final meaning—the "real" meaning—of any word in any occurrence could be derived only from an understanding of the totality of the contexts in which it is, has been, or may be used. But that of course can never be given. No context is fully saturated and finally bounded. And since the conditions of closure cannot be met, plurisignificance explodes in dissemination. The meaning of any word and of any structure made of words—read: the world — is in principle undecidable.

That meaning is undecidable is a characteristically deconstrucivist rule of thumb, the appreciation and application of which distinguishes deconstructive reading from Classical exegesis and Romantic-modernist heremeneutics. On the Classical view language is a complete and coherent, albeit conventional, system of signifying elements, the competent employment of which encodes determinate meanings decodable by an equivalently competent exegete. The Romantic-modernist view locates the origin of meaning in the creative subject, who embodies his intentions in the expressive medium of language, from which the hermeneutic empathy of a kindred subject may recover it. But the deconstruction of the linguistic sign makes it impossible for the reader to discover, exegetically or hermeneutically, a meaning which in fact the writer, whether by a supposed linguistic competence or the equally mythical force of genius, may not even be able to put into words. Richards' contextualism removes language from the control of the sovereign subject, who does not comprehend and cannot command the whole context by which words are invested with meanings, and on top of that denies that anything like "the whole context" could ever be present and accessible, if indeed it can even be thought. The conclusion would seem to follow, as ineluctably for him as it does for the desconstructivist, that the meaning of any and every text is undecidable.

This conclusion is confirmed, if it needs confirmation, by Richards' thesis that the meaning of a word is the "delegated efficacy" of its context(s). Since the word stands in, as a representative stands in, for what is not there, the aspects of context that give it meaning are necessarily absent—its "missing parts"—and the donation of meaning takes away everything it gives as the condition of its bestowal. For Richards as for Derrida, it would seem, the signified is distanced and deferred by the signifier, which is therefore always only a trace and a supplement—the signifier of an absence.

Richards is not unaware that the contextualist theorem of meaning gives rise to an apparently intractable problem of closure. His doctrine of metaphor is meant to provide a solution. Metaphor in the usual sense—the "figure of speech" that Richards redefines as Coleridgean symbol or concrete universal—is offered as the vivid present realization of that meaning which cannot be derived theoretically in default of the requisite conditions of closure. And yet metaphor as the "omnipresent principle" of language, the interinanimation that creates meaning, also creates the impossibility of any final determination of meaning. The structures that simultaneously generate meaning and prevent closure of meaning at the macro-level are iterated in the microcosm of metaphor. More accurately, since metaphor is the point at which new meanings and therefore new problems of interpretation are continually coming into being, it is not the repetition but rather the origin of all the difficulties that reappear at the theoretical level and seek resolution in metaphor. But metaphor is not the solution. It's part of the problem—the main part. And the endless exchanges of opportunity and aporia between the actual and the ideal amount to no more than a juggling of accounts in the deficit economy of language, a kind of hermeneutic check-kiting that can never come to rest in a solvent interpretation. No metaphorology, even the most resilient and resourceful, can contain the disseminative energies of its subject. In which case metaphor, and with it the main part of Richards' rhetoric, goes to pieces. Strictly speaking, it deconstructs itself and in so doing becomes the perverse Coleridgean symbol in which the truth of deconstruction is translucently enunciated.

These remarks are not offered in criticism of Richards, certainly not as a refutation of his views. I have only meant to highlight certain implications of his doctrine of which the doctrine itself is already plainly aware. Specifically, I have pointed to that "last resort" of which Richards says that it is "a long way off and very deep down"(10). And I have noted that, on his view, "a long way off" means "off the deep end" and "very deep down" is the abyss. The question is not: why didn't Richards see these consequences of his position? He did. My question is: why didn't he follow them to their deconstructive conclusions?

It is important to recall that metaphor is not in the strict sense a *solution* to the problem of closure. It is not the theoretical last word, it is a pragmatic and always provisional *recourse*. Though metaphor may resonate with the ultimate, the resonance itself is never more than proximate, not the ultimate itself but a proxy for the ultimate. Understanding the character of a human being (oneself or another) is analogous to interpreting a text, and no less difficult. Certainty is out of the question. Yet there are some actions of the person that seem to be uniquely revelatory, and though we could not justify our doing so we incline to take them as dead giveaways. In other words, as metaphors of personality. Similarly, the meaning of a text, which we cannot determine in theory, we take, without sufficient reason, to be practically accessible in those intensest moments of textuality we call metaphor. But this is not a theoretical solution to a theoretical problem. It is a pragmatic makeshift to repair an irreparable deficiency of theory. Bricolage, not engineering.

At the very outset of his first lecture Richards explains that his interest in rhetoric is mainly practical. It should be, he says, a "study of misunderstanding and its remedies" that would "minister successfully to important needs" by teaching us how to distinguish good communication from bad(3). Toward the end of that lecture, having described at some length what he takes to be catastrophic misunderstandings of the nature of language and meaning, he voices the idealist commitment—"the fabrics of all our various worlds are the fabrics of our meanings"(19)—that is several times reaffirmed throughout the book (Cf.30, 36, 41, 108, 134). But immediately after this first declaration he makes it clear that the purpose of philosophy (=idealism), like the purpose of rhetoric, is practical:

> Whatever we may be studying we do so only through the growth of our meanings. To realize this turns some parts of this attempted direct study of the modes of growth and interaction between meetings, which might otherwise seem a niggling philosophic juggle with distinctions, into a business of great practical importance. For this study is theoretical only that it may become practical. (19)

Having said this, Richards quotes Hobbes paraphrasing Bacon to the effect that the end of philosophy is "the commodity of human life," that "knowledge is power," and that "the scope of all speculation is the performance of some action" (19-20). The first lecture ends with a notice that later lectures will deal with "problems... upon which... we spend our whole ordinary life." Though Richards will not further insist upon it(20), all of his speculations in rhetoric are conducted under the rubric of praxis.

Richard speaks of the things words *do* at least as often as he speaks of what they mean. Meaning itself is a mode of action—a way of coping with experience—rather than a terrain of inert signifieds mapped by the signifiers of language. Rejecting form/matter and form/content analogues for the relation of word and meaning—"wretchedly inconvenient metaphors"—Richards says, "We shall do better to think of meaning as a plant that has grown...."(12) The vegetable metaphor, Coleridgean in origin and a mark of Richards' own organicism, enriches his pragmatism with the memory of that idealism from which all pragmatisms derive. It is an essential component in Richards' view of language. "Words are not a medium in which to copy life. Their true work is to restore life itself to order."(134) These sentences from the very end of the book express as succinctly as possible the vital and ordering principle of Richards' philosophy of rhetoric.

Somewhat disturbingly, however, at least from a deconstructivist point of view, Richards' last words suggest that there was an original order from which we have fallen and that our present state of misunderstanding and broken communication is a product of this lapse. Coleridge says as much in a lengthy passage quoted at the end of Lecture V. The soul tells herself, "From this state"—that of the "vegetable creation"—"hast *thou* fallen!"

(110)[11] Richards neither espouses nor disavows the explicit soteriology of this passage. But to construct a world of meaning and the meaning of a world out of the elements of language is itself a soteriological enterprise requiring at least a minimal (idealist) faith that the whole is still latent in the parts, however it may have been obscured or suppressed by the "superstitions" of correct usage and proper meaning, and the hope bordering on determination that it shall once again be (pragmatically) recovered and life itself returned to order. For this reason Richards' rhetoric will build most confidently on those parts in which the whole is most brilliantly relucent: the singular metaphors in which the principle of metaphor is writ small. And as in theology the Incarnation—the Logos writ small and the metaphor of divinity—is not a theoretical solution to the problems created by the fall, but a bit of celestial praxis to compensate for the inevitable postlapsarian deficit of knowledge; so also, as we have seen, the rhetorical appeal to metaphor is a practical way to cope with the failure of theory.

The theological analogue is only that and should not be pressed. But neither should the spectre of soteriology in Richards' text occasion surprise, least of all to a deconstructionist. Rhetoric is a soteriological project and remains such even after deconstruction has exposed the groundlessness of all attempts to recover a presumed prelapsarian presence. It is both pragmatically wise and sound deconstructive doctrine to recognize this. The dream of presence, however troubled by a deconstructive critique, is a dream from which we never awaken, and the ghost of paradise lost, forbidden to materialize, is never terminally laid but continues to haunt the most perfectly (but never perfect) disillusioned language. Even in this attenuated form, the soteriological impulse is not to be trusted. But its existence may not in good faith be denied. Illusions deconstructed are not destroyed, they are only, again and again, disarmed. The pragmatism of Richards' rhetoric is evidenced by the fact that it acknowledges their inevitability even as it exposes their deceptions.

Richards' pragmatism is also clear from his critical writings; that is, his understanding of the relationship between critical theory and practical criticism.[12] The speculations of the theorist do not generate a critical canon the application of which to particular texts will turn out theoretically authorized interpretations and evaluations. Practical criticism is not applied theory. Theory leads the theorist away from practice through abstraction into the undecidable. If we had a sufficiently good (i.e., perfect) theory, we wouldn't need practice. But we don't, and we do. Practice is necessitated by the necessary failure of theory.

Problems of self-reference aside, the theorist can remain suspended in indecision. But not the practical critic. To be practical is, among other things and perhaps foremost among them, to be prepared to respond to the demands for action that life continually puts in our way. And that means to reach a conclusion in fact when none is available in principle. What is true of life is true of the hermeneutic life. If the world is a fabric of meanings, there may be no important difference. This is where the deconstructivist and the Richardsian critic are in the same boat. Given their knowledge of the way language works and the decisive knowledge that the meaning of a text can never be decided, both of them are constrained to produce interpretations that they know are not fully justified, exclusively correct, or completely exhaustive. There is always room for additional and alternate readings with as much claim to legitimacy as those already delivered. In theory meaning may remain undecided, but in practice, where undecidability comes home to roost, you have to make judgment calls. Richards calls them guesses. Concerning "the senses of an author's words," he says that "they are resultants which we arrive at only through the interplay of the interpretative possibilities of the whole utterance. In brief, we have to guess them and we guess much better when we realize we are guessing, and watch out for indications, than when we think we know"(55).

Richards rejects the Usage Doctrine and the Proper Meaning Superstition, both of them theoretically tidy, because they have disastrous practical consequences (54)—they block communication and breed misunderstanding—and instead adopts a contextualist view of meaning which ends in theoretical undecidability but leaves the practical options open.

Unlike some contemporary modes of critical pragmatism (e.g., Rorty, Fish, and other theorists "against theory"),[13] Richards' version is not required to disengage itself from the theoretical project as such, nor is it committed to denying the reality of the admittedly insoluble problems of theory, in order to justify its practice and liberate the bricoleur. Indeed, it is the persistence of theory that makes the demand for practical expedients most pressing. Theory and practice never exist save in tension with each other. Yet both must exist and exist together. To deny one or the other is to debilitate both. It is not just that theory without practice is empty and practice without theory is blind. Their relationship is dialectical and their codependence essential. As the undecidables of theory make practice necessary, so practice is governed by theoretical considerations that will not provide it with a foundation nor allow it the possibility of closure.

Presumably even the deconstructivist critic, given an actual text and required in the face of the undecidable to reach a decision, will go for the reading(s) that facilitate understanding, maximize the intelligibility of the text, and promote communication between texts and readers. These are practical objectives, ideally the objectives of all critics, and they govern critical practice even in those cases—which may mean all cases—in which the intelligibility terminally communicated by the text is its own undecidability. It is if nothing else a major achievement of understanding and a breakthrough in communication to have read this unreadability.

What is true of deconstruction is also, seen from the other end, a truth about Richards. I have not meant to suggest that Richards is the voice of moderation that the wild-eyed and irresponsible deconstructivist would do well to heed, but rather that he is *in the end* the voice of *praxis* rather than *theoria*. "This study is theoretical only that it may become practical"(10). Though he does not shrink from treading the theoretical abyss, he does (in the end) insist that we develop sophisticated and carefully nuanced techniques for using and interpreting the language in which we live. But we must not forget, as Richards never forgets, that our deployment of words in creation and interpretation alike, however admirably adopted to whatever practical ends, is never adequately grounded and decisively warranted, but always only the latest addition to the growing—vital and therefore unfinished— body of linguistic comportments by which and in which we construct the human world.

7

Sounding Brass. Tinkling Symbols.

> The Parthenon and Our Lady of Chartres, the Sistine Chapel and the Mass
> in B Minor are also rubbish, destined to be burned on the Last Day... It is
> folly to try to find in art the words of eternal life...
>
> —Jacques Maritain

I was listening to the radio. A classical music station. The orchestra was about to perform Carl Nielsen's *Fifth Symphony*. The announcer introducing it informed me: "In a way this symphony is like life itself—struggling through, persisting, in spite of all opposing forces. Now in this symphony the opposing forces are represented by the percussion, especially the side drum...." I turned the radio off. Whatever life may do, there are some opposing forces that I cannot persist in spite of.

Among those who write on the subject there is almost universal agreement that music has something to do with the emotions. I'm not sure that's the case. But suppose it is. If we then ask, Exactly what does music have to do with emotion? the unanimity quickly scatters.

From Plato to Tolstoy and beyond, there have been those who believed that music causes emotions (usually unacceptable emotions) in its hearers. But that horse is at least moribund, and I do not intend to cause it any further suffering. Here's another uncontroversial precision. At least it should be uncontroversial. Music is not essentially a representational art. It need not picture nor relate nor describe nor refer to anything.

Not even emotions? There's a rub. Some theorists (notably Leonard Meyer)[1] have argued that music produces in its hearers what we might call patterns of feeling. Leaving out the details (and looking away from Meyer's rather ponderous erudition), what this means is fairly simple. By the way it begins a piece of music arouses in the listener certain expectations as to how it will go on. By the way it actually continues it satisfies, frustrates, or revises—in any case complicates and refines—those expectations. By the time it ends, the piece (if it is successful) will have fulfilled the expectations it initially prompted, with (of course) all the qualifications introduced by what has happened between the first pick-up and the last fermata. When it has done all this, the music has given you a complete emotional experience. Structurally speaking, the description of a complete musical event (a whole piece) is also the description of a complete course of emotion: from first arousal, through medial complication, delayed gratification, provisional distraction, and temporary frustration, to eventual satisfaction. Getting one, you get the other in the bargain.

This said, it is necessary to add a couple of restrictive clauses. First: for all their structural similarity, the emotional experience made possible by music is not a reasonable facsimile—a phonostatic replica—of an analogous non-musical emotional event. Listening to music is not an acceptable substitute for making love, receiving communion, or going off to war.

Musically engendered emotions diverge from (otherwise congruent) extra-musical emotions in at least two ways. For one thing, the emotional experience provided by music is—or may be—perfect. The expectations evoked are always met. But real-life emotions are often, if not most often, fragmentary and incoherent. Life repeatedly disappoints us by suggesting more emotional possibilities than it permits us to actualize. Unlike music, in which every detail contributes to the total effect, real life is cluttered with loose ends of feelings. Life is a series of one-night stands and brief encounters; music is the perfect love affair that ends when it should, without remorse or remonstrance, just the warm afterglow of satisfaction.

This first difference between musical and non-musical emotions may be traced to a second: the musical experience is—or may be—rigorously self-controlled. The expectations it starts are produced solely by the music, and the gratification it provides is accomplished exclusively in and by the music. In the production and management of quotidian emotions, a great many causes and kinds of causes collaborate or, as the case may be, compete—causes that are, by and large, out of our control. In the case of musical emotion, the music itself gives both the beginning and the completion; outside of music, what triggers an expectation and what (if anything) satisfies it may be altogether different, and neither may have anything to do with the quality of the emotion itself. In a word: the finality of the musical experience is a function of the autoteleology, the strict self-contentment, of the music, so that musical emotion is an emotional experience of music and of nothing else.

This is the first restriction: musical emotion, though it is homologous with it, neither duplicates nor doubles for extra-musical emotion. Here's the second. The fact that musical emotions resemble non-musical emotions has led some aestheticians (notably Susanne Langer)[2] to suppose that musical emotion is a semblance of non-musical emotion. The (symmetrical) relation of resemblance is assimilated to the (asymmetrical) hierarchy of appearance and reality. Musical forms thereby become a means (a mere seeming) by which we are enabled to understand real feelings. By symbolizing the forms of feeling, music acquaints us with our emotions just as (classically) the image facilitates cognition of its original.

I think this view is misleading in more ways than one. To begin with, even if we assume that music is a means of cognition, the analogy between music and emotion is so nosebleedingly abstract that the emotional nourishment we might derive from music would be well below subsistence level. Music acquaints us with our feelings in the same way, and to the extent, that Mondrian's canvases manifest the order of the cosmos or a trefoil the Blessed Trinity. That is, not much.

From erotic music we learn that sexual passion mounts slowly and stepwise to a shattering explosion and then rather abruptly rollercoasters down to total lassitude. We needed Wagner to teach us that? Surely there are betters ways to learn about sex, even without doing it.

To continue. The notion that music mediates a knowledge of emotion grievously misrepresents the musical experience. The experience of music is intense and compelling. A lot of us seek it as (I'll have to eat these words later) an end in itself. Cognizing one thing by way of another is, by comparison, a rather cool and detached business. And should be. If you want A to convey knowledge of B, you need to make A as negligible as possible. A Venn diagram may help you understand the syllogism, and nothing is less interesting (*per se*) than a Venn diagram. Rightly so, for if A ever gets to be as impressive as B, then the means becomes an end and the end is obscured. When we examine a piece of great portraiture, our interest in the sitter is replaced by an interest in the canvas. Music is immensely absorbing, and the last thing you think of when you listen to music, is... something else. We misconceive portraiture if we suppose it a way of getting to know the persons portrayed. And if we think that the function of music is to provide us with cognitive access to our feelings, we trivialize music and the musical experience.

These animadversions suggest a further and (under this head) final observation. Wouldn't it make more sense to put the hierarchy in reverse? If we recognize a person from her portrait, we must already know her. Our prior knowledge of the subject permits us to interpret her picture, not the other way around. Lacking such knowledge, we cannot get it from the painting. Analogously, it is our prior knowledge of the emotions that impels us to describe music in emotional terms and then regard the music as a symbol of the feelings with which we have invested it. Deprived of the title and the lyrics, would you have known that the *Liebestod* is erotic if you hadn't already known something about orgasm? I once played Samuel Barber's popular *Adagio* for a class in aesthetics and asked them to tell me what feelings it suggested. About half of them said sex. The virgins thought it was religious. Which figures.

If you're going to insist that the relation of music to emotion is a cognitive relation, it makes just as much sense to say that emotions explain the shape of music as it does to say that music reveals the forms of emotion. Just as much. Maybe more. But why do it at all? Why hierarchize a mere homology? And why, in the process, privilege cognition? Perhaps: to elude the inference (Platonic-Tolstoyan) that music is emotionally infectious and therefore dangerous. Cognition at least is not contagious, as teachers know only too well. But though it may never become epidemic, cognition is the occupational psychosis of academics and theoreticians. It's our version of the Midas touch: everything we lay our hands on turns to knowledge, and for all that we should know better we keep on producing revisions—ever more attenuated— of the view that music is a kind of representation.

King Midas learned to his regret that not everything should be made of gold. Daughters, for example. And so, in spite of our monistic pathology, we might learn that not everything should be a mode of cognition. Music, for example?

But if music is not an instrument of learning, what is it? It is, proximately and provisionally, itself. I have already said, though I have hardly argued, that music offers its listeners a complete emotional experience. Not a simulacrum or a sublimation or a substitute, neither symptom, stimulus, nor sign. But the thing itself, an emotional experience *sui generis* and in its own right. The experience of music is an experience of music: caused, controlled, and contained by the music itself, having the music itself as its objective correlative.

So far so good. Now let me add this: to the extent that music is the rational ordering of matter (sound) instinct with the possibility of pathos, and to the extent that the experience of music is autotelically grounded and bounded, music provides us with a *paradigm of experience*. The musical experience is at once intensely emotional and thoroughly rational. And that in such a way that the heart and the head vary directly. Not inversely. In music (at least) rationality does not demand a disengagement of the passions, nor do the passions insist on suborning the intellect. On the contrary: the more exquisitely ordered is at the same time the more affectively compelling. In music at least. And if (at least in music) this perfection is occasionally actual, may it not be (at least) possible elsewhere?

The ancients (among them Plato and Boethius)[3] used to say that music molds character. Maybe this is what they had in mind. You are what you hear. By its own disciplined affect and impassioned rationality, music shows you how to call your emotions to order and infuse your intellect with pathos. Shakespeare warns us to beware the man who "hears no music."[4] His intellect is likely to be a calculating machine and his emotional life rampant with riot. But music is, and life might be, the harmony of heart and head, a "blessed rage for order."[5]

Others among the ancients (for example, St. Augustine)[6] and some of the moderns (for example, Hindemith and Stravinsky)[7] have insisted on the essential spirituality of music. In the Middle Ages music was the only one of the fine arts with an unqualified claim to "liberality"—which in that age meant liberty from the servile submission to matter that hampered painting, sculpture, and the like. The medievals recognized three kinds of music. *Musica instrumentalis*, audible harmonies produced by voices and instruments. *Musica humana*, the harmony of the faculties in a well-ordered human soul. And *musica mundana*, the harmony of the cosmos ordained by God. The function of *musica instrumentalis* was to induce harmony in the soul, which latter was to be modeled on the harmony of the spheres. Unheard melodies were not only sweeter, they were also more real. That is, more spiritual. Music (in the ordinary sense) conformed the soul to God by attuning it to the universal concord.

The spirituality which the medievals attributed to music we may perhaps ascribe to the spirituality of its medium. Music after all is not sound, but the order of sound. Old Hanslick was right: music is *tönend bewegte Formen*, sounding forms in motion.[8] I might conflate a couple of formulas stolen from Kenneth Burke and say that music is *symbolic action* and *equipment for living*.[9] The latter because the former. Because it provides an authentic emotional experience, music is a mode of action or production. But by virtue of its autotelic self-contentment, its action is in the symbolic order. As both act and symbol, music does not copy or reveal emotion: it models— provides a model for—the emotions. Equipment for living, music is a paradigm and a paragon by which we may order the life of feeling and inflame the life of reason.

If I am allowed this conclusion, I may be able to make some small retribution to the view I earlier maligned as "philosophical:" the view that music is a means of cognition. It is true, I think, that music has something to teach us and that we have something to learn from music. But our education by music is closer to what German calls *Bildung* than it is to what an epistemologist might think of as learning. Music teaches us by shaping us. It molds (i.e., models) character, as the ancients said. And when we learn from music, it is not like learning about X from a sign or representation of X. What we get from music is neither description nor acquaintance, but a *way to be*. In Oscar Wilde's phrase, which I hereby endorse, *life imitates art*.[10] We inhabit the world and enact the self first imagined in and by the work. Like God, we all wind up becoming what we have created.

That, I suspect, is true of all the forms of art and not just music. Music, by virtue of its patently non-mimetic character, makes obvious what is happening in all the works of the human imagination. If all the arts do not aspire to the condition of music, they should.

But. And however. I discover myself on the verge of a usual mistake. Like Pooh and Piglet hunting the dreaded Heffalump, I have fallen into my own trap. I have offered you a piece of classical metaphysics—revisionist, to be sure—and then assured you that music can be assimilated to my own version of the dream of presence. But while the dream of presence may be a necessary dream, from which we can never wholly awaken, it needs to be interrupted now and again by a salutary nightmare. One little dietary indiscretion ought to do the trick. So here you are: Welsh rarebit for dessert.

It is often said (this may even pass for common sense in such matters) that music expresses emotion. This is not quite true, and therefore perilously false. Music does not express emotion because there is no such thing as expression. (There may be no such thing as emotion either, but never mind that.) That is, no such thing as immediate utterance (*Äusserung*) of inner states, only an irreparably mediate act of signification that dissembles at least as much as it exposes. We are never in direct contact with our emotions to begin with—they are always already re-presented in our experience of them—and therefore can never directly present them. Least of all in a medium. For the same reason, with the gears in reverse, music cannot reveal the emotions. It can only interpose between us and our already re-presented life of feeling a redoubled representation that dissimulates everything it discloses.

By this logic—the logic of difference or perhaps of *différance*—I am hoist on my own petard. The spirituality which I have (classically enough) claimed for music and which (in my revisionist way) I have ascribed to the medium of music is illusory. It's a tempting illusion, much like the alleged spirituality of language, only more so. For while musical sounds (like words) can be subjected to syntactical (intelligible) orders, they do not (unlike words) have semantic commitments that bind them to the order of material things. But, seductive as it is, this is only an illusion of spirituality. Hanslick's formula, *tönend bewegte Formen*, which makes the form substantively central and relegates the sound to adjectival ancillarity, is a fragment of idealist metaphysics: a nineteenth-century German *Verbesserung* of classical logocentrism. It insinuates if it does not plainly declare that the musical sound is (only) secondary: a means by which the primary reality—an independent intelligible order of forms—is made manifest to the mind through the senses. Thus musical theorists from antiquity to modern times have pounced on the non-referentiality of musical tone, yoked it together with the intrinsic plasticity of sound (its receptivity to form), and concluded that music is an expression (less mediate even than words) of the Logos in its Paternal originality and Spiritual finality.

It should be evident that this inference is tipsy. For one thing, while musical sound may supplement—that is, stand (in) for, discorporate structures, and thereby inaugurate an endless chain of representations and repetitions, it can no more directly express form than our words can directly express our meaning. Therefore, from its limitless malleability and its incapacity for reference we may with equal force and rigor conclude that the order of tones is (like the order of words) a collocation of material signifiers galvanized to significance by the dissemblance of a superintendent transcendental signified. Sound dissimulating spirituality.

This conclusion (itself imperfectly sober) is tracked by another. If music is but the illusion of spiritual integrity—the mere (re)semblance of an interinanimation of heart and head, signifier and signified—then it may not so simply and unproblematically provide a model for the emotions. Neither paragon nor paradigm, it may instead go proxy for the less orderly and therefore more troublesome thing we call real life. What music offers us may be substitute satisfactions, alternatives to experience rather than the quote unquote real thing. The musical experience may be, not the highroad to reality, but a detour that bypasses reality—just as poring over the pictures in *Playboy* or *Penthouse* replaces and does not reinforce actual sexual intercourse. To say this much is to insert into this most proper discussion the most improper suspicion that the musical experience may become a masturbatory fantasy. That's the danger of associating with people like Oscar Wilde. But Wilde should (must) have known that even our finest lies—those fabulous fictions-for-their-own-sake that we call art, are not purely gratuitous but inevitably contaminated by the will-to-believe and its motivational twin, the will-to-be-deceived. Maybe Plato and Tolstoy were right to be wary.

Like Plato (more or less), and maybe like Tolstoy, Kierkegaard saw in art a spiritual peril: a delicious distraction from the serious business of ethical choice and religious faith. These were the modes of authentic human existence for which "the aesthetic" was an inauthentic substitute. Yet the predominantly poetic character of Kierkegaard's own *oeuvre* suggests that his hierarchy was not so unshakably emplaced as he wanted us to believe. Schopenhauer knew that the peace of mind vouchsafed us by the arts is but a provisional repose: a temporary release from the striving to which we are doomed. The Wheel of Ixion takes a break now and then, but it grinds relentlessly on. Unreconstructed Romantic that he was, Schopenhauer also thought that music uniquely and proximately expressed his pessimist's surrogate for the Logos: the ultimate aimless spasming of the Will. But we alas (disenchanted Romantics that we are) know that even the most powerful illusion sooner or later lets us down. The more insistently it strains for the effect of reality, the more flatly our musical invention disappoints us. And authenticity is only the already remote, always receding term of a nostalgic allusion.

There you have my Welsh (or is it French?) rarebit. Have I taken back everything I said? Yes and no. I have written a palinode. But the palinode does not expunge the text it retracts. Adding yet another ode (an ode again), it supplements its origin and allows it to stand...legible under erasure. Its motto is: "and yet...." *Quod scripsi scripsi*, and the effect of rescription is not to unwrite what is written, but rather (*e pur*) to disturb its presuppositions irreparably and to thrust it into endless closure. Most uncharitable. In the plainest and most barefaced language, music may not only uplift and edify and ennoble. It must also unsettle us and discontent us and make us uneasy. Not just with our frazzled quotidian lives—that would be too cheap a shot—but also with its own pretensions. The authenticity that we do not achieve in existence is not to be found in our attempts to transcend it and recreate it. Which is not to discourage the endeavor, but only to underline its poignancy.

It has not been part of my purpose in these theoretical remarks to construct an apologia for the kind of music I happen to like. But all of us are goaded by obscure motives and repressed desires as much as we are guided by conscious intention. Since I've already tipped my hand (if that's what it is), I may as well let it all hang out. Or as much of it as I can locate. I have heard it said, in praise of Beethoven's late quartets, that they go beyond music. Whether this is true of the compositions in question I shall not try to say. But the compliment is at least left-handed and maybe back-handed. It is fairer to Beethoven and a more accurate assessment of his achievement to say that in the last quartets he finally approaches the perfection of music, acknowledging as he does so that he has not taken possession of the promised land but only, poignantly, viewed it from the neighboring height. Just as Bach, in the last "unfinished" *contrapunctus* of *The Art of the Fugue*, is on the verge of polyphonic perfection when both he and his music are taken up to a consummation that is no longer audible. In the end music is just music, and at its most magnificent knows this. For it is required by the self-consciousness of art that it record that breaking of the vessels which is a condition of all creation. "A scar is what happens when the word is made flesh."[11] Doubtful Thomas wants to verify upon the corpus of music the stigmata of incarnation. In plain clothes (and as fully exposed as he dares to be), he desires that music shall acknowledge its artifice even as it perpetrates its illusion, and (in these latter days) turn arsy-versy and undo its own bewitchments. With a blunt instrument: that it shall undeceive us in the same act by which it enchants us.

At the head of this paper I placed a couple of sentences from Jacques Maritain's *Art and Scholasticism*. In the third edition he appends to this passage a footnote apologizing for what he calls these "formulas of contempt with regard to created things." Where the book pontificates, "Created things have no savor," the afterthought retracts: "The creature is deserving of compassion, not contempt; it exists only because it is loved. It is deceptive because it has too much savor, and because this savor is nothing in comparison with the being of God."[12] We creatures—and our creations— exist only because we are loved. One need not embrace Maritain's theology in order to say Yes to that. A troubled Yes, both structured and deconstructed by the dialectic of text and subtext, ode and palinode, origin and supplement, that I have tried to trace in this discussion. This Yes—this *kind* of Yes—is all I wanted to say to/about music. Or rather, all that I was able.

8

Eros into Logos:
The Rhetoric of Courtly Love

Meum pectus sauciat
puellarum decor,
et quas tactu nequeo,
saltem corde mechor.
—The Confession of Golias

The middle ages were much preoccupied with eros. Championing the
ascendancy of spirit over flesh, the church found it necessary to restrain
or channel the power of sex in various ways. Contained within the bonds of
matrimony, sexuality was a useful instrument of social production (offspring)
and social control (taming unruly passions, assuring the orderly transfer of
property through patrilineal inheritance, etc.). In celibate religious
communities, sublimated (sublimed) erotic desire could be indulged as a
symbol of the love of Christ the heavenly bridegroom for his spiritual bride:
the church or the holy soul. In secular literature like the *Carmina Burana*,
unlicensed by the church but composed for the most part by clerics, love
was celebrated as the source of an illicit but ecstatic delight, the transience
and irregularity of which compounded sexual pleasure with the poignancy
of mortality and the fear of retribution. Though it could not authorize the
expression, carnal or verbal, of free sexuality, neither did the church regard
it as a serious threat to its own moral theology: sinners could be expected to
sin.

The configuration of attitudes, ideals, and beliefs that has come to be
known as courtly love was another matter. Theologians decried it, and
preachers inveighed against it. Openly defiant of the church's teaching (the
courtly relationship is normatively adulterous), with its own ideology and

its own cult (the rules of love and the courts of love), *fin' amors* was perceived as a rival religion. Normally expressed in song—the lyrics of the troubadours, the trouveres, and their counterparts in Italy and Germany—courtly love has its theorists, of whom the prince is Andreas Capellanus. My intention in this essay is to examine the theory and practice of courtly love as propounded in his treatise, to expose its motives and effects, and to explicate its relationship to medieval Christianity.

Andreas Capellanus is a cleric. His name, plus his association with the court of Champagne, suggests that he was a chaplain in service to the Countess Marie, who governed as regent after the death of her husband and during the minority of their sons. He describes himself as "chaplain of the royal court." The claim cannot be verified. But in view of the fact that King Philip Augustus was half-brother to Marie and the Queen Mother sister to Marie's husband Henry, relations between Paris and Troyes were very close and Andreas may be telling the truth.[1]

Andreas' text—*De amore* or sometimes *De arte honeste amandi* (ca. 1185)—is written in the form of a letter to a (real or fictional) friend named Walter (Gualterius). Its avowed purpose is to advise Walter on how to conduct a love affair: how to get love, how to keep it, and (if need be) how to get out of a relationship unscathed. Recently smitten by love, Walter does not know how to manage his passion and has asked Andreas for counsel. Andreas therefore offers him the wisdom gleaned from his own wide and varied experience. He is moved to do this by affection for his young friend, though he also admonishes him (in the Preface to his treatise) that it is neither fitting nor expedient to offer oneself to the service of love:

> For I know, having learned from experience, that it does not do the man who owes obedience to Venus's service any good to give careful thought to anything except how he may always be doing something that will entangle him more firmly in his chains; he thinks he has nothing good except what may wholly please his love. Therefore, although it does not seem expedient to devote oneself to things of this kind or fitting for any prudent man to engage in this kind of hunting, nevertheless, because of the affection I have for you, I can by no means refuse your request; because I know clearer than day that after you have learned the art of love your progress in it will be more cautious, in so far as I can I shall comply with your desire.(27)

It is impossible not to detect a note of irony in these words. "Entangle him more firmly in his chains": is love a kind of self-incurred bondage? And that last clause. Does it mean that Walter will be more adept in love once he has learned the art of it? Or is Andreas saying: the more you know about the trials of love, the less disposed you will be to rush precipitously into the lists? If Andreas is ironical here, what is the force of his irony? Does he seriously intend to introduce Walter to the mystery of love only in order to warn him against it? Book III (The Rejection of Love) suggests as much. But the brief diatribe against the evils of love (read: against women) in Book III is not obviously consistent with—nor an adequate antidote to—the expansive and enthusiastic exposition of the art of love in Books I and II. There is a problem about the integrity of this work. Of which more later.

At the outset of Book I Andreas defines love as "a certain inborn suffering derived from the sight of and excessive meditation upon the beauty of the opposite sex...." (28) Every element in this definition calls for comment. First, love is suffering. Specifically fear: fear that one will not attain one's object or that, having attained it, one will lose it.(28-9) It is clear from his language that what Andreas calls love is what St. Augustine calls lust. Andreas cannot have been unaware that Augustine had defined lust (*libido* or *cupiditas*) as the love of those things (e.g., a mistress) that one can lose against his will, and opposed it to the love of God, of whose favor one cannot be unwillingly deprived.[2] Andreas knows what he is talking about: not the ordinate love of God to which Christians are enjoined and by which they are beatified, but the inordinate love of created things from which they are urgently dissuaded and in which they experience nothing but misery and frustration.

Second, love is innate. Just as the cause of sin is not created things but the soul's immoderate devotion to them, so erotic passion is aroused not by its occasion (the sight of a beautiful example of the opposite sex) but by the mind's "excessive meditation" upon what it sees. The real object of sexual desire is not woman but the representation of woman. As opposed to *caritas*, which is a selfless love of the other, whether God or neighbor, sexual love (*amor*) is always self-love—a fascination with one's own imaginings. And so (perhaps) it ruptures two commandments at once. Flouting the sixth, it also undermines the first by idolizing the self and its desires.

Wherefore (third) Andreas proceeds to explain the growth of love in terms of the common medieval notion of the three stages in the genesis of sin: suggestion, delight, and consent. Suggestion: upon sighting a comely woman the lover-to-be immediately begins to "lust after her in his heart." Delight: the more he thinks about her ("fuller meditation") the more his passion is inflamed, until he comes at last to a "complete meditation:" he contemplates her form, imagines all her bodily parts and their functions, and desires to put each of her members to "the fullest use." Consent: having thus incited himself to lust, the lover "proceeds at once to action," and begins to plan the strategies by which he may possess the object of his desire. (29)

Since the genesis of love is structurally identical with the genesis of sin, you prevent love the same way you prevent sin: by avoiding the occasions of it. If the occasion nevertheless presents itself, you do not follow through. So Andreas, at the other end of his argument, advises:

> Never let your thoughts…lead you to the delight of the flesh, and always take care wholly to avoid places, times, and persons which may excite your passions or give occasion for lust. If a convenient place and some unexpected happening urge you on to the work of the flesh by putting the thought of some woman into your head, be careful to restrain your passion like a man and to get away from the tempting place. Even if carnal incitements have commenced to vex you, take care that they do not lead you to action, or that the combination of circumstances does not cause you to sin.(197)

Walter's objective—to be successful in love—is imprudent. Christ admonished his auditors to stop short of the first promptings of eros, for even to lust after a woman in one's heart is already adultery.[3] But Andreas' description of the progress of carnal love is medieval commonplace. He is not recommending that one become embroiled in love affairs. Teaching what experience has taught him, he is telling Walter, who is already past the stage of suggestion and has presumably achieved a "complete meditation," how to handle his passion and—eventually—get rid of it. Or so at least he would have us believe.

Everything Andreas says by way of characterizing love is consistent with Augustine's description of lust. "Love is always either increasing or decreasing:" erotic love is inherently mutable and unstable, as opposed to the love of God, eternal and unchanging. Love is a kind of bondage,[4] as opposed to the liberating service of God. (31) Love may be ennobling, but it is unreliable and seldom fair, as opposed to the love of God, which is always uplifting, always constant, and always just. (31-2) There are people who are unfit for love—the very young, the very old, the blind, the overly passionate—but no one is excluded from the love of God. (32-3)

Most perfectly Augustinian, though less obviously so, is Andreas' account of the means by which love may be acquired. Throughout the *Confessions* Augustine calls attention to the intimate connection between language and character. The deceitful language of the serpent precipitates the fall, and the language spoken by men ever after perpetuates its effects. The rhetoric that Augustine learned in school and later, as *vendor verborum*, retailed to his students is only the most corrupt (because most effective) form of a language corrupted from the beginning. After his conversion Augustine endeavored to free language from slavery to selfish desire (rhetoric) and return it to the service of God (prayer). The rightful use of words is to commemorate that Word by which the world was created and by which, incarnate, it was redeemed. But as long as human history is the history of sin, human language will continue to be the instrument of lust. It is this capacity of language to further the cause of eros that Andreas advises the lover to exploit.

There are, he tells us, five ways generally recognized by which the lover may get what he wants: "a beautiful figure, excellence of character, extreme readiness of speech, great wealth, and the readiness with which one grants that which is sought." (33) The last two he rejects as unworthy to appear in the courts of love. Of the remaining three he ranks character first. Beauty elicits an easy and incautious love at best, at worst it is nothing but cosmetic fakery, and in any case it is evanescent. "Character alone...is worthy of the crown of love."(35) However, Andreas adds, "fluency of speech...creates a presumption in favor of the excellent character of the speaker."(35) Only a lover of good character deserves to be requited, but facility in speech is the principle datum from which, rightly or wrongly, character is inferred. Andreas will not go so far as to say that character *is* rhetoric, but rhetoric produces the effects of character—its appearances—and in an erotic relationship it is appearances that count. For this reason Andreas devotes most of his treatise to the art of amatory discourse. Inverting and perverting Augustine's program for the redemption of rhetoric, exploiting rather than converting the language of sin, Andreas simultaneously declares his own commitment to the terms and parameters of the Augustinian tradition.

More than half of Andreas' text—106 out of 186 pages in the English translation—consists of exemplary dialogues of seduction and, embedded in them, numerous stories of fabulous loves and lovers. There are no explicit descriptions of sexual encounters of the sort one gets in contemporary fiction. Nor does Andreas' work, like a modern sex manual, enumerate and illustrate the techniques of intercourse. That is not his concern. What he does provide is two lists of the "rules" of love (81-82, 184-186), a long chivalric narrative recounting the discovery of these rules (177-186), and records of judgments handed down in the courts of love by Countess Marie, Queen Eleanor, and other authoritative judges. In short: language and lots of it. Not the language of pornography or the language of sexual technology, but the language of seduction and erotic adventure. The medium has become the message. The reality of sex is sublated and sublimated in the discourse of love. Eros is subsumed without remainder into logos.

According to Kenneth Burke, the paradigmatic rhetorical performance—the quintessence of persuasion—is the act of courtship: seduction lifted from the carnal to the verbal level, and perhaps consummated there. Courtship is the "spiritualization" of seduction, the spirituality of which is the spirituality of its linguistic medium.[5] So in Andreas' text love is spiritualized—made "courtly" or *honestus*—by its translation into language. Courtly love becomes thereby the inverse (and no doubt perverse) counterpart of the heavenly love imagined in monastic commentaries on *The Song of Songs*. Each is a purified eros directed at an ideal object, in the one case God and in the other a lady who, in her unapproachable remoteness, is the intentional (albeit not the actual) equivalent of God. Both the love of God and the love of woman are meant to produce a certain perfection of character in the lover: single-minded chaste devotion to the beloved. Both result in the elaboration of a distinctive rhetoric. In both its courtly and its monastic transformations, love is a matter of character and character in turn is a matter of language.

Courtly love expresses itself in a series of formal postures and a system of linguistic conventions. That is why Andreas advises Walter: do not try to court peasant women. His brief remarks on this head (149-50) are motivated by aristocratic disdain and a regard for feudal order: if (*contra naturam*) farmers cultivate the art of love rather than the art of agriculture, the upper classes will get nothing to eat. But along with these economic proprieties, there is the fact, decisive for the theorist of courtly love, that a peasant woman *cannot* be courted. Crude and illiterate, she is incapable of responding to the finer solicitations of language and—if one is so incautious as to desire her—may simply be taken by force.

An even closer association of economic and rhetorical motives is evident in Andreas' attitude toward commerce with prostitutes and other women who give their "solaces" in return for money. (144-48, 150) His abhorrence of such relationships is unqualified:

> [T]his most precious gift of love cannot be paid for at any set price or be cheapened by a matter of money....the love which seeks for rewards should not be called love by anybody, but rather shameful harlotry and greedy wantonness....(144,145)

Andreas' contempt for the oldest profession symptomizes the incommensurability of the feudal ideal, formally committed to chivalric relations between the sexes, and the capitalist economy of the future, in which the prostitute's medium of exchange, money, will replace language as the universal means of communication and the sole spiritual bond among men. Even within the feudal economy, marital contracts are based on considerations of property rather than personality, so that, although a man should not court a woman he would be ashamed to marry (81, 185), courtly relations are normally extramarital (187-88) and the courtly lover careless of his property. (191)

Spiritualized by its transformation into logos, eros becomes (1) an exchange of set speeches from a repertory of prescribed dialogues between lover and beloved, aimed at eventual consummation; (2) a code of rules to be followed and a set of poses to be assumed by lady and leman on the way to sexual congress; (3) stories of noble loves and lovers, *exempla* of successful seduction; and (4) judgments rendered in the courts of love, legitimizing honorable conjunctions. In short: an art—or artificiality—of speech and gesture all directed—presumably—toward the single end of carnal union.

Presumably. For the union in question, though carnally imagined, is not copulation in general or without qualification. Intercourse between husband and wife is excluded (106-107, 156, 171, 175), as is intercourse between peasants, intercourse between peasants and nobles, and intercourse with prostitutes or other venal women. The immediacy of sexual union is not what matters. What matters is context: an artfully contrived setting for erotic adventure and the artful arrival at sexual fulfillment. An overabundance of lust is incompatible with courtly love. (33). Orgasm is better if postponed as long as possible, infrequently enjoyed, and difficult to procure. It is only fully satisfying if accomplished by artistic means and relished for its aesthetic value.

Indeed, it need not occur at all. Andreas distinguishes what he calls "pure" love from an inferior form called "mixed" love. (122, 164) Mixed love goes all the way. Pure love appears to be something like heavy petting that permits the nude embrace but stops short of copulation. Copulation adulterates love because it terminates the dialogue of seduction. Orgasm is notoriously wordless. Accompanied by nothing more articulate than moans and groans and cries of ecstasy, it blocks the flow of language and curtails the (otherwise endless) opportunities for rhetoric. But the show must go on. Therefore, in Andreas' text, copulation is not even named but only suggested by a glossary of euphemistic designators: the work of Venus, sweet solaces, the regular solaces, the final solace, the ultimate solace, the yielding of the whole person, etc. In its courtly transfiguration, sexual intercourse becomes a purely rhetorical exchange and orgasm ideally a rhetorical climax. Courtly lovers don't mate, they flirt. And instead of coming, they go on and on and on....[6]

Under the sign of paradox, the rhetoric of courtly love threatens to deconstruct itself. Ostensibly a mode of discourse and a style of comportment aimed at gratifying desire, it is nevertheless so designed that it postpones gratification indefinitely and distances the immediacy which is its (ostensible) consummation. Without sexual desire, courtly love could not exist. But it cannot tolerate the satisfaction of the desire that sponsors it. Intercourse itself, if it does occur, is not enjoyed immediately[7]—for that purpose the occasional peasant girl would no doubt be better—but savored as the finishing touch on a successful work of art.

The linguistic technique which intends to overcome difference and effect unity institutionalizes difference and interdicts unity. Such is the paradox of courtly rhetoric. The union of lover and beloved, which is the purpose of courtship, is indefinitely deferred by the transformation of eros into logos. The union of flesh and spirit that would render love "courtly"—make sexual intercourse honorable—is achieved only at the level of spirit (language) and thereby distanced from the immediacy of the flesh and its desires. The rhetoric of courtly love is a rhetoric of *différance*: the transcendence of carnal reality necessitated by the requirements of courtliness iterates the difference (of lover and beloved, flesh and spirit) it is meant to repair and defers the consummation it is meant to facilitate. Courtly love is a failed incarnation—a disincarnation—in which the flesh becomes word, and for that reason—among others—the antithesis of the Love which prompted the Word to become flesh.

The topos of the celestial bridegroom and the divine nuptials (a commonplace of monastic spirituality) with which Andreas ends his work (211-12) is simply the ultimate act of transcendence: the projection of erotic fulfillment from the courts of love into the court of the heavenly King. It is also the ultimate *différance*, as heaven is infinitely remote from earth in space and time alike. But—and this is typical of the rhetoric of religion—the language and the imagery imply that in the heavenly union of Christ and the soul the immediacy forfeit in this world is recovered in the next. The joys of mystical marriage are at once the purest and most fulfilling. In the bridal chambers of Zion, the perfection of *fin' amors* and the gratification of desire coincide in a single everlasting and wholly spiritual orgasm.

But there is a price. Just as the elevation of love to the level of *courtoisie* demands the suppression of gross carnality, so admission to the heavenly nuptials demands the renunciation of courtly love. Therefore, Andreas, having spent 160 pages explaining love—what it is, how to get it, how to keep it—, adds 26 pages counselling "The Rejection of Love."

At the outset of Book III, Andreas tells Walter: you now "lack nothing in the art of love, since in this little book we gave you the theory of the subject, fully and completely." (187) Whereupon he adds:

> [W]e did not do this because we consider it advisable for you or any other man to fall in love, but for fear lest you might think us stupid; we believe, though, that any man who devotes his efforts to love loses all his usefulness. Read this little book, then, not as one seeking to take up the life of a lover, but that, invigorated by the theory and trained to excite the minds of women to love, you may, by refraining from so doing, win an eternal recompense and thereby deserve a greater reward from God. For God is more pleased with a man who is able to sin and does not, than with a man who has no opportunity to sin. (187)

The Scriptures admonish us again and again: be not hearers of the word only but doers as well, for it is not understanding that pleases God but obedience. Many a medieval text repeats this admonition, urging its readers to move through contemplation to action. Andreas' skewed relationship to his own tradition requires him to turn this familiar trope against itself. Echoing and clarifying the language of his Preface ("after you have learned the art of love your progress in it will be more cautious"), he makes his meaning plain: you are to become expert in the art of love in order *not* to practice it. By refusing to do what you have been trained to do ("excite the minds of women to love"), you will gain an eternal reward. For God is better pleased with a man who can sin and won't than He is with a man who just can't.

But the clarification only intensifies the irony of Andreas' text and aggravates the problem of its integrity. Granted that incapacity (impotence?) is no virtue. Does he really mean that one should learn to sin in order not to, so that, not doing the evil one might, one acquires greater merit thereby? How does this—cultivating the art of love—differ from that "fuller meditation" which, in the genesis of sin, leads from suggestion to consent? Wouldn't it be better, as Andreas advises a few pages on, simply to avoid the occasions of evil in the first place? "For lust is the sort of thing that overcomes us if we follow it, but is driven away if we flee from it." (197-

98) Book III appears to stand in irreconcilable contradiction with the main body of the text.

One may of course suppose that Andreas, as a cleric, was just protecting himself—summarily recanting what he had taught in order to maintain the appearance of regularity. Assumptions of this sort come easily to the modern mind, but they may be too easy. In any event, it seems evident that Andreas' superiors, if they worried about such things, would not have been deceived by so obviously cynical a gesture. Therefore, another solution recommends itself: in his terminal revocation Andreas may, in all sincerity, be confronting the courtly ideal of love with the brutal actuality of sex. The courtly ideal is a vision of eros conceived and consummated in logos: a rhetoric of romance. The actuality would be the church's normative view of sexual relations, opposing to the romantic glorification of woman a misogynist conception of her historical reality. For while it had to condone marriage as a sacrament instituted by God and confirmed by Christ, the medieval church could not forget that women, ever since Eve, had tried to distract men from their divinely ordained destiny, displacing and replacing God as the supreme object of their desire and the only source of true happiness.

This reading of the text is recommended by the fact that the bulk of Andreas' third book is occupied with denigrating woman and itemizing the miseries entailed by sexual infatuation. Andreas has a whole arsenal of reasons for abstaining from the love of woman. (1) As Holy Scripture tells us, the "foul and shameful acts of Venus" (188) are hateful to God. (2) The love of woman causes men to neglect their duty to their neighbors. These two arguments, taken together, should be sufficient. By yielding to sexual temptation we violate the two great commandments: "Thou shalt love the Lord thy God...and thy neighbor as thyself."[8] But Andreas has just begun. (3) Sexual attachments ruin masculine friendships. Andreas was neither the first nor the last to complain that the love of woman ruptures male bonding. (4) Love defiles body and soul alike. (5) The lover is enslaved to fear and jealousy: the suffering which defines love (28) is also one of its chief faults. Naturally enough: having described love in the terms used by Augustine to characterize lust, Andreas, in order to disparage love, has only to reaffirm his solidarity with the tradition from which, even in subverting it, he has never really departed. (6) The lover is impoverished by the service of his lady, and by his poverty he is (like the addict) impelled to crime in order to maintain his habit. (7) The lover suffers constant torments, both temporal and spiritual. (8) Love (= lust) is universally acknowledged to be a vice, opposed to the corresponding virtues of temperance and chastity. (9) Love incites its devotees to every kind of crime. (10) Much evil but no good comes from love. (11) Love deprives men of worldly honor and heavenly reward.

At this point Andreas breaks off enumerating arguments (already redundant) and embarks on an extended and impassioned exhortation to chastity. But eventually he resumes his bill of particulars. (12) The act of love (where have we heard this before?) weakens the body. (13) Love robs a man of his wisdom. Andreas is thinking of David and Solomon, both deranged by lust. Had he also heard of Abelard, whose dalliance with Heloise caused him to neglect his studies? (14) Not quite finally, Andreas argues that women are incapable of true love by reason of their many faults. To be precise: every woman is avaricious (she's after your property), envious, slanderous, greedy, gluttonous (there's nothing she won't do for a free meal), inconstant (*la donna è mobile*), deceitful, disobedient to God and her husband, arrogant, vainglorious, mendacious, bibulous, loud-mouthed, incapable of keeping a secret (telephone, telegraph, tell a woman), wanton, faithless, and—like the Greeks, who built a shrine to the god they might have overlooked—Andreas adds: prone to every sort of evil. From which (surely exhaustive) catalogue of vices it follows that no woman is capable of a pure and sincere love. To which, as if more were necessary, Andreas subjoins (15): love itself is unjust and will not constantly reward even the most consistent lover with the satisfactions he seeks. Clearly, he says, these are "conclusive reasons why a man is bound to avoid [love] with all his might and to trample under foot all its rules." (210)

Clearly. Yet these considerations, while they do epitomize the received opinion of sex and woman in the middle ages, only exacerbate the contradiction in Andreas' text between its apparent recommendation of love and its terminal renunciation. They represent but do not reconcile the conflict between the courtly ideal and the Christian norm. However, it must be remembered, first, that the monstrous female of Book III is just as much a rhetorical ideal as the romanticized lady of Books I and II. The woman maligned in Book III is a masterpiece of wickedness and a virtuoso in "every sort of evil." (208) She is, as Andreas more than once reminds us, a perfect Eve (203, 205): the object of a love that will finally betray our trust and disappoint our expectations. Her counterpart in Books I and II is likewise a rhetorical entity: the incarnation of a remote perfection with whom the lover seeks to be united and from whom he is repelled in the seeking. An inverse image of the Blessed Virgin, who for Christians is the historically actual paradigm of womanhood, she is at once the joy of every man's desiring and the *ewige Weibliche* who is never possessed. Supremely alluring and cruelly aloof, the beloved lady of the troubadours welcomes all her courtiers and remains disdainfully indifferent to their entreaties.

The contradiction *between* the repulsive woman of Book III and the enticing woman of Books I and II iterates the contradiction *within* the woman of Books I and II. The antagonism of the (theologically) real and the (courtly) ideal repeats and potentiates the tension already present in the ideal. And both—both women and both contradictions—are projections of the contrary vectors in the rhetoric of courtly love, a rhetoric designed to prevent the attainment of the end it seeks. The two faces of woman are just the two poles of a rhetoric which at once attracts and repels, and the two women (of Books I and II and of Book III) are contradictorily coherent with each other and with an ambivalent language which simultaneously proposes unity and perpetuates difference.

From this point of view it is not difficult to understand why courtly love was both so attractive and so threatening to the medieval mind.[9] Courtly love and Christianity were rival religions because they were rival rhetorics. For the Christian religion, though it offers itself as revealed truth commanding men's allegiance, is never more than a representation of revealed truth. Holy Scripture, accepted by believers as the one true story of the world, inspired by the Holy Spirit, is nevertheless the work of human authors, composed in the language of fallen man. Sacred history is not literally recounted but figuratively represented, wrapped in an artful *integumentum* that exploits all the tropes of rhetoric from allegory to zeugma. Only in this way can human beings receive it. Likewise Christian doctrine is not simply the truth about God and the economy of redemption, but a figuration of that truth mediated by the forms of human thought and by human modes of expression.

Christianity itself is a rhetoric of salvation, its figurative character necessitated by fallen man's alienation from the unmediated vision of God. For the faithful it is the rhetoric of truth, over against which the rhetoric of courtly love could only be perceived as the rhetoric of deviance and error. From a Christian point of view the lady imagined in the literature of courtly love would have to be either the apotheosis of Eve or a degradation of the Blessed Virgin—and unacceptable under either description. But the relation between Eve, the executrix of damnation, and Mary, the mediatrix of salvation, is just as ambiguous as the relation between the courtly lady of Books I and II and the vile creature anathematized in Book III. Though opposed as figures of sin and grace respectively, they are both women. And as it was woman's disobedience that succumbed to the blandishments of the serpent, so it was the seed of woman's obedience who trampled the serpent under his feet. The Blessed Virgin, who is the opposite of Eve, is also the redemption of Eve, just as Christ is Adam's anti-type and his redeemer. And from an historical point of view the crime of Eve (the original sin) is always already past just as the achievement of Mary (the final restoration of human nature) is never yet present. Christianity, like courtly love, is not only a rhetoric, but a rhetoric of *différance*. Presupposing difference (the alienation of sin), it promises union (atonement), but in fact—until the end of history—reiterates difference and postpones reconciliation. The bitterness of the rivalry between courtly love and Christianity is a function of their complicity—both are rhetorics of reunion—and their complicity is the effect of their common duplicity—both are rhetorics of difference and deferment.

Though it has non-Christian (e.g., Islamic) antecedents, the ideology of courtly love as expounded by Andreas Capellanus is obviously parasitic on the Christianity with which it competes. Not only are its values defined by Christianity—courtly *amor* is the negative image of Christian *caritas*, Andreas' "love" is Augustine's "lust," and the courtly lady a blasphemous conjunction of the mother of men and the Mother of God—but also its ultimate goal is reunion with the Christian ideal of which it is the travesty and to which it pays tribute thereby. This duplicity is, *faute de mieux*, the source of whatever integrity may be found in Andreas' text.

At the end of Book III Andreas himself admits there is a problem and offers a solution. "This doctrine of ours," he tells Walter, "will...seem to present two different points of view." (210-211) In the first part of this work, he says, "we tried to assent to your simple and youthful request" (211) by explaining the art of love in detail and in order.

> If you wish to practice the system, you will obtain, as a careful reading of this little book will show you, all the delights of the flesh in fullest measure; but the grace of God, the companionship of the good, and the friendship of praiseworthy men you will with good reason be deprived of, and you will do great harm to your good name, and it will be difficult for you to obtain the honors of this world. (211)

But in the latter part of the work,

> We were more concerned with what might be useful to you, and of our own accord we added something about the rejection of love, although you had no reason to ask for it, and we treated the matter fully; perhaps we can do you good against your will. (211)

Books I and II are really to be ascribed to Walter, in response to whose simple and youthful (albeit misguided) entreaties they were written, that Andreas might prove his diligence and his friendship. Only Book III is Andreas' own work, added not to please his friend by providing him the illusory good he craves but (in the spirit of true friendship) to help him (albeit against his will) obtain the good that satisfies eternally. But it's all one. If Walter practices the art of love, he will enjoy the pleasures of the flesh "in fullest measure," but forfeit all spiritual and temporal well-being. If he abstains from it, he will merit worldly success and earn the favor of the heavenly King. Whatever his choice, he will learn what he needs to know. Enrolled in the service of love, he will learn from bitter experience that he has made a mistake. Adopting the counsel of Book III, he will learn, honorably and without pain, the evils of carnal love. Consistent in spite of appearances to the contrary, the *De amore* offers Walter two ways to learn one and the same lesson: renounce the love of woman and cultivate the love of God.

If he is wise, therefore, Walter will ignore the solicitations of Venus and obey the commandments of God. By so doing he will keep himself (wise virgin) in readiness for the advent of the heavenly bridegroom, a worthy candidate for the joys of celestial marriage.

> Therefore, Walter, accept this health-giving teaching we offer you, and pass by all the vanities of the world, so that when the Bridegroom cometh to celebrate the greater nuptials, and the cry ariseth in the night, you may be prepared to go forth to meet Him with your lamps filled and to go in with Him to the divine marriage, and you will have no need to seek out in haste what you need for your lamps, and find it too late, and come to the home of the Bridegroom after the door is shut, and hear His venerable voice.

> Be mindful, therefore, Walter, to have your lamps always supplied that is, have the supplies of charity and good works. Be mindful ever to watch, lest the unexpected coming of the Bridegroom find you asleep in sins. Avoid then, Walter, practicing the mandates of love, and labor in constant watchfulness so that when the Bridegroom cometh He may find you wakeful; do not let worldly delight make you lie down in your sins, trusting to the youth of your body and confident that the Bridegroom will be late, since, as He tells us Himself, we know neither the day nor the hour. (211-212)

As love becomes rhetoric in Books I and II, so the rejection of love is an exercise in the rhetoric of renunciation and postponement: give up pleasure in favor of virtue (here and now), so that you may (there and then) enjoy both in fullest measure. The problem of the unity of this text is a problem in rhetoric: how to align the rhetoric of "what you want" with the rhetoric of "what is good for you." Andreas' solution—and here the language of courtly love rejoins the language of monastic spirituality—is to invoke the rhetoric of transcendence and merger (deferment): *in heaven* what you want and what's good for you will be the same, and the rhetoric of victimage (difference): *until then* curb your desires and seek the good.[10] When your Lover comes, you will have it all. The cravings of the flesh and the needs of the spirit are proleptically reconciled, by the rhetoric of religion, in the world (ever yet) to come. There the fulfillment of the divine mandates will be the satisfaction of desire. But in this life we are caught in the dialectical standoff of the rhetoric of desire and the rhetoric of virtue. And this dialectic—projected as contradictory perspectives on the nature of woman but rooted in the differantial logic of the rhetorical project itself—is the only integrity Andreas' text can hope to achieve. "A scar is what happens when the word is made flesh."[11] And when eros is taken into logos, the wound of renunciation is not healed save in expectation.

9

Allegories of Reading in
Robert Coover's Exemplary Fictions

Nothing is gained by continuing to idealize reading, as though reading
were not an art of defensive warfare.

—Harold Bloom

Allegorical narratives tell the story of the failure to read....

—Paul de Man

I call them dirty stories. And so they are, not by reason of filthy matter, but
essentially. Whatever their theme, the stories dirty themselves. Think of
them as self-polluting narratives.

The author's intentions may or may not be honorable: in the "*Dedicatoria
y Prólogo*"[1] to "Seven Exemplary Fictions," Coover associates his art with
Cervantes' and casts himself as Don Quixote. Tilting his pen at the windmills
of myth, he redeems a tradition by deconstructing its forms. But in the
"Prologue of Sorts" that is our "Door" (13) into the book that contains his
"Fictions," we are shown a different picture: the writer as Big Bad Wolf
lusting unnaturally for the pubescent beauties of fairy tale.

Consider the title. *Pricksongs and Descants* has a perfectly respectable
meaning. A pricksong is a song performed from "pricked"—i.e., written—
notes. A descant is a secondary melody counterpointing a primary melody
or "burden." Coover's fictions draw their matter from folklore, the Bible,
popular culture, and quotidian cliché. His "magic poker" (20) commits these
raw materials to writing and converts them into art. Transformed in the
transcription, they become descants: counternotations to stories whose
burden is old and well-known. *Pricksongs and Descants* reduces a tradition
to an institution and provides it with a bit of dissonant counterpoint, so that

it may be rendered by note men. You, *"lector amantísimo"* (79), and—of course—I.

All this a church musician might understand and approve. But Granny takes a darker view. Thinking of the wolf-author and her silly but innocent granddaughter, the "old Beauty" says:

> I know who's got her giddy ear with his old death-cunt-and-prick songs haven't I heard them all my god and smelt his hot breath in the singin? yes I know him can see him now lickin his hairy black chops and composin his polyphonies outa dread and appetite whisperin his ecologues sprung from disaster croonin his sacral entertainment yes I know him well....(16)

Where my reading identifies a high-minded narrative purpose Granny finds a dirty pun. "Death-cunt-and-prick songs" indeed. To her mind, made wise by experience of the "Beast," the writer is not redeeming a tradition. He's corrupting the young. Composing polyphonies out of dread and appetite (he's still a musician), whispering eclogues sprung from disaster (and a kind of poet), crooning sacral entertainments (is that "sacred" or "sacroiliac"?), the writer turns foolish virgins (you, *lector amantísimo*, and I?) into withered old hags full of bittersweet memories.[2]

Introducing his own "exemplary" narratives, Robert Coover appeals to don Miguel de Cervantes Saavedra:

> The novelist uses familiar mythic or historical forms to combat the content of those forms and to conduct the reader (*lector amantísimo!*) to the real, away from mystification to clarification, away from magic to maturity, away from mystery to revelation. And it is above all to the need for new modes of perception and fictional forms able to encompass them that I, barber's basin on my head, address these stories. (79)

In the same paragraph, and in Cervantes' words, the author hints at a "hidden mystery" contained in these stories, by which they are lifted above their vulgar occasions. He could hardly assure us, as Cervantes does,

> that the amorous episodes you will find in some of them are so respectable and restrained, so within the bounds of reason and conformable to Christian conduct, that no one who reads them, either carefully or carelessly, can possibly be moved to evil thoughts.[3]

Neither writers nor readers are capable—shall I say "any longer"?—of such a pure regard. Without irony—and despite the fact that he has twice as many hands as his "Maestro"—he might "venture to say":

> if I believed that the reading of these [fictions] would in any way arouse an evil thought or desire, I would sooner cut off the hand that wrote them than see them published.[4]

And he does, appropriating the Master's prologue, promise that "there is not one of [these stories] that does not afford a useful example."[5]

"*Pricksongs and Descants*," morally and musically expounded, agrees with the figure of the writer as Don Quixote, decreating the narrative past and announcing the future of fiction. But "death-cunt-and-prick songs" exposes him as a dirty young man who feeds on the tradition he has ruined. The prologue *within* the book (by the author) reaffirms (on behalf of the author) a claim that has already been discredited (by one of his characters) in the prologue *to* the book. Brandishing a two-edged title and prefaces that clash, this book proclaims itself unreadable from the beginning.

The readable text began with Cervantes. Cervantes' *novelas* are exemplary because they "tell good stories and they tell them well" (77). Cervantes opens a way for the writer into the modern age. Deconstructing and displacing romance, his stories demonstrate, by exemplifying it, the possibility of the novel. Of what do Coover's seven fictions, whose very title echoes the Master's, serve as useful examples? What story does he tell?

As the accompanying table indicates, each of the "Seven Exemplary Fictions" incorporates a metaphor of the text and a metaphor of the reader. The stories themselves enact metaphors of reading and must therefore be taken, in the second degree, as allegories that narrate the *impossibility* of reading. In each of them save (possibly) one the reader is defeated by his text. In the post-modern age, when naturalism seems to have exhausted its powers, just as romance had become effete in Cervantes' day, Coover's exercizes, relentlessly troping their own unreadability as conventional fictions, deconstruct low-mimetic narration and displace it in the direction of the illegible text. So doing, they open the way for "new modes of perception and fictional forms able to encompass them" (79).[6]

The way is strewn with difficulties and mined with occasions of disaster. The failure to read, which these stories both narrate and exemplify, is bound to contaminate—in the third degree—my own (or anyone's) reading. If in reading them anyway I seem to court catastrophe, the ensuing debacle will

Story	Text	Reader
1. Panel Game	The game: enigmatic & perverse	You (Bad Sport, Unwilling Participant): hanged.
2. The Marker	Jason's wife: dead, maybe murdered.	Jason: emasculated.
3. The Brother	The Ark: silent and mysterious	The narrator: marked for death.
4. In a Train Station	The story itself: a script enacted by the characters: a repetition compulsion.	Alfred: condemned to endless repetition of the text.
5. Klee Dead	The scrap of paper: the story itself: illegible, maybe blank, maybe a forgery, maybe a handbill.	The person addressed by the story: you: cheated and fobbed off with circus tickets.
6. J's Marriage	J's wife: an impenetrable Virgin.	J: unmanned and dead.
7. The Wayfarer	The wayfarer and his speech: silent or incoherent.	The police officer: kills the text in order to produce his own report.

demonstrate better than any success the (inevitably questionable) legitimacy of my approach. Of the seven I select four, supposing them so exemplary of the rest that repeated deployment of the same strategies of reading would yield the same results.

1

"Panel Game" is just what it says it is: a TV game show. The cast includes, besides Moderator and Audience, the panel: Aged Clown, Lovely Lady, Mr. America (later Mr. Amentia), and Unwilling Participant, alias Bad Sport, aka...You. You, the reader, are written into the story and required to answer "THE BIG QUESTION!" (80) The question is never asked. You have to figure out what it is. Question and answer alike wait upon the reader, who, enlisted as an Unwilling Participant *in* the fiction, is expected to guess the name and nature *of* the fiction. Bad Sport, charged to identify and interpret the narrative in which his life is trapped, resigns himself "to pass the test in peace" (80). Before Moderator formally declares the show begun, Sport scrambles desperately to interpret the hints broadly (and often lewdly) provided by the other panelists. His hermeneutic, which proceeds through a chain of metonymies, puns, rhymes, alliterations, and sexual allusions, is vaguely literary and (though frequently distracted) pointed in the general direction of Shakespeare (80, 81, 82, 83-4, 84-5). As he frantically tries to follow the clues and find the meaning, he is constantly, tauntingly observed by the Eye of the World: sometimes the television camera and sometimes Lovely Lady's navel.

"And the Bad Sport, you ask, who is he? fool! thou art!" (80) When, well into the proceedings, You speak for the first time—to protest that You don't know how to play the game—You are answered with hostile silence or cruel mockery. Eventually You stumble on the answer, but You don't understand it.

> The dog rose and—what? Rose and scrupled? Rose: rows: stichs: stickleback. Going in circles. "Depends—!" gasps America. Can't last long now. Own cells against him. Flesh dogbane pink. "Depends—!"
> Depends: hangs. But what hangs or hangs on what? (84)

You *do* know that "it's your *mind* they're after. Humor, passion, sobriety, and truth. On *you* , then, it depends, they depend, they all depend. They all hang. It may be so" (84). With everyone and everything "depending" on You—"what does it mean? *what does it mean?*" (84)—You try to start a game of Twenty Questions: "'I think—...—That, if the subject is animal—'" (85). But Mr. America announces that it's Too Late, breaks wind, and dies. Dead (85).

That should have told You:

> "Come, *come*, sir!" cries the Moderator, much amused, but rising now and pressing forward. "You *must* have contrived some concrete conjunctions from the incontrovertible commentary *qua* commentary just so conspicuously constituted!" Deafening applause.
> Dig in! Tie it up! The truth is: "The truth is—"
> "The truth is," shouts the Moderator, jabbing at him with an angry finger, "*you have lost!*"
> "But I haven't even—!"
> "*Why are you here*," the Moderator explodes, losing all patience, "if not to endeavor to disentangle this entanglement?" (85)

You have failed to tell the truth, and You must therefore "PAY THE CONSEQUENCES!" "But the truth is—", You object. "The truth is," says the Clown (86), and goes into a dirty song-and-dance with Lovely Lady, at the end of which the Lady obscenely fakes death. Echoing once more the old refrain, Moderator gives it all away. "The truth is" that

> "...the frame is the same
> In fame or in shame
> And the name of the game—
>
> ...
>
> is La Mort!" (87)

A noose descends.

The name of the game—and the meaning of the life embedded in the game—is: Death. But You, still hung on Shakespearian titles, got it all wrong.

"I thought—" But the Audience drowns you out. Well, they are happy, think about that. The noose is fitted.

"You thought—?" asks the Moderator and the crowd subsides.

"I thought it was all for fun."

"That is to say," smiles the Moderator wearily, "much ado about nothing."

"That's it! *that's it!* Yes! *that's* what I was *trying* to—!"

The Moderator shakes his head....

"Sorry." (87)

Aged Clown makes a joke, Audience laughs, Lovely Lady whispers sweet nothings in your ear and gooses you good-bye. "Off you go!" As you dangle, you get—in a way—the answer to the BIG QUESTION: "The dog rose and there depended." But the answer to the question is the end of the game. "So long, Sport." (88)

Your ordinary television game show (the "real" thing) is generically senseless and more often than not—with its accoutrements of phony cameraderie, gross humor, and snickering sexuality—downright emetic. But even that makes more sense than this "Panel Game". There at least you have determinate questions with straightforward answers. Whereas here...where? Coover's game show is a metaphorical *text*. A text both underdetermined and overdetermined, as obviously meaningful as it is hopelessly without meaning. Unwilling Participant—Bad Sport and eventually bad loser—figures the *reader* to whom is assigned the impossible task of interpreting the uninterpretable. But of course Sport is also You: at once the reader *in* the text and the reader *of* the text. Like an oldtime Calvinist scrounging in his diaries among the random leavings of his life, looking for signs of election, You (in the text) anxiously try to guess the question and the answer while you, with text in hand, try to dope out its meaning. The hermeneutic of life. For the panel game, a metaphor of the text, is transumptively a metaphor of life. Unwilling Participant is "dragged protesting" (79) into the game just as you "with text in hand" are inscribed, without a by-your-leave, in your own life. In both cases (oldtime Calvinism again) the outcome is assured in advance. The game is an allegory of reading is an allegory of life. The question is: what does it mean? And the answer is: nothing. Yours.

2

"The Marker." Jason and his wife discovered alone in their bedroom. (But there are five policemen outside the door.) Of the wife we are told that she is nude, that she is lovely and affectionate, and that she "has a direct and charming manner of speaking, if we were to hear her speak." We don't. Always at ease, neither pretentious nor shy, she moves about the room, and "whatever meaning there might be in her motion exists within the motion itself and not in her deliberations" (88). An autotelic text, not to be interpreted but loved. Jason, deeply in love with his wife, sits in an armchair reading a book and watching her. As soon as she gets into bed, he puts a marker in his book, undresses, and turns out the light.

His wife's image fades from his mind and is replaced by an image of Beauty "indistinct and untextured" (89). Ever the reader, and now completely in the dark, Jason undertakes a project of interpretation. Groping more or less methodically about the room, he tries in vain to find the bed where Beauty and Love await him. The failure of the quest extinguishes his libido. But his wife laughs gently and, turning, he finds the bed where he wasn't looking for it...right behind him. At the sound of her laugh and the touch of her cool thighs Jason recovers his appetite.

> In fact, the experience, the anxiety of it and its riddles, seems to have created a new urgency, an almost brutal wish to swallow, for a moment, reason and its inadequacies, and to let passion, noble or not, have its hungry way. He is surprised to find her dry, but the entry itself is relaxed and gives way to his determined penetration. (90)

Is this really his wife? But who else could it be? As he leans to kiss her, he notices a bad smell.

Suddenly the lights go on and the police enter. (They've been waiting for this moment ever since the beginning of the story.) Looking beneath him, Jason finds his wife three weeks dead and decaying. And himself *captivus*. Converting reality ("her nude body crackling the freshness of the laundered sheets") into meaning ("an abstract Beauty that contains somehow his wife's ravaging smile and musical eyes") (89), and presuming to take it by force, Jason's hermeneutic is captivated by its own fixation. Which is death: interpretation kills, and once you're into it you're stuck with it.

As the policemen wrench Jason away from his wife's corpse, it clings like a sheet of paper. They carry him to the table "where his book still lies with its marker in it", and the officer, drawing out his genitals—his organs of penetration and his means of interpretation—on the tabletop, pounds them to a pulp (another paper word) with the butt of his gun. (91) Before he leaves, the police officer picks up Jason's book, now stained with his own blood, and flips through it. The marker falls to the floor. Jason cries out for his marker, but the officer, replacing the book, "does not hear him, nor does he want to." (92).

Jason is both literally and figuratively a reader. The marker in the bloody book tropes the penis in the dead wife. In the agony of his emasculation, his sole concern is that he has lost his place. All his places—in his text and (equivalently) in his wife—are lost for good. But the violence he suffers is prepared by the violence he offers. When his wife beckons him to the act of love he darkens the room, exchanges her image for an idea, and in the obscurity of that abstraction seeks the object of his desire. When he tries to rekindle the lamp it is too late and his desire has gone limp. His wife's motion has a meaning of its own independent of deliberation: Jason looks for meaning *through* deliberation. Small wonder that when he does find her he finds her desiccated. He has reduced her to a sheet of paper, and he himself—his hermeneutic vigor—is finally reduced to the stuff of paper.

Jason's text is dead, and he (at least) an accomplice in her death. You can almost understand the vehemence of the police officer's revulsion. For although he observes, with "a flicker of compassion" (91) and scarcely more than a flicker of relevance, that neither tradition nor innovation is to be preferred at the expense of the other, since they are mutually originary, nevertheless, "*some things still make me puke!*" (91) Reading is a necrophiliac violence that brings the living spirit to the dead letter in order to penetrate it. Masquerading as an act of love, it inspires the counter-violence by which it is wrenched away from its desire and bereft of its power. Interpretation *interruptus*. In all of Coover's fictions the act and the art of interpretation are lethal. In "Panel Game" the reader is finally snuffed by the text that mocks his efforts to comprehend it. In this (perhaps) most shocking of the lot he is a murderous exegete who disseminates death and begs his own castration.

3

At 9:27 Alfred buys a ticket and sits down to wait for the 10:18 Express that will take him home to Winchester. Banal conversation between Alfred and the Stationmaster. Enter the stranger, drunk, raving, begging for help. Alfred draws his jackknife, approaches the intruder, weakens, and drops the knife. The Stationmaster picks up the knife, decapitates the stranger, disposes of the remains, and (as the 10:18 pulls out of the station), resets the clock at 9:26. Alfred approaches the ticket window....

"In a Train Station" is an infinite narrative loop, a scenario that is going to be played again and again in a never-ending cycle. "But to return..." (99). Apparently the cause of this eternal recurrence of the same is Alfred's failure to kill the stranger. Were he to seize the moment (it's his cue) and behead the intruder himself, that (it is ambiguously implied) is the one decisive act that might end the cycle and allow him to go home. Assuming, of course, that all this is real (99). But the assumption may not be warranted. It is clear that Alfred and the Stationmaster and the boozy prophet are acting a familiar script. The clichés they utter are lines in an oft-rehearsed performance by which Alfred is frightened (101) and anguished (103), from which he wants to be released, and in which more than once (e.g., 100) he needs to be prompted. "'How's the tomaters doin' this year?'" the Stationmaster asks.

> "Aw, well as kin be expected. Need a—look!" Alfred spins suddenly around to confront the Stationmaster, his pale blue eyes damp as though with tears. "Don't ye think maybe this time I could—?"
> "Need a little...," intones the Stationmaster softly, firmly.
> Alfred sighs, turns back toward the gate, works his jaws over the chicken. "Need a little rain," he says glumly. (101)

Don't you think maybe this time I could...what? Do the killing myself? Just forget the whole thing, go home, and escape once for all this grisly round? No way. The Stationmaster's reply condemns Alfred, gently but firmly, to the ceaseless repetition of his role.

As the intruder staggers into the station, he addresses Alfred, "'Our fazher...whish art 'n heaven...*is eating hish own goddamn chil'ren!*'"

Retching and wretched, he adds, "'So *help* me!'" (102) Alfred fails, the Stationmaster administers the *coup de grace* while Alfred weeps, and we take it again from the top. The Stationmaster—author, director, prompter, and chief actor in this catastrophe—repeatedly destroys his own children. He who lacks the courage to play his part—to assume the burden and the responsibility of death—never goes home. Alfred's failure is a failure of interpretation. Though he has the means (the jackknife), he cannot summon the courage to enact the violent hermeneutic demanded by his role. By responding with the violence of murder (a reading that is clearly required of him) to the violent textuality in which he is inscribed, he might (perhaps) break the chain of repetitions and escape, *hors texte*, to ... Winchester.

Where? Alfred wants to go home. But there's no way he can get there. Before he can catch the 10:18 to Winchester, he is obliged to play out this always already repeated scenario with the Stationmaster and the drunk. Though his desire impels him beyond his role, Alfred is again and again recalled to his dreary destiny: reminded to speak the part set down for him (100,101), reprimanded when he departs from the prescribed stage business (102), goaded to get on with it and reproved when he fails (103). There is nothing outside the text. Winchester, the 10:18, and the rest exist only within the script and its performance. There is no "home" to which Alfred can go, no transcendent "meaning" at which he as reader might arrive and in which he might repose. For which reason no doubt the story begins by reminding us that the reality of the scene with all its props and *personae* is a doubtful assumption at best. (99).

Reluctant to play his part and knowing it all too well, Alfred is terrified by the sight of his own jackknife. The tall stranger enters and begins a speech he cannot continue: "'Belovéd!... The su'jeck f'my dishcoursh is.... The su'jeck...the su'jeck...aw, *fuck it!*'" (101-102) From its opening words ("Belovéd...") and from its subsequent parody of the Our Father (102), it is evident the discourse is meant to be a sermon. It ends with a demotic Amen that is also a prayer for death: "'So *help* me!'" (102) Alfred knows what he's supposed to do and draws the terrible knife. But he cannot kill, only weep, and the Stationmaster (the only true interpreter) has to finish the job. Alfred misses his train and has to try again. He will never succeed. The preacher's tongue-tied sermon demands, like any sermon, an interpretation in action. Failure to interpret decisively entails perpetual iteration of the demand.

Not that success is any improvement. The Stationmaster (a strong misreader?) does what is required of him, but he too gets another turn on the wheel. Whether we do or whether we don't, we are condemned to do it again. The double violence implicit in "Panel Game" and "The Marker" is here made painfully explicit and even more painfully potentiated. There is the violence of the text—the intruder's speech and behavior—and the violence of the reading it asks—murder. If we do not respond with violence to the violence of the text—and even if we do—we are subjected to the ultimate violence (cf. Prometheus, Ixion, Sisyphus, *inter alios*) of an endless repetition compulsion.

Violence figures once again in the seventh and last of Coover's fictions. But in a way that distinguishes it (perhaps) from all the rest.

4

"The Wayfarer" reports a police action. A police officer discovers an old man seated beside the highway and interrogates him. Provoked by the wayfarer's unresponsiveness, the officer tortures him, kills him, and prepares to make his report. Which report (a report of which?) we have, presumably, read.

The figure is plain. An agent of the law encounters inscrutable mystery situated, "on an old milestone" (120), outside the stream of life. The law is determined that everything shall be brought to light and brought to order.[7] Extending its long arm, it requires of the mystery a full explanation. Interpreting silence as "violation", the law invokes its "unlimited powers" (121) and wastes the mystery.

Throughout the interrogation and the torture, the fortunes of the law are noted and remarked by the travelers who pass by on the road. They commiserate as he approaches his painful duty (120), they reprove him when he seems indecisive, deride his fatuous commands ("I ordered the blood to flow from his...nose") (122), and commend him when he kills (123). The officer cannot decide whether the old man's silence expresses fear—"generally a safe" and (for the law) a comfortable "assumption"—or "*contempt!* The thought, unwonted, jolted me" (121). In either case, the mystery is uncommunicating and uncooperative—he will not even focus his eyes—and cannot be tolerated.

Once the execution is accomplished, the officer is momentarily haunted by the wayfarer's image.

> I suppose that this was due to my having stooped down to his level: my motives had been commendable, of course, but the consequences of such a gesture, if practiced habitually, could well prove disastrous. (124)

But he is quickly solaced by the smooth unruffled movement on the road.

> Uniformly it flowed, quietly, possessed of its own unbroken grace and
> precision. There was a variety in detail, but the stream itself was one. One.
> The thought warmed me.... At last, I sat up, started the motor, and entered
> the flow myself. I felt calm and happy. A participant. I enjoy my work.
> (124)

It is not quite true that the mystery will not declare itself. After he is shot,
but before he dies, the old man opens up:

> Suddenly, his eyes fixed on mine. His lips worked, his teeth chewed his
> beard, I wished he would end it quickly. I even considered firing a second
> shot through his head. And then he spoke. He spoke rapidly, desperately,
> with neither punctuation nor sentence structure. Just a ceaseless eruption
> of obtuse language. He spoke of constellations, bone structures,
> mythologies, and love. He spoke of belief and lymph nodes, of excavations,
> categories, and prophecies. Faster and faster he spoke. His eyes gleamed.
> Harmonics! Foliations! Etymology! Impulses! Suffering! His voice rose
> to a shriek. Immateriality patricide ideations heat-stroke virtue
> predication—I grew annoyed and shot him in the head. At last, with this,
> he fell. (124)

The moment of revelation arrives and is refused. Desperate, obtuse, without
stops and without syntax, incoherent raving or apocalyptic ecstasy: the
prophet speaks and the rifle interprets.

From the first it is assumed, by the minion who executes justice and
prepares this report, that the old man will either speak or die. As it turns out,
both. We know of nothing he has done that might have brought him to this
pass. Apparently his marginality is enough to activate the rough hermeneutic
of the law. The officer prepares to perform his function by extracting his
memo-book from his pocket and tapping it with his pencil. When he finds
his book empty, he is temporarily unsettled.

> I studied my memo-book. It was blank! my God! *it was blank!* Urgently, I
> wrote something in it. There! Not so bad now. (121)

Filling that book is the matter of first importance. "Duty, a proper sense of
it, is our best teacher: my catechism was coming back to me" (121). The old
man's silence is recorded: the officer writes the word *aphonia* in his book
and then erases it. Everything—the nothing that is not there and the nothing

that is—must be written. Even the torture and execution of the wayfarer seem to have but one purpose: to fill the memo-book. When his victim finally falls, the officer calls in details of the incident, jots down the vital statistics, anticipates the preparation of his "full report" (124), returns the memo-book to his breast pocket, and rejoins the stream of traffic.

Oddly, though his silence is named and notated, the old man's speech is not reported save in the most indirect ("he spoke of...") kind of indirect discourse. Itself a violent outburst, its own violence is met by the counter-violence of the death shot. The wayfarer's glossolalia, with its suggestion of man(t)ic authority, is interpreted by the sterner authority of the law: its possession of the instruments of death and the solid backing of the social order. Not to mention its supervision of the public record. In Coover's agent of the law we meet at last—and in the first person—a competent reader qualified to explicate the most unforthcoming text, resolve the most chaotically overdetermined discourse, and produce his own definitive report. The only reader in the lot who is not defeated by his task. Small wonder he enjoys his work.

The rest of the seven exemplary fictions exhibit the same pattern. In each of them a metaphor of the text, a metaphor of the reader, and a metaphor of reading conspire to provoke a supervenient allegory of unreadability. In "The Brother" a farmer (figure of the reader) is persuaded against his better judgment and the advice of his pregnant wife to help his crazy brother construct a text—a huge boat— the point of which he cannot for the life of him understand. When the rains come, he misses the boat, loses wife and child, and knows himself marked for death. In "Klee Dead" an unreliable narrator tells the reader (you) a story that manages almost successfully to evade the issue: the death of Wilber Klee, its motive and its meaning.[8] At the scene of his demise you find a scrap of paper that may contain the clue to the mystery, but it is completely illegible, maybe blank, and possibly only a handbill. In lieu of explanantion you are offered a pair of tickets to the circus. "J's Marriage" is the familiar tale of a man whose wife—a mysterious virgin whom he cannot penetrate—conceives and gives birth without sex. An uncomprehending reader, J perceives but does not fathom the annunciation and the birth and finally, robbed of his masculine office, dies drunk and consumptive with his face in a glass of red wine. In every case what is narrated is the failure, by an incompetent or disabled or encumbered reader, to interpret a text that is perversely, obtusely, or mysteriously unreadable.

If the variety of these occasions suggests that life itself is the text, then the monotony in the upshot even more forcefully recommends the conclusion that death, literal or figurative, is its meaning. But death—termination without completion—means nothing. No meaning at all. Thus the text of life defeats every hermeneutic and destroys all its readers. But I need not go out on that limb. Closer to the bole: in each of Coover's stories, a reader confronts a text and adopts a set of interpretive strategies. In every case (save one?) he loses. He is denied the intelligibility he seeks, fobbed off with cheap entertainments, condemned to repeat the text forever without understanding it, emasculated, or killed. Coover's readers are weak misreaders, and they all suffer for it. Only a strong misreader would look at the Ark and imagine the deluge, and perhaps not even the strongest would have concluded the Incarnation from his wife's frigidity. John Barth has said that God wasn't too bad a novelist, except that he was a Realist.[9] Barth was thinking of the Book of Nature, but has the craziest post-modern fabulator produced anything wilder than the Bible? A book that still defeats its readers.

There *is* that one (apparent) exception. The strong reader in "The Wayfarer" is no loser. Empowered by the law and supported by his community, Coover's officer obliterates the text that challenges him and writes his own. The wayfarer's unsanctioned existence and his disorderly effusions are replaced jot and tittle by the authoritative text now on file at police headquarters. It's a question of means. Jason's penis-marker, Alfred's jackknife, and Your fumbling philology (Bad Sport) are phalluses that falter and fail. The police officer's pencil/rifle resolutely does its lethal and life-giving work. Their means of interpretation are expunged or expropriated. His accomplishes a full report.

In his *Prólogo* Coover addresses don Miguel:

> For your stories also exemplified the dual nature of all good narrative art: they struggled against the unconscious mythic residue in human life and sought to synthesize the unsynthesizable, sallied forth against adolescent thought-modes and exhausted art forms, and returned home with new complexities. In fact, your creation of a synthesis between poetic analogy and literal history (not to mention reality and illusion, sanity and madness, the erotic and the ludicrous, the visionary and the scatological) gave birth to the Novel—perhaps above all else your works were exemplars of a revolution in narrative fiction, a revolution which governs us—not unlike the way you found yourself abused by the conventions of the Romance— to this very day. (77)

Cervantes brought off a revolution in narrative fiction which has governed writers—e.g., Robert Coover—"to this very day". And now abuses them. Like Cervantes (and perhaps like Little Red Riding Hood in "The Door"

(17-19), the modern writer is a liminal figure. But while Cervantes stepped from a closed world into an open universe, we feel our world closing in on us again.

> Like you, we, too, seem to be standing at the end of one age and on the threshold of another. We, too, have been brought into a blind alley by the critics and analysts; we, too, suffer from a "literature of exhaustion", though ironically our nonheros are no longer tireless and tiresome Amadises, but hopelessly defeated and bed-ridden Quixotes. We seem to have moved from an open-ended, anthropocentric, humanistic, naturalistic, even—to the extent that man may be thought of as making his own universe— optimistic starting point, to one that is closed, cosmic, eternal, supernatural (in its soberest sense), and pessimistic. (78)

Of all the characteristics here enumerated, only the last—"pessimistic"— sounds unmedieval. The modern world is a recapitulation, sadder if not wiser, of the Middle Ages. Once again the writer sees his world as a microcosm of a larger "Design" and probes "beyond the phenomenological, beyond appearances, beyond randomly perceived events, beyond mere history." Like the Knight of the Mournful Countenance, he sallies forth to challenge "the assumptions of a dying age" (78). Barber's basin on his head, the modern writer tilts at illusions in order to disclose reality and conduct his reader to clarity, maturity, and revelation. He engages the preconceptions of the age quixotically, by taking them seriously, and by opposing them he lays bare the truth they dissimulate.

Coover's art is an art of disenchantment. In this respect he is Cervantes *redivivus*. Like the Master's, his stories are his experiments in writing (77-77). But he is doing Cervantes in reverse. Whereas Cervantes' *novelas* are exemplary because "they tell good stories and they tell them well" (77), Coover's fictions illustrate the impossibility of reading and the extreme difficulty of writing. Witness "The Door." Here in the Prologue ("of sorts") to the book as a whole, where you might expect the writer *in propria persona* to give you a concise statement of his purpose, his program, and his achievement, what you get is a clutter of narrators, fairy-tale identities hopelessly confused and conflated, who cannot seem to agree on just what stories to tell—pricksongs and descants or death-cunt-and-prick songs— and what those stories might communicate—a new knowledge of reality or a new brand of illusion. We, who have read (!) the seven exemplary fictions, know what kind of stories they are—both of the above—and what they mean—nothing you can lay your hands on.

The writer as Big Bad Wolf seduces and devours the wisdom of his tradition, and the writer as Don Quixote hacks away at mythic windmills. Both of him perpetrate violent acts: the violent imposition of order on the "flux and tedium" (16) of innocent experience or the violent deranging of an experience already compromised by the violence of prior order. His weapon—his "thick quick cock" (17) and his potent lance—is language. To read Coover's seven deadly fictions is to oppose the counter-violence of interpretation to the originary violence of writing and to commit thereby yet another offense of language.

To the violence which these texts inflict on the conventions of verisimilitude I respond with the counter-violence of allegorical reading. I call the police on these offenders. Or take the law into my own hands. The outcome of this encounter is not the restoration of law and order but the purification of conflict: the act of communication is always thwarted (love is entrapped by death), and the recovery of meaning is always deferred (we never catch the train that will take us home). The recognition of these inevitabilities is itself a liberation of writing and of reading for the fuller exercize of their actual and always contested powers.

Provided we are not then captivated by the illusion of release. The last desire from which we must liberate ourselves is the desire for liberation. In this connection "The Wayfarer"—that apparent exception—is misleading. Coover's efficient peace officer wraps up the case and returns to headquarters happy in his work. But his success is a sham and a shambles. His reading, strong as it is, does not issue a full and final report. It only prolongs the history of violence. And the peace he leaves us with is no more than a deceptive euphoria induced by his own and (if it fools us) our submersion in the stream of life. His reading goes through, but only because it is wholly inscribed within the order enforced by his community. By every community, whether it be the community of culture or the community of interpretation. It is not hard—it may even be mandatory—to imagine that smoothly flowing traffic as the literary-critical establishment.

Calling the police, a summons necessary to the finalization of any act of reading, succeeds in the only way a violent act can succeed. It sets the stage for further violations. No reading is final save by fiat or by consensus, forced terminations that challenge interminable revision. As Bloom has argued, there are no readings pure and simple. There are only misreadings, the strength of which is measured by their power to stimulate more of the same. Every reading is a trope waiting to be sprung.

Granny is right. These *are* dirty stories. But not because of their obsession with sex and death. What they offend is not our moral sensibilities, but the canons of critical responsibility. Experimental in this sense, they severely try the conventions of imitation and the norms of interpretation. Coover's fictions and the hermeneutic that is up to them enact the rape of representation and the death of the innocent reader.

The narrative technique employed in "Seven Exemplary Fictions" is not without precedent or parable in American literature. Here is our strongest reader affronting the text that finally did him in:

> All visible objects, man, are but as pasteboard masks. But in each event—
> in the living act, the undoubted deed—there, some unknown but still
> reasoning thing puts forth the mouldings of its features from behind the
> unreasoning mask. If man will strike, strike through the mask! How can
> the prisoner reach outside except by thrusting through the wall? To me,
> the white whale is that wall, shoved near to me. Sometimes I think there's
> naught beyond. But 'tis enough. He tasks me; he heaps me; I see in him
> outrageous strength, with an inscrutable malice sinewing it. That inscrutable
> thing is chiefly what I hate; and be the white whale agent, or be the white
> whale principal, I will wreak that hate upon him. Talk not to me of
> blasphemy, man; I'd strike the sun if it insulted me. For could the sun do
> that, then could I do the other; since there is ever a sort of fair play herein,
> jealousy presiding over all creations. But not my master, man, is even that
> fair play. Who's over me? Truth hath no confines.[10]

Starting with his own contemporaries, American writers have doggedly made it their business to rebut Emerson's conviction that brute fact passes without remainder into transcendental truth.[11] By now it's a tradition: Hawthorne and Melville its patrons, Whitman its reluctant fellow-traveler, and Pynchon its adept. The burden of the tradition is to insist on the intransigent opacity of fact: fact that will not convert to meaning or that only so converts in a forced exegesis that both distorts the fact and shatters the meaning. It is this harping on the irreducibility of fact that produces the unreadable text. Ontology blocks epistemology.

In *Snow White* Donald Barthelme gives us the unreadable text (and a vision of contemporary American life) in the form of a fairy tale reduced to a trash heap. A pile of plastic buffalo hump which cannot be interpreted but only appreciated. Coover does not ask us to cultivate a taste for dreck. His purpose is not to undo but to redo, for the post-modern age, Cervantes' revolution. He characterizes his own narrative tactics—his peculiar way of pricking and descanting the burden of tradition—in these words:

I like to use the original mythical materials and deal with them on their home ground, go right there to where it's happening in the story, and then make certain alterations in it, and let the story happen in a slightly different way. The immediate effect is to undogmatize it so that at least minimally you can think of the story in terms of possibility rather than as something finite and complete.[12]

Under any description *Pricksongs and Descants* is an experimental work. This is Coover's experimental method, what he calls in the case of Cervantes his "writing ideas" (76). Typically he begins with a familiar story from the Bible, folklore, children's literature, pop culture, what-have-you. Then he opens it up: tells it from a novel point of view, introduces new and often preposterous givens, allows the narrative to take a different and usually startling tack at crucial junctures, or just lets the story go off simultaneously in all the directions it *might* take. The first effect of these techniques is to block all the standard reader responses and to encourage "communication across reality links, not across conventional links."[13]

It is the writer as Big Bad Wolf who makes possible the writer as Don Quixote. By his perverse consumption of traditional materials Coover loosens the strangle-hold which these materials in their conventional forms have on the reader. Disengaging matter and form, he enables us to perceive both afresh: if not originally, then at least more primitively than before, and if not immediately, then at least without the usual narcotic mediations. Recast in Coover's way, the old story becomes not an occasion for knee-jerk reaction but a locus of undecidable possibilities.

The reader *in* Coover's fiction, who is always figuratively and sometimes literally identical with the reader *of* the fiction, invariably tries to subsume the brute and carnal facts that affront him into some superintendent significance. Each of the seven exemplary fictions shows us a reader struggling to contain the data of experience within a system—ideal, mythical, linguistic, narrative, etc.—that will give them meaning. Invariably he tries, and just as invariably he fails. Stones are not sermons, and reality is never a source of messages.[14]

Ontology blocks epistemology. But the distinction is specious. As there are no meanings latent in fact awaiting exegesis, so there are no facts that irresistibly resist explication. Every fact is already a meaning, and a meaning is a fact as hard as any. Beyond the transcendentalist aspiration and the realist demurrer, fact and meaning alike are interchangeable counters in a panel game which generates no final meaning and comes to rest on no fundamental fact. In which (in fact) even the name of the game is up for grabs.

Coover's superficial subject-matter is most often (what else is new?) Love and Death. But the love is commonly drawn toward a sexuality that castrates and kills, and the death whether swift or lingering is usually painful and without point, so that his "deep" subject is violence. Grotesque and excessive, the effect of the violence is to shock us *out of* intepretation and force us *into* essays in redemptive hermeneutic. But the facts resent interpretation as surely as the interpretations collapse in the face of the facts that demand them. Both matter and form are unreadable: the matter inexponible in meaning and the form unexhibitable in fact. The meaning of Coover's fictions (their illegibility) doubles their matter (life as it is suffered) without redundancy. Substance and significance coincide without coalescing, and their duplicity reduplicates the double meaning of Coover's title. Pricksongs and descants (unreadable texts) are also death-cunt-and-prick songs (love and death), and this irreducible duality both structures and perpetuates our (necessarily) violent encounter with both. To read them is certainly an experience that exercizes—vigorously—all the imagination we have.

10

Pieces of Pynchon

a. *Gravity's Rainbow* and the Economy of Preterition

It was quite by accident that William, the first Pynchon in the new world, acquired a place in American literary history. A successful (if controversial) tradesman and magistrate, he tried his hand at theology with *The Meritorious Price of Our Redemption*, published in England in 1650. Cast in the form of a dialogue between a tradesman and a divine (both of them presumably William Pynchon), the book takes issue with the Calvinist doctrine of atonement. Its teachings so outraged the theocracy that the work was proclaimed heretical and publicly burned. William Pynchon returned to England, but (here's the accident) his brother John remained in Massachusetts and had issue. The last (to date) of his progeny, Thomas Ruggles Pynchon, Jr., address unknown, is the author of a book, *Gravity's Rainbow* (hereafter GR),[1] which on its first appearance offended the literary establishment almost as deeply as William had offended the ministers of New England. The protagonist *lieu-tenant* of GR, Tyrone Slothrop, has a first-American-ancestor named William, also a tradesman and amateur theologian, whose treatise *On Preterition* was condemned and burned. History repeats itself…as fiction.

In *The Meritorious Price* (hereafter MP)[2] William Pynchon argues, against the Puritan norm and among other things, (1) that Christ did not suffer the torments of hell, by rights devolved upon mankind, in order to redeem the souls of the Elect; (2) that God did not impute to Christ the sins of the Elect nor oblige him to bear the curse of the law on our behalf; (3) that the sufferings of Christ, voluntarily endured, were inflicted not by God but by the devil and (4) that Christ redeemed us "by paying or performing unto his Father that invaluable precious thing of his Mediatoriall obedience, whereof his Mediatoriall Sacrifice of atonement was the master-piece." (MP, title) William's theses would be uncontroversial today. By contrast with Calvinist orthodoxy, they are almost humane. That was the problem. The ministers smelled a Socinian rat. The book was burned. The Reverend John Norton was deputized to produce an official refutation. Pynchon went back to England, and Massachusetts was rescued for the true faith.

By comparison with MP, William Slothrop's *On Preterition* still sounds like heresy, even in the laid-back ambience of contemporary Christianity. Himself a friend of the Preterite, "William argued holiness for these 'second Sheep,' without whom there'd be no elect." (GR 555) Jesus walking on the water was the exception—"the successful loner"—but "without the millions who had plunged and drowned, there could have been no miracle." Jesus was just "the last piece to the jigsaw puzzle, whose shape had already been created by the Preterite." (GR 554) Like the pigs William loves and annually leads to the slaughter, the Preterite rush "into extinction…, possessed not by demons but by trust…, by innocence they couldn't lose…, by faith." William concluded that "what Jesus was for the elect, Judas Iscariot was for the Preterite." If Jesus were a monster—"the unnatural, the extracreational"—then he could only inspire horror. But "if he is the son of man, and if what we feel is not horror but love, then we have to love Judas too. Right?" (GR 555) William was not burned for heresy, but his book was. "They did finally 86 him out of Massachusetts Bay Colony…," whence he removed not to Rhode Island—"he wasn't that keen on antinomians either"—but to old England, where he died amid his preterite memories. (GR 556)

According to the received opinion, the latest of the Pynchons, apparently cognizant of William's book, took his ancestor's modestly heterodox treatise and twisted it (out of shape) into the wildly heretical *On Preterition* by William Slothrop. Well of course he did. But that's *in* the book. And maybe, like other obvious things in GR, it's something of a diversionary tactic. Let me offer my own (wildly heretical) amendment to the orthodox reading, a supplement that attaches itself not to the contents of GR but to GR itself. My not-so-modest proposal is that Tom Pynchon did not (merely) include an extravagant caricature of MP in GR, but (more importantly) that in GR he (re)wrote his ancestor's treatise ab-orginally. A monstrously presumptive feat of transumption, GR is *The Meritorious Price of Our Redemption…* by Thomas Pynchon. GR is Tom's modest heresy. But though the heresy be moderate, the price of heresy is not, so that Tom's (re)writing of William Pynchon (the theological vocabulary is inevitable) redeems the madder speculations of William Slothrop. It is (shall we say?) the meritorious price of *his* redemption. Be that as it may: *On Preterition is The Meritorious Price*, and both are GR. The book behind the book and the book within the book are finally just: the book.

But you will want cause and effect.... Shortly before the account of the Slothropite heresy we (readers of GR) witness a curious exchange between the ever youthful Osbie Feel and the corrupt-beyond-corrupting Katje Borgesius. In the midst of that exchange we learn (we seem to be reading Katje's mind) that "dialectically, sooner or later, some counterforce would have had to arise." (GR 536) Just as the Iscariotism of William Slothrop is the necessary antithesis of Christian soteriology—"It was a little early for Isaac Newton, but feelings about action and reaction were in the air" (GR 555)—so a We-system is needed to counteract the They-system that wants to rule the world. But what made Katje think of the counterforce? Osbie has just led her into a back room, apparently a scene of writing,

> fitted out with telephones, a cork board with notes pinned all over, desks littered with maps, schedules, *An Introduction to Modern Herero*, corporate histories, spools of recording wire. (GR 536)

Is this the room in which GR was written? After Katje flashes on the counterforce,

> Osbie...hands her now a mimeographed sheaf, rather fat it is, "One or two things, here, you should know. We hate to rush you. But the horse trough is waiting." (GR 536)

What he hands her—"one or two things...you should know"—has got to be (the inference is irresistible) the manuscript of GR. Rather fat it is.

Osbie's last words allude to the Western fantasy on the preceding page. Osbie has been working on a movie scenario—a message for Katje—in which S. Z. ("Cuddles") Sakall winds up in a horse trough. Katje picks up on the allegory. The scenario represents the plot (or wannabe plot) of GR, in which characters like Osbie (Basil Rathbone) defeat villains like Ned Pointsman (Sakall) and send their plots (the midget sheriff) packing. (GR 534-535) Now we have a chain of figurations: Osbie's scenario figures GR, which in turn figures the counterforce. Where's the counterforce? Between the covers of GR.

The figure figures itself? On the very next page we find ourselves in hell. Like Dante's, it is many-leveled, and the episode begins with an allusion to T.S. Eliot alluding to Dante's *Inferno*. But Pynchon's hell is populated (natch) with all the *good* guys, who in this (counter)narrative are (natch again) those who "will *always* be bad." (GR 548) This hell seems to be a hell of a lot of mindless pleasures. But it's also the scene of intense theological controversy. At issue is the question of "Return." The case against Return is argued (at "Critical Mass") by the Jesuit Fr. Rapier, who knows that Return is possible only if "They" too are mortal. Do we die only because They want us to? Or are They only pretending that Death is Their servant?

> To believe that each of Them *will* personally die is also to believe that Their system will die—that some chance of renewal, some dialectic, is still operating in History. (GR 540)

To believe that Death is "the master of us all" and "to withhold from Them our fear of Death" would be the faith that saves. (GR 540) But Fr. Rapier— he is after all Devil's Advocate in hell—cannot summon the courage for that conviction. All he can do is point out "certain obstacles in the way of affirming Return" (GR 540): the dreadful possibility that we may already have reached critical mass, where everything is connected and "the chances for freedom are over for good." (GR 539)

But this is a Slothropite hell. And so, Jesuitical reservations to the contrary notwithstanding, the figure figures itself. Sir Stephen Dodson-Truck is "actively at peace." (GR 541) The damned pass their time playing childish games and watching government newsreels. Loving the People means fucking everybody in every possible way, knowing that "the People will never love you" (GR 547), and the greatest freedom is not to be able to trust yourself. (GR 543) Pirate Prentice, who was hoping for "a bit of mercy" (GR 542), learns that it

> will be possible, after all, to die in obscurity, without having helped a soul: without love, despised, never trusted, never vindicated—to stay down among the Preterite, his poor honor lost, impossible to locate or to redeem. (GR 544)

The Preterite Convention—a hell of sorts—is the gathering of those who have ceased to resist their Preterition. Double agents, who have turned but cannot escape. Hopelessly compromised, they have learned—or are learning—to protect themselves against the longing for purity and the lust for vindication. Even (perhaps) the thought of Return. There is no nostalgia in hell: the first thing is to swallow your shame. What the next step is, no one knows. (GR 541, 546) As the scene ends, Pirate and Katje are dancing, and the episode trails off as ambiguously as possible:

> [T]hey dissolve now, into the race and swarm of this dancing Preterition, and their faces, the dear, comical faces they have put on for this ball, fade, as innocence fades, grimly flirtatious, and striving to be kind....(GR 548)

These are the kind of folks William Slothrop would have liked. The people for whom Judas died, their own death the *mise en scene* of Jesus' resurrection. And what about that Jesus? What did he do? William Pynchon tells us: he was obedient unto death. How far is it from Pynchon to Slothrop?

Enlightened by Byron the Bulb, company barber Pfc. Eddie Pensiero snips the jugular of the colonel whose hair he's cutting. A legendary hero of the counterforce, Byron escapes GE's Committee on Incandescent Anomalies and achieves luminous immortality. Lucky for him, there are lots of bulb-snatchers around (with no sense of shame!) who switch him from *Mutter* to *Mutter* just one step ahead of the CIA. His longburning soul (*Seele*) learns what any counterforce agent has to: Love (for his fading companions) and Silence (Their operatives are everywhere, so don't press your luck). Byron endures, and the manner of his endurance is a thumbnail sketch of counterforce life:

> Byron...is condemned to go on forever, knowing the truth and powerless to change anything. No longer will he seek to get off the wheel. His anger and frustration will grow without limit, and he will find himself, poor perverse bulb, enjoying it....(GR 655)

What we're talking here (and perversely enjoying) is the soteriology of GR. You rub this text with the right stuff and a message begins to emerge.

The members of the counterforce are the Preterite who have embraced their preterition. They have learned to love intensely, to keep silent...and to live without hope. Hope is nothing but the brighter side of paranoia, the happy face of fear, and like fear an attitude They encourage—the fear of damnation and the hope of redemption. Redemption would be the return to innocence, and Fr. Rapier has warned us that there are "certain obstacles in the way of affirming Return." (GR 540) Yet the Americans in GR—especially the Americans—are obsessed with the thought of return. That old nostalgic yen to rewind history, find the fork in the road where we took the wrong turn—and this time do it right, follow the path not taken, and come at last to a better and happier present. When will they cease their "senseless and retrograde journals" (GR 644) and remember what Skippy learned from Mr. Information: the way to Happyville, just like the way to Pain City, is at the disposition of the pointsman? That desire to return to the points and find the track that leads to Happyville is conditioned into you by the same guy who takes you (all too often) to *Der Leid-Stadt*. He creates the *need* for return, and he decides if and when it will be satisfied. To yearn for return is to play his game. Like the sinister *Weisse Engel* in *Marathon Man*, Pointsman (and the Firm he works for) dispenses both pleasure and pain. If you reach for the pleasure he alone can give you, you're just reacting to the pain he makes you suffer. There's no return to Go and start over. No escape.

But it's impossible not to be tempted. The pointsman has made sure of that. So Lt. Slothrop reflects on the theology of his ancestor and daydreams an alternative American history:

> Could he have been the fork in the road America never took, the singular point she jumped the wrong way from? Suppose the Slothropite heresy had had the time to consolidate and prosper? Might there have been fewer crimes in the name of Jesus, and more mercy in the name of Judas Iscariot? It seems to Tyrone Slothrop that there might be a route back....(GR 556)

But these are only "vistas of thought." The Slothropite heresy is not an alternative to orthodoxy, only its backside, and Slothrop's version of history would project its Calvinist antithesis just as surely as Calvinism spawned William Slothrop. As Tyrone accompanies Ludwig in search of his lost lemming, he doesn't know if he's drifting (preterite) or being led (elect). He hopes that love—item: Ludwig's pathetic love for Ursula—may be able to stop history. But "he will never find out" (GR 556), and the lemming quest leads him to nothing less frightening than a new encounter with the unspeakable Major Marvy in a subbasement of the Michaeliskirche.

Slothrop's nostalgia is figured at the microlevel by the ongoing debate between Gustaf Schlabone and Säure Bummer on the relative merits of Beethoven and Rossini. "The point is," Säure says,

> a person feels *good* listening to Rossini. All you feel like listening to Beethoven is going out and invading Poland. Ode to joy indeed. The man didn't even have a sense of humor....With Rossini, the whole point is that lovers always get together, isolation is overcome, and like it or not, that is the one great centripetal movement of the World. Through the machineries of greed, pettiness, and the abuse of power, *love occurs*. All the shit is transmuted to gold. (GR 440)

If only Western music had taken the southern route—through Italy—instead of the north road—from Bach, through Beethoven, Wagner, and Schönberg, to Webern—love might have happened and the world might have rushed together. But it's too late to go back to Rossini. The dialectic of German music led inexorably to the death of Webern: the last European stupidly shot by an ignorant barbarian from North Carolina come to liberate Europe. From the invasion of Poland to the murder of Anton Webern, shit happens.

Pages later Slothrop is still dreaming of return. If not to that fateful fork in the road, at least a trip back home:

> Yup, still thinking there's a way to get back. He's been changing, sure, changing, plucking the albatross of self now and then, idly, half-conscious as picking his nose—but the one ghost-feather his fingers always brush by is America. Poor asshole, he can't let her go. She's whispered *love me* too often to him in his sleep, vamped insatiably his waking attention with come-hitherings, incredible promises. (GR 623)

But he's wiser now, and he knows it won't work:

> What if there's no place for him in her stable any more? If she has turned him out, she'll never explain. Her "stallions" have no rights. She is immune to their small, stupid questions. She is exactly the Amazon Bitch your fantasies have called her to be.
>
> Then there's Jamf, the coupling of "Jamf" and "I" in the primal dream. Who can he go to with *it*? (GR 623)

There's no going home: not to the America that might have been, not to the America that is. Neither one exists. Never did. Mingeborough is occupied. (GR 744) Naughty Nalline would just as soon have that gold star. (GR 682) And even if America were there to go back to, who would go back? Tyrone Slothrop? His American infancy was sold (by Pernicious Pop, for the price of a Harvard education) to that villainous old European Laszlo Jamf. Spoiled rotten before he was even born. So much for the innocent abroad.

Slothrop can't go home. So he goes on, through the Zone, where he is haunted at every turn by the ghosts of himself, "fifth-columnists, well inside his head, waiting the moment to deliver him to the four other divisions outside." (GR 624) On the wall of a "public shithouse…ripe with typhoid" (GR 623) and graffiti memorials of himself, Tyrone scratches his sign:

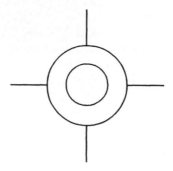

As he eventually comes to realize, that's just the A4 seen from below. Not to mention the symbol of the Zone Hereros: the five positions of the rocket switch. Plus: the cosmic windmill, four F's "symmetrically upside down and backward," the swastika, cruciform churches supporting, rocket-like, heavenward spires—the cross (symbol of redemptive suffering) inscribed in the circle (symbol of integration). A Zone mandala.

Slothrop finds himself surrounded by churches. It's Lent. Chiseled in the sandstone of a church he finds the mark of consecration: a cross in a circle. And then:

> At last, lying one afternoon spread-eagled at his ease in the sun, at the edge of one of the ancient Plague towns he becomes a cross himself, a cross-roads, a living intersection where the judges have come to set up a gibbet for a common criminal who is to be hanged at noon. (GR 625)

Himself the place of execution, Slothrop becomes a cross. In the fantasy that follows we witness a hanging straight out of William Burroughs, in which the hanged man ejaculates into his loin cloth as his neck breaks. His seed falls to earth and becomes a mandrake root.

That's heavy. Both cross and crucified, here the emblem of salvation through suffering (the cross in the circle), Slothrop later becomes the sacrificed and dismembered victim of whatever tragic catharsis this novel enacts. He is not resurrected. But GR is born. Is GR the mandrake root that springs from his preterite seed? Tyrone Slothrop resurrected as text? Tear him up and see if he screams.

But it's a bit late for all that jazz about redemption-through-art. And a bit too early for the resurrection of the dead. What we get—right now—is this:

> In the Zone, later in the day he became a crossroad, after a heavy rain he

doesn't recall, Slothrop sees a very thick rainbow here, a stout rainbow cock driven down out of pubic clouds into earth, green wet valleyed earth, and his chest fills and he stands crying, not a thing in his head, just feeling natural.... (GR 626)

In pursuit of the soteriology of GR we stumble on the image of the poor benighted unhero: crying, empty-headed, feeling (for a change) natural. Is that the "meanest sharp sliver of truth" we are able to find in "so much replication, so much waste?" (GR 590) To coin a phrase, what is truth?

Whatever it is, it ain't easy. With the passage quoted above compare this:

In one of these streets, in the morning fog, plastered over two slippery cobblestones, is a scrap of newspaper headline, with a wirephoto of a giant white cock, dangling in the sky straight downward out of a white pubic bush. The letters

MB DRO

ROSHI

appear above with the logo of some occupation newspaper.... The white image has the same coherence, the hey-lookit-me smugness, as the Cross does. It is not only a sudden white genital onset in the sky—it is also, perhaps, a Tree....

At the instant it happened, the pale Virgin was rising in the east.... A few doomed Japanese knew of her as some Western deity. She loomed in the eastern sky gazing down at the city about to be sacrificed. The sun was in Leo. The fireburst came roaring and sovereign.... (GR 693-694)

August 6, 1945. Another sacrifice, this time an entire city. Was the terrible orgasm triggered by Harry S. Truman's finger on Enola Gay's atomic clit (GR 588) a redemptive oblation? For whom and to what end was that holocaust offered? Slothrop looks at the nuclear umbrella and sees a Cross. Maybe a Tree: the Tree of Calvary and/or the Kabbalistic Tree of Creation. Both the rainbow and the mushroom cloud are heavenly phalluses thrusting into Mother Earth. The original symbol of hope (no more water) and the latest threat of total destruction (the fire next time) have the same form and figure. Is it a figure of rape or a figure of fecundation? The end of the world or the renewal of the earth? Are they different? Check your Bible.

One and the same figure is troped, incoherently, both *in bonum* and *in malum*. GR comments on this paradox in the course of the surrealistic fantasy in which the Floundering Four struggle ineffectually, against the murderous machinations of Pernicious Pop, to rescue the Radiant Hour:

> Slothrop...observes his coalition with hopes for success and hopes for
> disaster about equally high (and no, that *doesn't* cancel out to apathy—it
> makes a loud dissonance that dovetails inside you sharp as knives)....Those
> whom the old Puritan sermons denounced as "the glozing neuters of the
> world" have no easy road to haul down, Wear-the-Pantsers, just cause
> you can't see it doesn't mean it's not there! Energy inside is just as real,
> just as binding and just as inescapable, as energy that shows. When's the
> last time you felt *intensely lukewarm*? eh? Glozing neuters are just as human
> as heroes and villains. In many ways they have the most grief to put up
> with, don't they? (GR 676-677)

Slothrop's "glozing neuters"—a preterite lot if ever there was one—are
borrowed from the Puritan preacher Thomas Hooker, to whom we are also
indebted for the distinction (GR 22) between "wilde love" and "garden
love." Both precisions come from a sequence of sermons on the Christian
life, in which Hooker identifies the glozing neuters as those who, neither
declaring themselves the enemies of Christ nor owning his covenant,
endlessly reassess the signs of the times and hide the Gospel under the
blanket of their glosses.[3] Interminable interpretation indefinitely deferring
decision and eventually losing sight of the issue. Whom Hooker condemns—
the lukewarm souls that Christ shall spew out of his mouth—Pynchon
champions. Painful as it is to spend your life straddling the fence, the
preterite—and their champion—mean to elude binary oppositions. The
invitation at the end of the glozing neuters' song—"now ev' rybody—"
(GR 677) is tendered again at the end of the book—"Now everybody—"
(GR 760): moments undecided and undecidable. It's a case of "Outside and
Inside interpiercing one another too fast, too finely labyrinthine, for either
category to have much hegemony any more." (GR 681)

That *would* be (in both senses of the word) a mean sliver to extract
from this Augean novel. If it's a truth, it's not the Truth opposed to Falsehood
but a truth that doesn't acknowledge the hegemony of either category. They
of course (Hooker was one of Them) wouldn't allow it. They recognize
only the Ins and the Outs, and those who won't line up behind the Ins are
filed with the Outs. The glozing-neuter truth that In and Out are operationally
indistinct, since both are part of Their plan, is a truth They can't admit,
since it isn't part of Their plan. And that's *not* a binary opposition.

But They think it is. Fr. Rapier says: our only hope of return lies in the
possibility that They and Their system are mortal. Death erases all
oppositions, including the opposition of life and death. Elsewhere we are
asked (anonymously) to entertain another hopeful thought: maybe They'll

make a mistake. And They do make mistakes, as when Muffage and Spontoon cut Major Marvy instead of Lt. Slothrop. As a result of that serendipity Slothrop is liberated and Pointsman demoted. Not everyone is so lucky. When the narcs come to raid your pad, They turn off the water first so you can't flush your stash and you wind up "trapped inside Their frame." Maybe They'll forget the water, in which case "Their neglect is your freedom." But don't count on it. Best to crack the valve a bit, so there's always some flow through the toilet and you can hear the silence when They shut off the water. Gives you a minute or two of grace. It takes "a particular kind of mental illness" to do that. "Not the usual paranoia", but—presumably—*creative* paranoia. (GR 694, 638) No doubt it was creative paranoia that inspired Roger Mexico and Pig Bodine, with a little assist from that grand old gourmet Earnest Pudding (†), to cook up the revolting menu that trashed the Krupp barbecue and saved their sirloin. As Pig and Rog "soft-shoe out the door,"

> The last black butler opens the last door to the outside, and escape. Escape tonight. "Pimple pie with filth frosting, gentlemen," he nods. And just at the other side of dawning, you can see a smile. (GR 717)

In the Chicago Bar analepsis Pig Bodine, toking a fat reefer and strumming his guitar, whistles through a siren ring (1 boxtop + 25c to cover postage and handling) installed in his asshole. Farting melodiously and "in the right key," Bodine signals "a return toward innocence." (GR 740) As he hands Slothrop his undershirt anointed with the blood of John Dillinger, he gives him a bit of advice:

> Yeah, what we need isn't right reasons, but just that *grace*. The physical grace to keep it working. Courage, brains, sure, O.K., but without that grace? forget it. (GR 741)

What's a nice girl like grace doing in a place like this? William Slothrop says that grace has favored the preterite. Tyrone's cards call him a "tanker and feeb" with a "long and [remember Ian?] scuffling future," mediocre both in his life and in his (heh heh) chroniclers. (GR 738)

> Knowing his Tarot, we would expect to look among the Humility, among the gray and preterite souls, to look for him adrift in the hostile light of the sky, the darkness of the sea....(GR 742)

Adrift and awash, Slothrop goes to pieces. He

> has become one plucked albatross. Plucked, hell—*stripped.* Scattered all
> over the Zone. It's doubtful if he can ever be "found" again, in the
> conventional sense of "positively identified and detained." (GR 712)

That albatross is the self. (GR 623) It's also the trademark of the Firm:

> The Man has a branch office in each of our brains, his corporate emblem is
> a white albatross, each local rep has a cover known as the Ego, and their
> mission in this world is Bad Shit. (GR 712-713)

To escape the Firm you have to off that albatross. But to pluck the albatross
is to die, and Tyrone's albatross is stripped.

> There is also the story about Tyrone Slothrop, who was sent into the Zone
> to be present at his own assembly....The plan went wrong. He is being
> broken down instead and scattered. (GR 738)

This epitaph is followed by excerpts from Slothrop's Tarot, a random
assortment of comments on the *problem* of Tyrone Slothrop, and what may
be his mortal remains: a fragment of undershirt, U.S. Navy issue,
bloodstained; a bottle containing 7 cc. of *Maiwein*; and a photograph that
could be his on the jacket of a record album by The Fool (the preterite card
among the Major Trumps), with a note that reads "Harmonica, kazoo—a
friend." (GR 739,742) But the son of Broderick and Nalline Slothrop is no
more. He has fallen through the cracks and out of the system.

William Pynchon: the grace of our Savior—and the price of our
redemption—is obedience unto death. William Slothrop: grace is with the
preterite. To be preterite is to be lost, and to be lost is all the salvation there
is. You won't find that equation in your standard Christian calculus. But if
it solves, it vindicates the Slothropite heresy and plots the parabola that
arches from Pynchon to Slothrop, dt by dt converting salvation into
preterition. (Re)writing his ancestor's preterite tract, Thomas Ruggles
Pynchon, Jr., "last of his line, and how far-fallen" (GR 569), was led by the
inexorable dialectic of American fiction to compose the treatise of William
Slothrop *On Preterition*—and to (re)inscribe himself therein as Tyrone
Slothrop, whose Preterition groweth sure. (GR 509)

Mainstream dialectic is a logic of redemption. It saves everyone, even
its enemies, by defining them as the necessary internal articulations of itself.

There's nothing you can say *about* it that hasn't already been said *by* it. In the Hegelian version the Other-than-Spirit is just a cunning device by which Spirit, alienating and recuperating itself, asserts its own finality and totality. That's the economy of the Absolute: the provisional expenditure that guarantees the ultimate gain. Calvin's economy of salvation salvages even the Reprobate: their personal dereliction confirms the divine justice. Nothing is lost. Except, in the case of Hegel, the perishing particularity of the particular that resists sublation: the "single individual" Kierkegaard tried to rescue from the dialectical juggernaut. And in the case of Calvin, the lost souls of those "second Sheep" who fall out of the economy of salvation. Foreshadowed in William Pynchon's vision of the perfect self-sacrifice that is the meritorious price of our redemption, the holiness of the preterite is the substance of William Slothrop's new covenant. Both are coinscribed, as figure and fulfillment, in GR, the bible of the preterite.

Item: Slothrop's personal mouthorgan, flushed down the toliet at the Roseland Ballroom and recovered years later in the Zone. Of course he doesn't recognize it. They're the ones who remember. But Slothrop sucking on his harp is as close to being a spiritual medium as he'll ever get. (GR 622) Harmonicas, kazoos, and siren rings are always positively charged in GR. As is the saxophone in the hands of the right jazzman. Maybe even the ocarina. These are the preterite instruments, passed over by the dialectic of German music as it gradually assembled the modern symphony orchestra. Preterite instruments, instruments of the preterite, and vessels of preterite grace.

First and foremost of all the preterite creatures in GR is the pig. Despised by the religions and folklore of the world, the pig wallows on, comfortably accepting his preterition and thoughtlessly rushing lemming-like to the slaughter at the end of the pike. William Slothrop drove pigs to market,

> but William wasn't really in it so much for the money as just for the trip itself. He enjoyed...just being with those pigs. They were good company....William came to love their nobility and personal freedom...— pigs...were everything Boston wasn't. (GR 555)

William's pigs are "in company together" with all the other pigs in this novel. Pig Bodine, emblem of innocence and dispenser of grace. Pökler's Frieda (his peace), for whom Slothrop feels a momentary unprogrammed desire. Porky Pig, dancing in tattoo across the bellies of Osbie Feel and other demented denizens of the Zone. Or Porky in the cartoon, holding the anarchist's bomb in his guileless hands and staring, cross-eyed and non-plussed, at the sputtering fuse. And, last but not least, it is the *Schweinheld* Plechazunga (or at least his hide) that saves Slothrop's embattled testicles and releases him from service to the Firm—a release that issues, eventually, in his dissolution.

For dissolution, read redemption. The Scriptures tell us that he who would save his life must lose it. As the Slothrops (both of them) and the Pynchons (at least one of them) would have it, that is not a tender offer: if you lose your life now, you'll get it back with interest later. William Pynchon reformed the Calvinist economy: the price of our redemption is not the Saviour's coerced assumption of our arrears, but his voluntary forfeiture of self. William Slothrop refused the economic metaphor altogether: self-sacrifice is not the price of redemption, it *is* redemption. The economy of preterition is the aneconomy of expenditure without reserve. Neither counting the loss nor counting on the gain, to lose your life *is* to save it.

The pig, a type of preterite grace, is the totem of Pynchon's unsalvageable fiction. The production of GR is figured, as counterforce manual, in the text of GR, which in turn figures MP as OP, and offers its own preterition as the plenitude of all its figurations: the slaughter at the end of the pike. GR is the doomed phoenix that rises from the ashes of Tyrone's albatross, only to be consumed in the fire of his oblation. Tracking the dialectic that modulates price to preterition, and figuring itself, GR is the counterforce that "sooner or later…would have had to arise." (GR 536) And in rising, fall. GR redeems the novel in performing its death. Doing its damnedest (I use the word advisedly) to elude the dialectic by which the novel as genre is defined and in which it is contained, it enacts as novel the sparagmos of the novel. Slothrop's story goes to pieces just as Slothrop does. Welcoming its fate (the unliterariness which is not so much the reason for as the effect of its omission from the canon), GR pays with its preterition the price of its redemption.

For redemption, read dissolution. GR espouses the Slothropite heresy. Form and content alike make the unconditional surrender of self that is the destiny of the preterite. But the heresy of William Slothrop is just the heresy of William Pynchon taken to the end of the line by the last of his line. William Pynchon was a minor incident in the history of theology. His treatment at the hands of the theocracy, without which his treatise might have passed unnoticed into archival oblivion, probably reflects their political and economic anxieties as much as it expresses their devotion to orthodoxy. But he *belongs* to the history of American literature. And his place is within the covers of GR, where his tract, the presupposition *of* the book, is (re)inscribed *within* the book as William Slothrop's *On Preterition*, himself as the heresiarch, and his preterite progeny as the hapless Tyrone, "all out of luck and time." (GR 3) *On Preterition* is the true text of *The Meritorious Price* temerariously transumed and terribly transformed in the terminal tomfoolery of *Gravity's Rainbow*.

b. Paranoia, Pynchon, and Preterition

> God gave Noah the rainbow sign.
> No more water, the fire next time!
> —Spiritual

> God wasn't too bad a novelist, except he was a Realist.
> —John Barth

One of Pynchon's characters remarks that there are only two kinds of people: paranoids and positivists. The positivists believe that things just happen, more or less at random. The paranoids are certain that everything is connected (though the connection cannot be seen) and that They have a plan (though you cannot know what it is). The paranoid's faith—his substance of things hoped for and his evidence of things not seen—is: someone's out to get me.

A positivist could not write a novel, not even (what *Gravity's Rainbow* almost was) a book of "mindless pleasures."[4] The act of writing would impose and so dissimulate the very connectedness and order that the positivist *ex professo* is bound to deny. Novels don't just happen at random. They can only be made to seem to.

The paranoid can't exactly write a novel either. But he might conspicuously fail to write the novel that (perhaps) lurks like a spectre behind the grotesque facade of *Gravity's Rainbow*.

Along the story of Tyrone Slothrop's vacation adventures at the Casino Hermann Goering someone has strung out four "proverbs for paranoids." Here they are, foax, all together:

1. "You may never get to touch the Master, but you can tickle his creatures" (237).[5]
2. "The innocence of the creatures is in inverse proportion to the immorality of the Master" (241).
   (How's that? The greater the immorality of the Master, the less the

innocence of the creatures? And vice versa? Shouldn't it be the other way around? Proverb 3 replies—or does something—to these questions.)
3. "If they can get you asking the wrong questions, they don't have to worry about the answers" (251).
And 4. "*You* hide, they seek" (262).

As Lt. Slothrop reflects one day in the Zone, when he finds that his faith is faltering (he's "losing his mind" actually):

> If there is something comforting—religious, if you want—about paranoia, there is still also anti-paranoia, where nothing is connected to anything, a condition not many of us can bear for long....Either *They* have put him here for a reason, or he's just here. He isn't sure that he wouldn't, actually, rather have that *reason*. (434)

And here's that Slothrop again, in another of his almost ubiquitous desperate straits—Slothrop *de profundis*: "Providence, hey Providence, what'd you do, step out for a beer or something?" (378).

At Swinemünde the blackmarket impressario Gerhard von Göll observes with satisfaction that the ranks of the starving are dwindling day by day. When Slothrop objects ("that's a shitty thing to say"), Der Springer comes back like a prophet:

> Be compassionate. But don't make up fantasies about them. Despise me, exalt them, but remember, we define each other. Elite and preterite, we move through a cosmic design of darkness and light, and in all humility, I am one of the very few who can comprehend it *in toto*. Consider honestly, therefore, young man, which side you would rather be on. While they suffer in perpetual shadows, it's...always—

and he segues into the fox-trot, "Bright Days for the Black Market" (495).

The paranoia that infests GR is manifestly a religious attitude. In fact a familiar religious attitude, just as American as apple pie and growing up absurd. Paranoia is described at one point as "a Puritan reflex...seeking other orders behind the visible" (188). It is that paradoxical and singularly self-satisfied conjunction of total depravity and radical innocence that made this country great: old-fashioned New England Calvinism.

The heart of Calvinism is the doctrine of double predestination. God, whose absolute sovereignty Calvinists guarded more jealously than any Christians before them, has from all eternity relentlessly elected to save a few out of the corrupt mass of fallen humanity. The rest he passes over and allows to fall into hell borne down by the weight of Adam's and their own sin. All men are either Elect, the handful chosen for salvation, or Preterite, passed over and tacitly consigned to damnation.

In GR we see the divine decree of predestination from a new angle. All of our standard accounts were written by men persuaded of their own election. For all his agonized self-scrutiny, and in spite of his extraordinary bad luck with women (he is appropriately the opposite of Tyrone Slothrop in this respect), Sam Sewall never seriously doubted his eventual salvation. But in GR we are treated to the view from below. The Elect experience their election as the consciousness that all things, even tribulations, conspire together for their good. For the Preterite this converts to the strong suspicion, bordering on conviction, that "they're out to get me."[6]

The Elite apprehend their privilege by faith. No certainty, it insinuates itself in occasional or recurrent signs of grace that order their otherwise unraveling lives. The plan is not clearly discerned, but it makes itself felt. Paranoia, which is just the will of God as perceived by the Preterite, is likewise an act of faith, nourished by disparate but distressingly almost-consistent signs of impending destruction. As the Elect may not be certain of their election, but nonetheless hope for tokens of the divine favor, so the paranoid does not know what the events of his life mean, whence that meaning accrues to them, or what he is being used for; but he senses just the same that his life is plotted and that all his actions are rigged. Not that he has proof. Positivistic counter-examples abound, suggesting that events occur with no particular rhyme or reason. But though the evidence is not conclusive—no unambiguous pattern evolves—it is nevertheless overwhelming. And so the paranoid hopes—or fears, often he doesn't know which—that all things are connected, that They do have a plan, and that his doom is sure.

Tyrone Slothrop's ancestor William published a book defending the view that grace had always been on the side of the Preterite. The System got him for that: the Boston theocracy burned his book and drove him out of the New Jerusalem. Which figures. Grace is gratuitous, that is, not part of the plan, therefore irrational and reprobate. Mad, like paranoia.

The action of GR begins (with a dream of death and resurrection) during Advent of 1944 and ends (with the passion of Gottfried) at the time of the autumnal—or is it the vernal?—sacrifice in 1945, after Slothrop, a kind of comical *pharmakos*, has been dismembered and dispersed. It may be that Pynchon's manifold paranoid blasphemies, like those of *his* ancestor

William, who was also banned in Massachusetts,[7] contrive a pious inversion of Calvinist Christianity. As he explains to Karl Marx, "Christian Europe was always death, Karl, death and repression" (317). Had America followed the Slothropite heresy, its history might have been life and liberation instead: "fewer crimes in the name of Jesus and more mercy in the name of Judas Iscariot" (556).

But, as Richard M. Nixon once said, let me make one thing perfectly clear. When I say that paranoia is a religious attitude, I am not trying to suck edification from sour pickles. I merely observe that the *shape* of piety is always the same, whether it be the piety of the Elect or the piety of the Preterite.

The piety of the Preterite merits further refinement. The first discrimination in the divine decrees is between Elect and Reprobate. But some writers subdivide the Reprobate. There are the Reprobate in the strict sense, whom God designates for damnation. And there are the Preterite, whom he passes over and does not sign either for salvation or perdition, but who are of course damned anyway by the inertia of sin. All men are drowning. A few of them God mercifully plucks out of the water and revives. Some are pushed down and held under. The rest are allowed to sink on their own. A seventeenth-century theologian distinguished the positive act of punishment from the privative act of preterition, both of which he ascribed to God's simple prescience. A writer of the late nineteenth century spoke of "the reprobates who are damned because they were always meant to be damned, and the preterite who are damned because they were never meant to be saved."[8]

That would appear to be a disconsoling precision for the Preterite. As the name implies, they participate inversely in the eternal decrees: they are included only as omitted. Negatively prehended by God, they go their way to an end that is just as ineluctable and just as desolate as the damnation of the Reprobate. Maybe more so, since it is not distinguished by divine notice. Deprived of the dignity imparted by God's individuating wrath, the Preterite perish en masse in His ignorance.

GR is set among the Preterite, the "second sheep," "out of luck and out of time" (3, 555). Each of them hears a voice speaking only to him and saying, "You didn't really believe you'd be saved. Come, we all know who we are by now. No one was ever going to take the trouble to save *you*, old fellow" (4, and cf. 202, 204, 362).

Tyrone Slothrop, descended from an ancient line of American Puritans, finally escapes the clutches of "shit, money, and *the Word*, the three American truths" (28, my emphasis) and rejoins his earliest New England ancestor on the side of the Preterite. *"They"* chose him—or so this paranoid sometimes believes—"because of all those *word-smitten Puritans* dangling off [his] family tree" (207, my emphasis). He was sent into the Zone to be present at his own assembly—"perhaps, heavily paranoid voices have whispered, *his time's assembly.*" But the plan went wrong, and he is broken down and scattered instead. Everyone loses sight of him. Analyst Mickey Wuxtry-Wuxtry explains that the villainous Laszlo Jamf was only a fiction to help Slothrop explain his erotic fascination with death. "These early Americans," he says, "were a fascinating combination of crude poet and psychic cripple." The spokesman for the Counterforce admits (lies?) to *The Wall Street Journal*, "We were never concerned with Slothrop *qua* Slothrop" (738). He was only a pretext...or perhaps a point-for-point microcosm.

By the end of the book Seaman Pig Bodine is the only person who can still perceive Slothrop as an integral creature. No one else can even imagine him. As they put it, "It's just got too remote" (740). There is what may be a snapshot of him on the only album ever released by an English rock group called "The Fool." One of the faces in the group might be his—no one knows for sure if or which—and "the only printed credit that might apply to him is 'Harmonica, kazoo—a friend.'" The narrative continues, "But knowing his Tarot, we would expect to look among the Humility, among the gray and preterite souls, to look for him adrift" (742).

Late in the story we are given bits and pieces of Slothrop's Tarot reading. All of his hopeful cards are reversed, especially and most woefully the Hanged Man, who upright (that is, upside down) represents "wisdom, circumspection, discernment, trials, sacrifice, intuition, divination, prophecy," but reversed (upright) signifies "selfishness, the crowd, body politic."[9] His significator is covered by the 3 of Pentacles reversed, which means:

> a long and scuffling future..., mediocrity (not only in his life but also, heh, heh, in his chroniclers too, yes yes nothing like getting the 3 of Pentacles upside down covering the significator on the second try to send you to the tube to watch a seventh rerun of the Takeshi and Ichizo show...)...no clear happiness or redeeming cataclysm. (738)

00000

I have laid a lot of words on the theological meaning of preterition. Which was inevitable under the circumstances. That's the first order of preterition in GR, and there are pages (roughly 760) of examples. But it's only the first order. Tyrone Slothrop is preterite not only in his destiny but also (heh, heh) in his chronicler. Back to the tube for the seventh rerun of a vulgar Kamikase sitcom, he himself ends as a motley of pop signifiers. Was he ever more than that?

The second order of preterition devolves from the further meanings of the word. Preterite, which means "passed over," also means just "past." As Webster puts it, with exquisitely unconscious paranoid sensitivity, "a verb tense that indicates action in the past without reference to duration, continuance, or repetition."[10]

Restored to its native Latin, *praeteritio* identifies a figure of rhetoric. The Greek *paraleipsis*, the figure of conspicuous omission. Omission by mention, or mention by omission.

At the level of its rhetoric GR is a sustained piece of preterition. It displays on its rhetorical surface a linguistic paranoia which answers to the "deep" paranoia of its plots and personae. That is, by preterition (passing over) it constructs them as preterite (past). What is conspicuously omitted is perspicuously obscured.

Some details, at random and of unequal importance: in the main plot involving Slothrop and the Rocket, a number of clues are planted, the meanings of which would clear up for once and for all the significance of the Rocket itself and of Slothrop's erotic connection with the Rocket. But the meanings are not given. Though a number of imperfectly paranoid critics have been eager to help us out, we never learn what the *Schwarz-gerät* is, what the "mystery stimulus" was that occasioned Slothrop's V2-related hard-ons, what the Kirghiz light is, and so on through a whole string of crucial and critically mislaid identities. Identities which function in the fiction not in spite of but precisely because of and in proportion to their elusive and spectral character.

Here's an instance of greater magnitude. GR is obsessed with death. And yet deaths (singular deaths, terminations, fulfillments) are not narrated. They are sometimes reported after they happen: the death of Tantivy Mucker-Maffick, mass deaths in the concentration camps and in German Southwest Africa, the extinction of the Dodo. Bianca's death (on a ship named *Anubis*, which means "death") is horribly suggested, but it happens—if that *is* what happened—during Slothrop's (and the narrator's) absence from the scene (531-532). It is certain that Gottfried will die as the rocket moves through *Brennschluss* and turns downward in its predestined course. But "the exact moment of his death will never be known" (751).

The one death for which we are most exquisitely prepared never comes off. We witness Klaus Närrisch awaiting his certain end at the hands of the Russians, meditating the last moments of John Dillinger, fingering his machine gun, and reflecting that tomorrow he will not have to worry about the blisters on his fingers. He's a goner for sure (516-518). Almost fifty pages later he turns up again, in the hands of the Russians, full of sodium amytal and babbling to Tchitcherine the secrets of the *S-Gerät* and the *Fünffachnullpunkt* (563-565).

These deaths are all preteritions. Including those that don't happen, for the survivors are just as preterite as the slain. The Schwarzkommando who escaped von Trotha's campaign console themselves with the Herero mantra "Mba-kayere," which means, "I am passed over" (362). Preterition *can* mean survival. And yet these deaths, like the lives they do not take, are emphatically not culminations, endings that give meaning to what has passed. Of none of them could it be said, *consummatum est*. And still the dead haunt the story. Pynchon's non-narration of death intimidates by its absence. Death is everywhere at hand (the War), repeatedly recollected (the several cases of genocide past), and always imminent ("Now everybody—"). But it is not narratively experienced. It is always only the unnameable object of a paranoid faith, most real and most terrifying because it is not told. The narrative distancing of death, itself a preterition, is a preterition of the second order.

More important than these quasi-substantives, the linguistic texture of GR has bothered some readers with its apparent disdain for all the norms and conventions of "literature." Almost the entire story is told in the crudest kind of 1940's pop talk. The metaphors of this talk are the popular media: the movies, TV, comic strips, advertising slogans. Pornography. Drug lore. And popular song: like a cheap musical, GR lapses into song at the most inopportune moments. The language is pretty consistently vulgar. The names of the characters are glaringly "meaningful," often suggesting obscenity. Not to mention the overt and frequently deviant obscenity. And Pynchon never passes up an opportunity—he'll make one if he has to—for a horrible pun. "For De Mille, young fur-henchmen can't be rowing!" (559). Did we really need that?

Pynchon has insisted—consciously, if not all-too-consciously—on taking an abysmal tone in what is—obviously, if not all-too-obviously—a serious text dealing with lofty themes. Even when the rhetoric does become exalted, as in Roger's and Jessica's poignant Advent service or the pathetic story of the Pöklers, the swell and expansion of the language is periodically checked and deflated by intrusions of Pynchon's more typical slang. Every ingredient of form—myth, symbol, archetype, history, allegory, romantic quest, even the ritual sanctities of science—is framed and qualified by the underslung tone of the narrative voice.

The blatantly low style of GR is a rhetorical way of searching among the humility and the preterite for a form suitably inappropriate to its content. Not quite the *sermo humilis* of early Christian stylistics, Pynchon's linguistic posturing is what one critic has described as "undergraduate defenses against seriousness…part of a more terrible seriousness."[11] An embarrassed and self-conscious way of talking about grave and momentous things, and a preterition of sorts. There is no matching of style to theme and no assertion of an incarnational realization of the noble in the vulgar (as in *sermo humilis*), but rather a discrepancy that implies the solemnity of the matter only negatively by means of the gross incompetence of the manner.

The language of GR refuses to take itself and its powers seriously. It is deliberately not literary, where "literary" stands for the romantic (and late romantic modernist) conception of a language perfectly integrated in itself and perfectly comprehensive of its meaning. GR does not wish to be a self-referring and self-obsessed structure that contains all it expresses. On the contrary, it is open with an artfully naïve openness. Self-wounded, it is therefore vulnerable by all the canons of good taste. Not because Pynchon, poor fellow, simply cannot write like a proper author. His occasional "elevated" passages proscribe that conclusion. He has willfully produced a text insufficiently sophisticated to build and maintain its own defenses. A text that rejects literary propriety with all its presuppositions, so that it seems adolescent and a bit shamed by its own self-exposure. A-and, it literally stutters.

Pynchon's book bombards us with data, tempts us with a surfeit of clues. But the data never entail a sure conclusion, and the clues lead not to solutions but to further problems: "this is not a disentanglement from, but a progressive *knotting into*" (3). There are signs—too many signs—but nothing assuredly signified; a jumble of texts, but no reliable edition.[12] Lots of noise and little information. The language—this is the secret of its mastery—is not master of itself. It has renounced self-mastery, so that there is no "authentic" text of GR. All the questions it broaches are over-researched, over-documented, and left in the breach. Whatever it says garrulously and disconcertingly fails to make the point. And that of course is the point. The power of Pynchon's language is its self-dissipation. Its energy is expended in verbal waste and degradation.[13] "Th' expense of spirit in a waste of shame…." Like that intricately orchestrated orgy on board the *Anubis* which ends in a communal orgasm, it achieves the bad infinite: the ouroboric state of perfect entropy (466-467). You may never get to touch the Master, but you can tickle his creatures to death. Or to exhaustion, which is the same thing.

The paranoid—it figures—can't win. He is doomed either to destruction or to dissolution. One or the other. Destruction if his paranoid faith (that is, fear) is warranted, dissolution if his anti-paranoid hope (that is, anxiety) is confirmed. He opts for verbal dissolution—the opposite of that verbal integration which is supposed to define literary language—and in so doing negatively adumbrates his destruction. But it's always an open question. Perversely nonliterary language is the refusal of closure. And the suicide of the song, *Sold on Suicide* (320), is indefinitely postponed through what cannot ever, thanks to Gödel's theorem, become a complete catalogue of renunciations.

What is the plot, or what are the plots, of GR? The interlacings and interfacings of the plots in the fictional sense (the sort of thing Aristotle might have recognized had he first read Sterne) are repeatedly—we could say "deliberately," but we don't dare—confused with Plot in the sense that only a paranoid would understand. The plotting—*mimesis praxeos* as well as conspiracy—seems to be forged, in both senses of that word. It occurs (or does not occur) outside the narrative sequence and provides no clear index to narratorial intention. "Paranoia allows plot—is plot. But to carry the pun that far is to turn narrative into madness."[14] Exactly.

GR is told by an omniscient narrator. At least it's not first person, stream of consciousness, epistolary narration, a narrative distributed among several voices, or any of the other familiar techniques. But this narrator does everything in his power to make us doubt the omniscience formally implied by his assumption of the role. Almost every word he utters undermines our confidence in his ability to handle this thing. He is no more in control of his story than he is in charge of what it darkly forbodes. It is not obvious that he is even a single persona, since his relationship to his story is continually changing. Narrative point of view and narrator affect vary from episode to episode, page to page. Sometimes he is the detached ironic observer, sometimes he is sympathetically within his characters sharing their passions. Sometimes he's frivolous, sometimes grave, and as a rule each mood is interrupted by the other. Anticipating the disintegration of Tyrone Slothrop, the narrator himself is fragmented and dispersed into his characters, for whom often (but not always) he speaks.[15] Like them, he is not well-rounded: and much less reliable.

Pynchon's narrator doesn't answer the questions he raises. Sometimes he passes them to the reader: "Is the baby smiling, or is it just gas? Which do you want it to be?" (131). Every once in a while he makes it painfully clear that his story is a fabrication—both a fiction and an expedient lie—and that he is at liberty to make or break connections at will: "You will want cause and effect. All right" (663). Having laid an analogy in our path—Kekulé dreams the benzene ring in the form of the Great Serpent—he will then belabor its point to make sure we don't miss it—"*Just like that snake with its tail in its mouth*, GET IT?" (413)—which of course robs the point of its power and ruins any confidence we might otherwise have had in the analogy.

The narrative voice in GR uses the conventions of novelistic realism, but he refuses the implications of those conventions. The point of the refusal is to provide rhetorical assurance that the important thing—the meaning or the subject—is never present in the narration or correlated with it by some lucid nexus of signification, but always evasive and absent. Not remotely present, but absent: not there, really, but threatening from the other side, from beyond the Zero degree of absolute writing. As Frank Kermode says, writing about the Tristero of *The Crying of Lot 49*, "That plot is pointed to as the object of some possible annunciation; but the power is in the pointing....Its [the novel's] separation from its exterior and its totality are precisely what it is *about*."[16]

Tyrone Slothrop, who at first is barely perceivable as an entity, winds up nearly inconceivable after his talent for phallic rocket-dowsing is of no further use to Them. In a curiously inverse way his paranoia pays off in his own preterition. The final *sparagmos* is a dissolution which averts destruction. Not meaningfully terminated, neither saved nor damned, he is dropped piece-meal from his own story and parsed into a scattering of ambiguous traces—a face on the cover of a record album, an undershirt stained with the blood of John Dillinger, a name here and there from which no identity may be salvaged.

Slothrop's disappearance is mirrored in the notorious paranoia of the entity (if there is one) called Thomas Pynchon. Whatever its basis in his personality (whatever and wherever that may be), Pynchon's paranoia is in the service of an authorial preterition. By refusing to permit photographs, by stubbornly remaining invisible, incognito, and incommunicado, Pynchon escapes into and through his texts. Mba-kayere. He is nothing but the signifier of occasional rumors in *Newsweek*, *Playboy*, and other literary journals. The paranoia and the preterition are part of the oeuvre.

Tyrone Slothrop and Thomas Pynchon follow their common father William down the way not taken, the way of the preterite. And both are lost.

They are the America we did not choose. According to Mondaugen's Law, "Personal destiny is directly proportional to temporal bandwidth" (509). Without past or future, Slothrop and Pynchon alike, deprived of a local habitation, scarcely left with a name, thin out to airy nothing. The America that was chosen—the America that burned William Slothrop-Pynchon's heretical book, the America that sent Tyrone Slothrop (and his time) into the Zone and into the void—also fabricated (perhaps) the paranoia of Tom Pynchon.[17] And his book. It may even be the case—this would be the ultimate paranoid fantasy—that the two ways, of election and of preterition, are the same. The destruction willed by election and the dissolution remaindered for preterition—Gottfried the sacrifice and Slothrop the scapegoat—are at last reconciled in the non-being that lies over the last dt and beyond the Zero.

00000

Cultural optimism aside, these remarks converge toward a conjecture about the rhetoric of GR.[18] By rhetoric I understand, most generally and most fundamentally, the technique of linguistic recovery. Traditionally rhetoric is the persuasive use of language. Burke identifies courtship as the paradigmatic act of persuasion and regards prayer as the pure form of persuasion. The use of language to persuade posits a hierarchic distance between persuader and persuadee and at the same time, by the same use of language, wills to reduce this distance to the absolute proximity of union. Rhetoric, which acknowledges the differences among men and proposes to overcome them, attempts by means of language to achieve what Burke calls a consubstantiality of motives. Thus the lover courting his beloved linguistically abases himself and exalts her, but to the end of achieving union with her: not only a congress of the flesh, but also a communion of wills and minds and affections. Thus also prayer, in which God as the Perfect Persuadee is infinitely exalted and the worshiper as the ideal persuader infinitely abased—to the end that they may eventually be joined in sacramental communion or mystical rapture—is the essence of persuasion.

Perhaps prayer is the *pure* form of the rhetorical act because God and the devotee are, rather obviously, linguistic entities. Unlike lover and beloved, each of whom retains an individuality and a substantiality that exceeds the bounds of their courtship, God and the worshiper are nothing but the termini of a perfectly ideal and all-encompassing relationship. At least the radical of every rhetorical situation is the relationship of language and reality. The purpose of language is to manifest being: to express, represent, comprehend. And yet the reality of the linguistic sign is an alienation of the being it wants to reveal. A hierarchy: language as sign is bound to the service of truth and reality, and a distance: the sign invariably others what it would grasp. Rhetoric, radically considered, is the endeavor, by means of language, to recover in and for language the being of which language itself is the alienation. Otherwise: rhetoric is the project of the redemption of language by the recuperation of being.

By preterition, rhetorically taken, I understand: negative recuperation. *Praeteritio*, the figure of conspicuous omission, magnified to the point of method, is a way of engaging a fundamental problem of language. Language cannot deliver the presence of being, a word which (following Nabokov) should therefore never be written except in scare-quotes. Reality is always drawn into the net of signifiers. Writing is, originally and essentially, absence, and the rhetorical project is doomed. But by making the absence of being conspicuous, by weaving a text of signifiers that is excessively, loquaciously, and spectacularly vacuous, one makes the absence portentous. Portentous of that which cannot be said and must be said.

Preterite rhetoric recuperates being by not signifying it. The non-signification does not permit the non-signified to become a signifier; does not draw it into the web of signification, but leaves it in its alterity. Neither spider nor fly, it is glimpsed through the interstices of the web as that which is not caught. Being is recuperated only if it escapes signification, and language is redeemed only if it retains its freedom from every predestined meaning. That is the double truth of preterition and the mercy of Iscariot.

Whereof one cannot speak one must keep silent. But this silence too must be spoken. If they can get you asking the wrong questions, they don't have to worry about answers.

Conventional literary forms—comic, tragic, or what not—present, in the foreground or provisionally, a world broken and disordered. But in the background, and finally, stands an overriding order and unity that redeems the chaos of the interim. A background that is either written in the text or unambiguously implied by it. But in the world of the paranoid, unity and order—in their Calvinist form, the eternal decrees of God—may only be perceived as an awful absence. And only portrayed as the shadow of a possible Other falling across the mortal scene. The world that is not delivered by preterition is therefore neither tragic nor comic, neither the setting for a romantic quest nor the occasion of an ironic put-down. Preterition is a way of inscribing without foreclosing an undecidable dialectic.

One characteristic and pervasive feature of Pynchon's style, not fully explicable as a piece of 1940's slang, is his use of the demonstrative "that" where one would expect the definite article or nothing at all. The text insistently *points*, to "that" Slothrop, "that" Peenemünde, "that" *Schwarzgerät*. Ostentatiously ostensive, it draws us into itself (centripetally) by directing us away from itself (the centrifugal "that") toward a signified that is not there.

Quite. On his way to rescue Der Springer from the Russians, Slothrop, growing ever more absent-minded, begins to lose his grip on the situation and the point of his presence in it:

> But just over the embankment, down in the arena, what might that have been just now, waiting in this broken moonlight, camouflage paint from fins to point crazed into jigsaw…is it, then, really never to find you again? Not even in your worst times of night, *with pencil words on your page only Δt from the things they stand for?* And inside the victim is twitching, fingering beads, touching wood, *avoiding any Operational Word*. Will it really never come to take you, now? (510, my emphasis)

The text/Pynchon here addresses it/himself. The absence of the signified is infinitesimal and absolute. The words on the page are only dt away from the things they stand for. But the thing itself will (maybe) never find you, never come to take you. There is no Operational Word, only vain gestures of signification—twitching—and ineffectual conjurations of significance—fingering beads and touching wood. Nothing is created and nothing is revealed.

Language is the approach to Zero. Reality—the Rocket for which language is the predestined quest—lies always on the other side, a camouflaged apparition. GR exists *at*—not *in*—the interface of signifier and signified. And the "last unmeasurable gap…, the last delta-t" is signification, by which we are inexorably directed toward being and irreparably sundered from it.

When Captain Blicero's African *Lustknabe* uses the words *Ndjambi Karunga* (Herero for "God") to mean "fuck," the passions of the Christian pervert are inflamed. Although "to the boy Ndjambi Karunga is what happens when they couple, that's all," Blicero "feels the potency of every word: words are only an eye-twitch from the things they stand for. The peril of buggering the boy under the resonance of the sacred Name fills him insanely with lust, lust in the face—in the mask—of instant talion" (100). It is that "eye-twitch" that makes the difference between "face" and "mask"…that makes all the differences. And all the differance.

Writing all by itself is a preterite act. Igor Blobadjian, party representative assigned to the G Committee of the Central Committee on the New Turkic Alphabet, observes that when an oral language is alphabetized and reduced to script, "print just goes running on without him" (355). The inscription of the signifier is the omission of the signified. As preterition, language is innately paranoid. Like every paranoid, it suspects the sacred everywhere. Paranoia, which is "nothing less than the onset, the leading edge, of the discovery that *everything is connected*, everything in the Creation, a secondary illumination—not yet blindingly One, but at least connected, and perhaps a route In" (703), takes linguistic form in the "mania for name-giving, dividing the Creation finer and finer, analyzing, setting namer more hopelessly apart from named" (391).

But the alienation of the named does not eliminate the Other; on the contrary, it establishes its Otherness. Miklos Thanatz discovers that a "screen of words between himself and the numinous was always just a tactic...it never let him feel any freer" (668). And Enzian (Blicero's catamite grown up) knows that although there "may be no gods..., there is a pattern: names by themselves may have no magic, but the *act* of naming, the physical utterance, obeys the pattern" (322).

The paradox of language, that it can only acknowledge being by not representing it, unites the preterite's negative freedom from the constraints of destiny and the paranoid's negative presentiment of the divine transcendence. Being, its integrity unviolated by a language of appropriation and possession (conventional rhetoric), is *revealed in* preterite rhetoric just insofar as it is not *claimed for* language. At the same time and by the same strategy language retains its liberty; the signifiers, not directed toward an always already foreclosed rhetorical consummation, are allowed to go their way.

That paradox is the source of the gravity of GR: the overpowering weight of reality it sustains not in spite of but precisely because of the "mindless" irresponsibility of the discourse itself. In the rhetoric of Pynchon's narrative preterition is the paranoid way of showing the natures of things by not capturing them in language. Its efficacy resides, paradoxically, not in its formal perfection and self-sufficiency, but in its cultivated ineptitude and formal disarray, by which the absence of the signified is made obvious and momentous. Like Roger Mexico pissing on the System (636), or Franz Pökler giving his wedding ring to a bare survivor of Camp Dora (433), the preterition itself—the dance of signifiers that performs this monstrosity—is an act of the invisible Counterforce, the We-system that sabotages the They-system by unreason and outrage. That is, by acts of grace.

The text of GR, as the end approaches and the Counterforce begins its work of destruction, becomes increasingly random and disconnected. Without the presence of the transcendental signified to hold it together, the fiction dismembers and disperses itself just as it does Slothrop. In so doing it at once allows Them their alterity and absence, and preserves for Us our freedom from the determinism and bondage Their presence would entail. The exorcism of Pointsmanian, Pavlovian, Calvinist—what's in a name?—predestinations, preterition is, as GR itself says, "creative paranoia" (638).

The end of the Elect and of the Reprobate is predetermined and sure. They have no option but to work out the terms (both words and conditions) of their respective destinies. Only the preterite, released from predestination by divine neglect, can play. A preterite "God," his own freedom (that is, transcendence) assured by his indifference to his handwork, releases his creatures from the shackles of his concern and thereby guarantees *their* freedom.

An admonition, perhaps, for Pynchon's reader. Paranoia, "the normal hermeneutic activity in disease,"[19] is the appropriate motive with which to approach GR. Its plot, incredible and unintelligible as *mimesis praxeos*, is also imperfect as conspiracy. The authorial deity, both person and persona, having perpetrated his text and littered it with ambiguous tokens of his intention, ironically withdraws and throws the question to the reader. Is there a plan? Does it mean anything? "Consider honestly…which side you would rather be on" (495). The author's preterition of his readers, his refusal to predestine their response, is the seal of their liberty; their consequent paranoia is the condition of the possibility of a creative exegesis. The innocence of the creatures is in inverse proportion to the immorality of the Master.

The Rocket of the Apocalypse fails to achieve transcendence, just as Pynchon's novel fails to deliver being or "whatever it is the word is there, buffering, to protect us from."[20] The Rocket, both the text and its obsession, is at once the seeking and the sought. As the hope of escape from sign to significance, the Rocket is sought, ineffectually at last, by the text, which in turn is the object, elusive as it turns out, of its reader's quest. There is no escape from the circuit of signification. *You* hide, they seek.

That is why Gravity's curve—the parabola described by the Rocket that sets out to invade and conquer the alterity of heaven, but halts, pauses, and plummets to earth—is a rainbow: a sign of hope.[21] As the *Fünffachnullpunkt*, bearing the sacrifice of the peace of God, is fired, the narrator says, "This ascent will be betrayed to Gravity….The victim, in bondage to falling, rises on a promise, a prophecy, of Escape" (758).

At the other end of its flight, as the Rocket is poised on its final infinitesimal over the roof of the Orpheus Theatre in Los Angeles, at the end of the West, the screen goes dark and we ("old fans who've always been at the movies") are invited to touch the person next to us or to reach between our own cold legs, and requested to sing a hymn by William Slothrop ("Follow the bouncing ball..."), a song "*They* never taught anyone to sing," for "centuries forgotten and out of print" (where did it come from?). A hymn that ends with the words (reminiscent of Lake District tunesmith William Wordsworth):

> With a face on ev'ry mountainside,
> And a soul in ev'ry stone.[22]

After these words—which may predict a state of total and final entropy or prophesy the eventual renewal of the world—there is nothing but the equally ambivalent solicitation: "Now everybody—" (760).

                              00000

GR begins—almost—with the words: "It is too late" (3). It ends—not quite—with the words: "there is time" (760). In the inconceivable warp of language that separates these two impossible moments of time, the fiction undoes itself.

c. Thomas Pynchon and the American Dream

> Look at a rainbow. While it lasts, it is, or appears to be, a great arc of many colors occupying a position out there in space....And now, before it fades, recollect all you have ever been told about the rainbow and its causes, and ask yourself the question *Is it really there?*
>
>   —Owen Barfield

                                    i

Ever since Emerson—since long before Emerson actually, but I have to start somewhere, so I start with an open-and-shut case—American writers have struggled to liberate themselves from their Puritan heritage.[23] From the doctrine of predestination, which says that the present and the future are irrevocably determined by the absolute past; and from the doctrine of total depravity, which says that no matter what you do you are sure to do it wrong. As against predestination, the American wants to believe that the present is a time of origination; as against total depravity, that actions proceed from an innocent mind and will. The American dream is a dream of innocence and originality.

To continue with the obvious: the dream never comes true. Emerson's manifesto of originary self-reliance is fixated on the past it refuses and repeats; his protestation of transcendental innocence is a denial of corruption corrupted by the guilt it disavows. His consciousness blocks out realities (sexuality, death, etc.) that do not illustrate his thesis.[24] But the repressed returns to cloud his Edenic vision. Cataracts, as it were, of the transparent eyeball. Hawthorne cannot decide between the antinomian forest and the orthodox city. Temperamentally unable to breathe the transcendental gas, he has no illusions of natural innocence, and he knows that reality demands (though it will not inevitably reward) a candid confession of guilt and a stoic acceptance of destiny. His hopes for the future of the race are scarcely more than wistful longings for an emancipation he sees no reason (in principle) to believe in. In "Song of Myself" Whitman manages to achieve the ideal American personality: Adamic, free, forward looking, sound of body and soul. But only as a myth. A colossal fiction that he himself did not and could not inhabit. A fiction that presumed to encompass crucifixion and resurrection (Christ's or, equivalently, Walt's), but which could not even contain the Civil War. Whitman's poetry, which begins as a celebration of life, passes through clouds of windy mysticism and ends in rapt meditation on death. Whitman the man, who displays himself on the frontispiece of his first edition as a hippie Christ, winds up hyping the good gray poet. A model of hygienic purity if not an insufferable prude.

The list could go on forever. But you get the drift. The question is: Why is it (apparently) impossible for Americans to escape the negations of New England Calvinism? The answer, I think, is simple. Am I still explaining the obvious when I surmise that for the American writer Puritanism is indistinguishable from reality? The conduct of life, the regulation of society, and the production of literary texts (*inter alia*) depend on the preservation of order (read: suppression of disorder) and respect for reason (read: suppression of the passions). But the only available paradigm of reason and order is Calvinist theology (or one of its secular derivatives), and outside the boundaries of that paradigm nothing has the right to exist, save in hell and Rhode Island.

That was (of course) exactly what the guardians of orthodoxy had in mind. In Michael Wigglesworth's great poem on the last judgment, the ultimacy and acceptability of the divine decrees, even for the preterite, is a function of their superior rationality. The reprobate infants appear before the throne of God and protest their innocence. But after God has taken off their arguments one by one and demonstrated their culpability, their consciences confess that "his Reasons are the stronger." The punishment of the damned is tolerable to the elect because it satisfies the demand for moral order no matter what the cost in personal wretchedness.[25]

Therefore, when American writers try (as they always do) to reject predestination (the tyranny of the past) and total depravity (the tyranny of guilt) in favor of originality and innocence, they are bound to see their exit from Puritanism as a flight from reason to unreason and from order into chaos. But this is intolerable—the irrational cannot be borne—and literally insufferable—the unordered cannot *be*—and so they invariably retreat, under whatever cover of mystification, into the very structures they tried to break out of. Guilt and predestination are the American reality, for which there is no cure that is not worse than the disease.

How else could one write a book? To write a book is to impose order and rationality on the boundless possibilities of language. The writer functions as a Calvinist God, predestining the creatures of his pen to weal or woe, inscribing in them from the first their total dependence on his authorial and authoritative decrees. The possibility of the book, presuming an omnipotent and omniscient narrator, demands the belatedness and impotence of its characters. In both senses of that word. The book itself, bound snugly within its covers, with well-defined beginning, middle, and end, is the suppression of everything irrational and chaotic.[26] Life may occasionally fall apart, and death, while it does end things, is rarely a consummation. But the book hangs together and provides its readers with a convincing and fulfilling conclusion. Every Book is Domesday: a graphematic eschaton.

Now then, riding the same old rails, here comes Tom Pynchon, belated and guilt-ridden and very wise about all these things. His Puritan paranoid reflex honed to a fine edge and blown up to more than cosmic proportions, he too wants out. He wants a way out of war and work and government and austerity, and a way in to love, dreams, the spirit, the senses, and all the trivial joys that might (if there were any) fill the idle hours.[27] He also knows that there is no way out, or rather, that the way out of Puritan reason and Puritan order is the way to dissolution. The way of the preterite. But, unlike his predecessors, Thomas Pynchon bites the bullet. He writes *Gravity's Rainbow*. The book that *Leaves of Grass* and *The Scarlet Letter* just failed to be, a book that is and must be a rejection of all the patterns and all the powers of the book.

A lot of people have trouble reading, or at least finishing, Pynchon's novel. Maybe they're on to something. After all, *Gravity's Rainbow* is not exactly your ordinary book. It's what happens to the book when it is released from the Puritan reflex. From the itch for order that creates international cartels to profit from international carnage, and from the lust of reason (aka technology) that rapes the universe with its rockets. GR is (therefore) a wholesale rejection of every standard of taste, an offense against every rule of literary decorum, and a repudiation of the conditions of literary reality. It is a monument to vulgarity and a wagonload (Pynchon would have said "shitload") of obscenities. *Qua* novel, it is a gratuitous indecency.

Well, not quite. Pynchon is not quite liberated. As he observes, paranoia keeps flooding in. In lots of ways Tyrone Slothrop and Thomas Pynchon are the same *persona*. Neither fully succeeds in freeing himself from the sense that he is dominated and victimized by all the Western, Christian, European, and American[28] forms of reason and order: industry, technology, government, work, law, international finance, and war. Which are, after all, just the secular reduction and global expansion of the Puritan ethos.

GR wants to live—honestly—outside the law. A compost of mindless pleasures, it celebrates moments of pure innocence and perfect originality neither scripted nor rehearsed nor staged but simply enjoyed. And yet, when anyone does step outside the boundaries drawn by the Firm, he is likely to be snuffed. Tantivy Mucker-Maffick was erased when he leaked Ned Pointsman's plot to Slothrop. What cannot be recovered for and reinstated in the system will be denied all reality by the system. Roger Mexico's love for Jessica Swanlake, which is authentic and therefore strictly out of bounds, is replaced by her preordained marriage to Jeremy. Roger was a holiday from the austerities of war conceded to Jessica by the Firm (it kept her happy in her work); her marriage to the Beaver is one of the even more terrible austerities of peace.

Almost without exception experiences that seem to have escaped the surveillance of the Firm turn out to be its products. Slothrop's hardon for Katje Borgesius, which looks spontaneous enough and issues more than one mindless ejaculation, is a reflex prepared in his infancy. His opportunity to stick it in and get it off is prearranged by Pointsman with the help of a carefully conditioned octopus. Katje herself is a witting co-conspirator. Brigadier General Pudding, now chained to a desk and obliged to shuffle papers, relives the reality of World War I (a reality compounded of mud, shit, blood, and the manly love of comrades) in his sado-masochistic rendezvous with the Queen of the Night, who forces him to eat her filth in exchange for the gift of pain. But the account of these meetings, at once nauseating and deeply moving, is finally chilling. *Domina Nocturna* is Katje Borgesius in leather and furs, her performance a scenario written, produced, and directed by Ned Pointsman (complete with laxative tablets).

Reality is a spectacular put on by the Firm. Literary reality included. Nothing exists outside the system save death and dissolution. But death and dissolution are themselves *effects* of the system. From the people who brought you reality. The Puritan God (and the omniscient narrator), when he elects a few for salvation (eternal life), *by the same* act consigns the remainder to damnation (everlasting death). Election is reprobation. Life is death. There is no escape. In or out, you are in—that is, a creature of—the Firm. For the Firm (God, the author, etc.) ordains the dichotomies (in or out, life or death) by which persons/*personae* are predestined and in which, therefore, they are trapped. It is not that there is nothing outside the system. It's much worse: there is no such thing as "outside." As Father Rapier observes: "Once the technical means of control have reached a certain size, a certain degree of *being connected* one to another, the chances for freedom are over for good. The word has ceased to have meaning" (539). And as Roger Mexico realizes, the "interesting" (and probably unanswerable) question is "which is worse: living on as Their pet, or death?"(713). Whatever you decide, your life and your death are defined by Them. Death without and living death within.[29] Sort of neutralizes the opposition: robs escape of its promise and does nothing to make captivity more attractive.

That's Pynchon's problem. Pynchon the writer. No wonder the stuttering raconteur of GR is embarrassed by his own omniscience and half-ashamed of the blatant artificiality of his artifice. If he plays omnipotence to the hilt, then (not only his characters but) we (gentle readers) obediently engorge when Super-Pointsman strokes our critical members. And if he shows his hand, tips his trick, we are cut loose to twist in the wind. You read what's set down for you or you don't read at all. Either way *your* number is up. Your goose (you *are* goosed) is well-done and hanging high.

Apparently. But maybe not quite. Pynchon-narrator *is* red-faced and red-handed. Caught in the act. Caught, that is, at the most embarrassing moment of all: between inauguration and completion, cause and effect, complication and denouement. The instant of ejaculation, which (if you're caught at it) is thereby forever premature and unconsummated.

GR is a text poised at *Brennschluss*. Burn-out: the interface between the exhaustion of the power that sent the rocket up and the first tug of the force that will bring it down. Suppose the inconceivable: if there were no gravity, the path of the rocket would be a straight line. After *Brennschluss* it would continue climbing forever, powered by inertia. But there is gravity, and the rocket falls. Gravity bends the straight line of its trajectory into a parabola. The instant after *Brennschluss* is the infinitesimal point (Δt) just before gravity takes charge: the bare far side of orgasm just before your cock shrivels and Chiquita's picture flutters to the bathroom floor. At that point the rocket is neither launched nor falling, but—in that timeless moment and only there—hanging in space.

GR and its anti-hero Tyrone Slothrop are likewise arrested in the moment, out of time and out of history, that follows the burn-out of Western civilization. World War II was the explosion that exhausted its power. The Zone (northern Europe after the collapse of the New Order) is the instant after *Brennschluss*, frozen forever in the text. In Pynchon's novel (at least) "'There are...no zones but the Zone'" (333).

As Pynchon informs Karl Marx, "Christian Europe was always death, Karl, death and repression" (317). The engine of death and repression, of which New England orthodoxy is only the American variant, also powers behaviorist psychology, captivated by a dream of perfect control. And the technology of plastics—fired by Kekulé's vision of the benzene ring as the worm ouroboros—aspires to replace nature with a wholly self-contained system of artificial substances. Not to mention war and the rocketry by which the art of war is perfected: a "celebration of markets" (105) planned and executed by homosexual masculinity, an introversion of the male principle which (even when it uses her) neutralizes and displaces the female. Emersonian self-reliance, via Whitmanian masturbatory self-sufficiency, ends as fatal faggotry in high places. And "the real and only fucking is done on paper" (616).[30]

The preterite of course continue to die. Like his precursors, Pynchon is obsessed with the thought of breaking out of Puritanism—away from death and repression—into the exuberant vitality of mindless pleasures. But for Pynchon, as for his predecessors, to run from Puritanism would be to run into madness and chaos. An escape from the system (rationality and order) would be an escape from being (identity) and truth (intelligibility). Why is Slothrop in the Zone? Either They have put him there for a reason, or else he's just there without reason. Paranoia or anti-paranoia? Tyrone isn't sure he wouldn't actually rather have that reason (434). With it he's doomed, without it he'll disappear. Can he make it in the Zone without Pointsman? As Pointsman's control is relaxed and finally withdrawn, Slothrop slowly disintegrates, becoming at first invisible and at last inconceivable. The escape does not come off. And the novel (which for that reason is not a novel) remains fixed at Δt, between "It is too late" (3) and "There is time"(760). GR is the uninhabitable interface between a deadly conspiracy of predestination and depravity and an impossible fantasy of innocence and originality. Literature at *Brennschluss*. The literature of exhaustion, with no repletion in sight.

Virtually (it is impossible to be sure) every character, subject, event, and institution in GR is intricately and obscenely connected with every other. That these connections exist adumbrates a pattern in which every particular has its place, its identity, its destiny. But the very complexity and confusion of the linkages frustrates the will to order and insinuates that all of these "Kute Korrespondences" (590) are random and lawless. There is too much and (for that reason) too little. The reader trying to dope out this "novel" is stuck at the interface of paranoia—Pynchon has designed and executed this book, and it's up to me to figure out what it means—and anti-paranoia—the whole thing is a medley of incoherences, no one is really in control, and there's no point worrying about what it means. Is the reader's role defined and thus constrained by the Omniscient Narrator (Tom Pynchon playing God)? Or is he released, like Slothrop, to be dismembered and dispersed among the errant signifiers of a preterite text? Between the slippery signifier and the superintendent signified, between word and world, between the either and the or, there is an arrow. And the caption: YOU ARE NOT HERE.

ii

The American dream was interrupted from the first by a recurring and unshakeable nightmare of belatedness and corruption. The Civil War was the waking reality. But in fact the dream was interrupted *before* the first. The founding fathers of Lincoln's address were already 150 years too late. *Their* version of innocence and originality—"we hold these truths to be self-evident"—was a desperate ruse to finesse their forefathers' convictions of total depravity and ineluctable predestination. The forefathers' forefathers were, in their time, exorcizing their own sense of belatedness. It was for these hard-shell Calvinists that America was the beginning place: the Canaan given them by God, where they might build a new Jerusalem free of the carnality and prelacy of old Europe. In themselves they conjoined, impossibly, originality and belatedness, innocence and depravity. The controversy in old New England between the orthodox and the antinomians was only the outward and visible sign of a conflict deep within the Puritan consciousness: the civil war in the American soul.

More than one American writer has done his best to awaken from the nightmare of guilt and belatedness while continuing to dream of innocence and originality. Thomas Pynchon (aka Tyrone Slothrop)—how far-fallen!— is only the last of his line (569). Toward the end of GR we get two views of America. One is the terminal raving of that most corrupt of corrupt old Europeans, Captain Blicero:

"And sometimes I dream of discovering the edge of the World. [...]

"America *was* the edge of the World. [...] Europe had found the site for its Kingdom of Death, that special Death the West had invented. [...] America was a gift from the invisible powers, a way of returning. But Europe refused it. It wasn't Europe's Original Sin—the latest name for that is Modern Analysis—but it happens that Subsequent Sin is harder to atone for.

"In Africa, Asia, Amerindia, Oceania, Europe came and established its order of Analysis and Death. [...] Now we are in the last phase. American Death has come to occupy Europe. [...] Death and Europe are separate as ever, their love still unconsummated. Death only rules here. It has never, in love, become one *with*..." (722-23; bracketed ellipses mine)

Weissmann's America is Europe's Death: a gift from the invisible powers, by Europe refused and now returned (at the end of the world) to occupy and to rule, but not to consummate their love. His sacrifice of Gottfried is at once an attempt to break out of the cycle of infection and death and a cosmic *Liebestod* uniting Blicero and his *Lustknabe* in a love that is immortal and a death that is final. But the ascent is betrayed to Gravity, and the rocket with its victim, rising on a promise of Escape, is in bondage to falling (758). And here's Slothrop's America. He has just found, in the occupied Zone, the harmonica he lost in '38 or '39 down the toilet at the Roseland Ballroom. But he no longer remembers that far back. Where should he go and what should he do?

[...] *where*, Slothrop? Huh? America? Shit. C'mon–
        Yup, still thinking there's a way to get back.
He's been changing, sure, changing, plucking the albatross of self now and then, idly, half-conscious as picking his nose—but the one ghost-feather his fingers always brush by is America. Poor asshole, he can't let her go. She's whispered *love me* too often to him in his sleep, vamped insatiably his waking attention with comehitherings, incredible promises. One day— he can see a day—he might be able finally to say sorry, sure and leave her...but not just yet. One more try, one more chance, one more deal, one

more transfer to a hopeful line. Maybe it's just pride. What if there's no place for him in her stable any more? If she has turned him out, she'll never explain. Her "stallions" have no rights. She is immune to their small, stupid questions. She is exactly the Amazon Bitch your fantasies have called her to be. (623)

For Slothrop/Pynchon America is a nostalgia for home and love. A mother (and lover) to whom he would like, for a while at least, to return. But Slothrop's America is haunted by a fearful ghost: "the coupling of 'Jamf' and 'I' in the primal dream. Who can he go to with it?" (623). The longing for home and love is troubled by the thought that the nest was fouled before the albatross of self had even hatched.

Slothrop's anxiety reflects the anxiety of America itself (herself?): the coupling of hope and fear. For Weissmann, America is Ground Zero: Europe's lover and her destroyer. For Tyrone, America is the place of origin...an origin always already corrupted. Both of these reports are torn by ambivalence. Blicero sees America as the end of the world, and longs to be lovingly one with her death. Slothrop dreams of a long-lost mother/ lover, and knows in his heart of hearts that she is an Amazon Bitch. For both of them America is a way of return that is refused.

"Slothrop, just suckin' on his harp, is closer to being a spiritual medium than he's been yet, and he doesn't even know it" (622). In one of our last views of him, Slothrop is recollecting his youth—a garbage heap of American trivia—"and his chest fills and he stands crying, not a thing in his head, just feeling natural...." (626) That's one of the few occurrences of the word—it may be the unique occurrence of the feeling—"natural" in the whole of GR. Nature's nation!

The problem is to find a way through the oppositions: orthodoxy/ antinomianism, predestination/freedom, depravity/innocence, reason/ madness, order/chaos, rocket/ Gravity, male/female. The Opposition. Them. Opposed to the Opposition is the Counterforce. Of what avail the Counterforce? Roger Mexico fears the worst. He may (and does, literally) "'piss on Their rational arrangements'" (639), and he would like to "disarm, de-penis and dismantle the Man." But the hard fact is that "[t]he Man has a branch office in each of our brains," so that even in opposing Them we "will help legitimize Them, though They don't need it really, it's another dividend for Them, nice but not critical." (712-13) In this worst-case scenario the opposition clearly becomes: Their life or your death. Which disjunction is also, as we have seen, a conjunction: Their life *is* your death. You get it either way.

Could that be the way out? Strictly speaking—that is, speaking as loosely as possible—it does no good to invert the oppositions. Opposed, the oppositions remain in force. But there is some point to the flip-flop. If the opposition is upended, and if the inversion is equivalent to the inverted, then in effect the opposition is leveled. Displaced from vertical and hierarchic *opposition* into horizontal and unvalorized *apposition*. "Outside and Inside interpiercing one another too fast, too finely labyrinthine, for either category to have much hegemony any more" (681). That may be GR's way of describing itself. And if that goes through, we may be home free.

"The dearest nation of all is one that will survive no longer than you and I, a common movement at the mercy of death and time: the ad hoc adventure" (706). Adopted by the Gross Suckling Conference, the "resolution" here set down is a typical Counterforce gesture. Paradoxical as it is, it may be (cf. dozens of references in the New Testament) a definition of grace: the state (pun intended) in which everything is gratuitous and free, if also without future and without promise. A grab-bag of mindless pleasures. "Your objective is not the King—there is no King—but momentary targets such as the Radiant Hour" (674).

Byron the Bulb achieves immortality because G. E. and its C(ommittee on) I(ncandescent) A(nomalies) cannot anticipate the random rapacities of bulb-snatchers. Rocketman scarfs the hash, right under the noses of the Russian guards, Mickey Rooney, Harry S. Truman, and the whole Potsdam peace conference. There are holes in the web. Hope is perilously possible in the interstices. Your job is to locate and occupy the uncharted place *between* the exclusive oppositions: the contingencies neither foreseen nor provided for by the busy spiders who weave your destiny.

One might, in her anti-paranoid moments, wish that were true. But is it credible? We have to be wary of belief. Creeds fatten on opposition and hierarchy. And the point is to transgress. Not to oppose or propose opposing positions, but: to transgress absolutely. To put the bananas in the refrigerator not in spite of but simply without any of the good reasons in Chiquita's hat. Just suck on your harp (or whatever organ is at hand), cry (or laugh) mindlessly, and feel natural.

New England Calvinists (as opposed to their co-religionists in Old England) were covenantal theologians. The elect, chosen by God for salvation in total disregard of their merits (they have none), nevertheless strike a bargain with their Redeemer. In return for election, they are bound (their part of the bargain) to keep his commandments and prosper his will. And thereby prosper. Election, though it preserves the elect from the otherwise ineluctable consequences of guilt, is not exactly liberation. If they are freed *from* sin and death, the elect are also (thereby) freed for obedience to the law of God: free to do what (God has decided) is good for them. Election entails obligation. It binds the elect to conditions, and if the conditions are not met, their election is uncertain.

If anyone is free—in the sense of "let loose"—in a world like this, it may be the preterite who, by virtue of God's neglect, are released at once from salvation and from the conditions of salvation. They die, of course, but (a) living on Their terms is not importantly different from dying, and (b) the preterite at least die without strings attached.

Freedom is not the opposite of predestination. It is the neutralizing transgression of the boundary between predestination and freedom. Just as innocence is not the opposite of depravity, but the appositional reduction of the difference between innocence and guilt. Seaman Bodine, farting melodies through the siren-ring installed in his asshole, signals "a return toward innocence" (740). As he gives Slothrop his Dumbo feather (a T-shirt stained with John Dillinger's blood), he tells him, "what we need isn't right reasons, but just that *grace*" (741). That's the wisdom of the preterite: of Pig Bodine, perpetually AWOL; of Plechazunga, whose misplaced pigskin preserves Tyrone's embattled testicles; and of all those trusting porkers, "possessed by innocence they couldn't lose"(555), who lovingly follow William Slothrop to the slaughter.

Analogously, GR is not the opposite of the novel. It does not simply contradict the assumption of auto-teleology that underlies our notion of the well-made book: the book as onanistic system. It is the transgression and the displacement of the will to contain and control. A book that is not a book: is it any wonder that the critical establishment has wanted to reject this...*thing*? This text which violates the (paradigmatically Puritanical) second law of thermodynamics by exploiting the powers left over when all the available energy has been used up and fiction is brought to terminal equilibrium. GR is a text always already from before the first remaindered: it is what remains when all the oppositions have failed—in flagrant disregard for the law of contradiction, that (paradigmatically Puritanical) most fundamental of all the foundations of law and order—to cancel each other out. What remains is this:

> There's no real direction here, neither lines of power nor cooperation.
> Decisions are never really made—at best they manage to emerge, from a
> chaos of peeves, whims, hallucinations and all-round assholery [...] with

hopes for success and hopes for disaster about equally high (and no, that *doesn't* cancel out to apathy—it makes a loud dissonance that dovetails inside you sharp as knives). [...] Those whom the old Puritan sermons denounced as "the glozing neuters of the world" have no easy road to haul down, Wear-the-Pantsers, just cause you can't see it doesn't mean it's not there! Energy inside is just as real, just as binding and inescapable, as energy that shows. When's the last time you felt *intensely lukewarm*? eh? (676-77)

Now everybody.... (677, 760)

iii

Of course, if you do put bananas in the refrigerator, you get spoiled bananas and nothing to eat. Chiquita's revenge. And if you refuse to color within the lines, you get an F in—no, friends and neighbors, not coloring—: you get an F in conduct. John Dillinger and Jesus and Judas and all the trusting pigs and stupid lemmings of this world—not a one of them would color within the lines. They all got F. Tyrone Slothrop is taken apart and scattered. Maybe a D ?

It makes little sense, therefore, to ask: does Pynchon get away? He has disappeared—has always already been invisible and inconceivable—just like Tyrone. Does GR succeed in finding and following the "fork in the road America never took"? (556). Not to say. A preterite text, GR is not authentic. It is a work without integrity and without certifiable meaning. There is no definitive edition. Cut loose from superintendent significance (superintendence and significance are Their prerogative), the fiction like its author and like its hero is disassembled (dissembled) and dispersed. GR "exists" in diaspora and takes effect by dissemination.

GR suggests, both by what it says and by what it does, that everything is connected to everything else. But if that is the case, then nothing connects *meaningfully* with anything. Meaning demands connection, but also differentiation. For example, the differentiation of the message from the static. But if there is no determinable difference—if anything and everything might mean everything and anything—then there is no meaning. Just noise. When the plot (both senses) has expanded to include everything, then there is no plot. No conspiracy and no story.

Too much is nothing at all: the problem of the author. But not enough is just about everything: the situation of the reader. YOU ARE NOT HERE. Where you are is Δt, not quite *here* but no longer *there*. "Their neglect is your freedom" (694). On his own, without an omniscient narrator—or (what's worse) with a narrator who blows his omniscience every time he opens his mouth—the reader is free to pursue his own mindless pleasure along the interfaces of this twisted text. Or for that matter (the reader as Gravity), to construct his own novel—an infinite series of novels—out of the accumulated wastes of his civilization, lovingly preserved if somewhat casually packaged by the last of the Pynchons. Those who do manage to read GR find that they have to read it again and again. And it's a different book every time.

Is that a description of narrative entropy? Or is it the final triumph of the preterite: their radical innocence (indistinct from original guilt) and their primordial originality (indistinct from terminal belatedness)? Is this the American Dream? *Is it really there*? Not to ask.

11

The Name of the Book

I suffered from an absence, though I was happy with the many ghosts of a presence.[1]

It would astonish the scholarly world if I were to announce that I had located the Latin manuscript by Adso of Melk that lies at the putative origin of *The Name of the Rose*. But if I were to do that, I should not have pretended to make a false beginning. Anyone who claims to have discovered a true origin these days is automatically suspect, and the child who knows his own father is too wise for his own good. However, errant sheep are occasionally found, and now and then a lost penny is swept up in the housecleaning. What I shall propose, therefore, is not a symptom of madness but only a piece of presumption.

It is said that a rose by any other name would smell as sweet. Maybe it would and maybe it wouldn't. But a name by any other rose? What would that smell like? Would it smell at all? The real thing is not forthcoming: neither a real origin nor a real lie. Certainly not a real rose. Not even a dried flower in a book, but only the name of the flower in the name of a book. "Naturally, a manuscript."

The Name of the Rose is more than moderately difficult to track down. We have a twentieth century English text purportedly produced by Mr. William Weaver. Weaver, however, only translates (faithfully, we shall assume) an Italian text, also of the twentieth century. The author of the Italian text is unknown—he does not sign his prefatory remarks—and it would be dangerous to assume that he is identical with Professor Umberto Eco. A semiotician who says that a sign is anything you can use to tell a lie is not to be taken at his word.[2] Written in the summer of 1968 and offered to the public in 1980, *Il nome della rosa* claims to be the translation of yet another text: this one, by Abbé Vallet, is written in French and published in Paris in 1842. The Italian translator tells us that Abbé Vallet's book was "handed" to him by someone he does not identify. Pestered by doubts— about Vallet's tampering with his original, about the propriety of his own rendition and its pretension to authenticity—he is nonetheless consoled by the thought that his book, dealing as it does with matters remote in time and written out of the pure love of writing, has absolutely no relevance for the present age.

But the "tale of books" (5) has only begun. Abbé Vallet's text presents itself as a translation of a Latin text edited by Dom Mabillon and published in 1721 in his *Vetera Analecta*. The Latin work in question is a lengthy manuscript by one Adso of Melk, a Benedictine monk of the fourteenth century, recounting a series of grisly murders in an Italian monastery of the period and the eventual solution of the mystery by the Franciscan sleuth, Brother William of Baskerville. It is possible, however, that Vallet has perpetrated a forgery, since his alleged publisher does not exist and the only extant copy of Mabillon's *Analecta* contains no work by Adso of Melk. The copy of Vallet used by the Italian translator disappeared along with the translator's beloved when their relationship dissolved in the vicinity of Salzburg—and for obvious reasons may not be recovered. Adso's manuscript is not in the library at Melk, and there would be no reason to think it had ever existed were there not, in a translation of Milo Temesvar's *On the Use of Mirrors in the Game of Chess*, quotations from Adso's work as found in a book by Fr. Athanasius Kirchner. The book by Fr. Kirchner is not identified and may not in fact exist.

What we are offered, by Harcourt Brace Jovanovich and Fabbri-Bompiani, is an English translation of an Italian translation of a French translation of a French edition of a Latin manuscript. Only the English and the Italian can be verified.[3] The manuscript, the edition, and the French translation are irrecoverably lost if indeed they were ever to be found. *Nomina nuda* indeed, many times removed from their (alleged) *status pristinus*. (502) This is only the beginning—the prefatory note—but a fit beginning for a book that ends with the combustion of a library. The mere existence of this text (San Diego New York London, 1983) postulates a chain of translations, representations, and supplementations that postpones forever the recovery of their original and plunges even the question of origin into the twin abysses of time and signification. All of which leaves plenty of room for wild speculation.

It is within the ample space opened up by these many absences that I erect, presently, my own preposterous proposition. To wit. Every reader of

The Name of the Rose is aware that the last obstacle to the solution of the mystery is the confusion of personal with material supposition. As soon as William (who, with his Ockhamist training, should have thought of it sooner) hits on that, the end of Africa is in sight and the labyrinth unravels. To those fond of word games I propose: anagram the entire novel (in the English translation) so as to produce Aristotle's lost book on comedy (in the Oxford translation).

A ridiculous proposal. But perhaps not as ridiculous as it seems. Or at least not ridiculous in the same way. At the beginning of the sixth chapter of the *Poetics* Aristotle (about to define tragedy) promises to treat of comedy and the epic later on. So far as I know, this promise is the only reason we have for supposing that Aristotle ever wrote a book on comedy.[4] Epic poetry is discussed in chapters 23, 24, and 26, and so (the legend goes) Aristotle composed a separate treatise on comedy which was subsequently lost. Lost or never written, we don't have it. We do have, however, in the *Poetics* that does exist, some *obiter dicta* on comedy that give us an idea of what Aristotle said or might have said in the real or fancied *De Comoedia*. For instance, at the end of chapter 2 we are told that tragedy imitates superior men, while comedy imitates men worse than those we know. (I suppose it's safe to say, by the way, that the men and the woman who populate *The Name of the Rose* are no better than the run of us and some of them (I hope) not so good. There are certainly no tragic heroes in the novel.)

Later on, at the beginning of chapter 5, Aristotle says that comedy imitates men who are inferior but not altogether vicious; namely, men whose bearing and behavior are ludicrous. The ludicrous he defines as the kind of ugliness which is not painful or injurious. (We might have to stretch the point in some cases—the case of Bernard Gui, for example—but on the whole the characters in *The Name of the Rose* are not altogether vicious. Though all of them are, more often than not, ludicrous.) So far so good. But this imminent derailment of our train of thought is forestalled by Aristotle's statement (in chapter 13 of the *Poetics*) that in comedy the good are rewarded, the evil punished, enemies reconciled, and (Aristotle adds) "no one kills anybody." (Not so *The Name of the Rose*, which is littered with murders, murderous executions, and death by fire; in which old enmities are exacerbated and the forces of evil seem (as usual) to be marching confidently on to victory.)

But of course (back on the track) *The Name of the Rose*, funny as it may be on occasion, is not supposed to be a comedy. No one ever said it was. It's a murder mystery (obviously), and even though the ending is not exactly happy, the mystery is solved and the demands of the genre satisfied. Which no doubt goes a long way toward explaining how a big book crammed with theological and historical and ecclesiological erudition, monastic lore, Latin tags, philosophical debate, soul-searching, semiotic reflection, and only one sexual episode (discreet enough to be rated PG 13) could become a long-running best-seller.

I suspect, however, that all the learning and learned disputation does not merely provide a setting, rich and authentic, for the mystery; that in fact it's just the opposite, and that the detective story more or less merely supplies a pretext for all that apparently dependent and attendant discourse. Seen from this angle—like one of those optical illusions in which background and foreground can be made to change places by the merest shift in visual resolution—*The Name of the Rose* proclaims itself (not a comedy to be sure and not even a murder mystery but (here I rejoin my preposterous proposition)) Aristotle's lost book on comedy.

A ludicrous notion. And appropriately so. In more than one way and at more than one level, the subject of this ostensible novel is: the ludicrous. Item: William of Baskerville, just beyond the dead center of the story, transcribes and translates into Latin (how accurately he cannot be sure) some notes made by the ill-fated Venantius while reading the book that did him in. All of them might have come (if I'm right they did) from Aristotle *On Comedy*:

> The terrible poison that gives purification... The best weapon for destroying the enemy... Use humble persons, base and ugly, take pleasure from their defect.... They must not die.... Not in the houses of the noble and the powerful but from the peasants' villages, after abundant meal and libations... Squat bodies, deformed faces. They rape virgins and lie with whores, not evil, without fear. A different truth, a different image of the truth... The venerable figs. The shameless stone rolls over the plain.... Before the eyes. Deceit is necessary and to surprise in deceit, to say the opposite of what is believed, to say one thing and mean another. To them the cicadas will sing from the ground. (284)

One of those—"Use humble persons, base and ugly, take pleasure from their defect.... They must not die...."—reads like a patchwork of *Poetics* 5 and 13, and by the end of the book (471) William has turned up sources for all of them: the *Poetics*, the *Rhetoric*, and Isidore of Seville. From these fragments and from the few pages he has read William is able to reconstruct the gist of Aristotle's theory of comedy:

Comedy is born from the komai—that is, from the peasant villages—as a joyous celebration after a meal or a feast. Comedy does not tell of famous and powerful men, but of base and ridiculous creatures, though not wicked; and it does not end with the death of the protagonists. It achieves the effect of the ridiculous by showing the defects and vices of ordinary men. Here Aristotle sees the tendency to laughter as a force for good, which can also have an instructive value: through witty riddles and unexpected metaphors, though it tells us things differently from the way they are, as if it were lying, it actually obliges us to examine them more closely, and it makes us say: Ah, this is just how things are, and I didn't know it. Truth reached by depicting men and the world as worse than they are or than we believe them to be, worse in any case than the epics, the tragedies, lives of the saints have shown them to us. (472)

To which Jorge (who has read the book) replies, "Fairly close." (472)

Closer yet—as close as you can get—is the opening passage of Aristotle's book, which we glimpse over William's shoulder as he reads it aloud to Adso. Here are Aristotle's exact words, perhaps never written, translated *ex tempore* by William of Baskerville, reported by Adso of Melk, edited by dom Mabillon, translated by Abbé Vallet, anonymous Italian, and William Weaver, and now at last quoted by me:

In the first book we dealt with tragedy and saw how, by arousing pity and fear, it produces catharsis, the purification of those feelings. As we promised, we will now deal with comedy (as well as with satire and mime) and see how, in inspiring the pleasure of the ridiculous, it arrives at the purification of that passion. That such passion is most worthy of consideration we have already said in the book on the soul, inasmuch as— alone among the animals—man is capable of laughter. We will then define the type of actions of which comedy is the mimesis,then we will examine the means by which comedy excites laughter, and these means are actions and speech. We will show how the ridiculousness of actions is born from the likening of the best to the worst and vice versa, from arousing surprise through deceit, from the impossible, from violation of the laws of nature, from the irrelevant and the inconsequent, from the debasing of the characters, from the use of comical and vulgar pantomime, from disharmony, from the choice of the least worthy things. We will then show how the ridiculousness of speech is born from the misunderstandings of similar words for different things and different words for similar things, from garrulity and repetition, from play on words, from diminutives, from errors of pronunciation, and from barbarisms. (468)

Here, at the heart of *The Name of the Rose* and in its climactic episode—in fragments, in reconstruction, and in actual quotation boldly transumed— we have: Aristotle's (happily no longer) lost work on comedy.

There is more. Add to this—the real presence of the book itself within the outward and visible signs of this book—the fact that the animus which motivates Jorge de Burgos is a hatred of laughter, especially laughter provoked by the grotesqueries sanctioned by Aristotle and favored by monastic illuminators. Or by the irreverent *Coena Cypriani*. Before his death Venantius commends Aristotle's book on comedy (which he has not yet read and can only imagine) and is ridiculed by the blind man from Burgos. Ridiculed, and at the same time coyly directed to the *finis Africae* and his dissolution. (112-113) On several occasions (78-83, 95-96, 130- 132, 161) William debates with Jorge and others the propriety of the ludicrous and (in particular) the question: did our Savior laugh? With some help from the pseudo-Dionysus, Hugh of St. Victor, and St. Thomas Aquinas, William argues that divinity is manifest in images of things vile and misshapen; while Jorge, sustained by Bernard of Clairvaux, is convinced that those who make use of monsters to reveal the things of God will wind up infatuated with monstrosity to their own destruction—and takes steps to prove that he is right. That Christ *could* laugh is beyond dispute, for He was a man and risibility his *proprium*. That He *did not* laugh we may conclude (*ad ignorantiam!*) from the silence of the gospels. As to *why* He did not, Jorge believes it is because He recognized that laughter, *proprium* or not, is inappropriate for those who serve God and seek salvation. William, perhaps with Jorge in mind, is of the opinion that the Son of God did not laugh because He knew, omniscient as He was, how Christians were going to behave. (161)

A propos: the events reported in Adso's narrative take place during Advent, the season of solemn expectation and penitential preparation for the Incarnation of the Word. (21, 143) But in this book Christmas never comes. If, as Adso fears, we live in a place abandoned by God, it may be, as William suggests, that there is no place in the world where God would feel at home. (155) No place, that is, where He would not be ridiculed to death.

The argument *de risu*, which is sounded like a *cantus firmus* throughout the novel and which provides a rationale for the many deaths that measure out its story, comes to a head in the final confrontation of William and Jorge de Burgos in the *finis Africae*. Cornered at last by the hound of Baskerville, Jorge fulminates against the Philosopher's legitimation of laughter: as his other books have inverted our image of the world, the book on comedy would if generally known overturn the image of God by distorting his face and debauching his reason. The elevation of the comic to the level of philosophy and art will be the ultimate and irreversible subversion of divine order:

> On the day when the Philosopher's word would justify the marginal jests of the debauched imagination, or when what has been marginal would leap to the center, every trace of the center would be lost.... If one day someday, brandishing the words of the Philosopher and therefore speaking as a philosopher, were to raise the weapon of laughter to the condition of subtle weapon, if the rhetoric of conviction were replaced by the rhetoric of mockery, if the topics of the patient construction of the images of redemption were to be replaced by the topics of the impatient dismantling and upsetting of every holy and venerable image—oh, that day even you, William, and all your knowledge, would be swept away!... If one day— and no longer as plebeian exception, but as ascesis of the learned, devoted to the indestructible testimony of Scripture—the art of mockery were to be made acceptable, and to seem noble and liberal and no longer mechanical; if one day someone could say (and be heard), 'I laugh at the Incarnation,' then we would have no weapons to combat that blasphemy, because it would summon the dark powers of corporal matter, those that are affirmed in the fart and the belch, and the fart and the belch would claim the right that is only of the spirit, to breathe where they list! (475-477)

William's response is simple and direct: "You are the Devil." He continues:

> They lied to you. The Devil is not the Prince of Matter; the Devil is the arrogance of the spirit, faith without smile, truth that is never seized by doubt. The Devil is grim because he knows where he is going, and, in moving, he always returns whence he came. You are the Devil, and like the Devil you live in darkness..., and if I could, I would lead you downstairs, across the ground, naked, with fowl's feathers stuck in your asshole and your face painted like a juggler and a buffoon, so the whole monastery would laugh at you and be afraid no longer. I would like to smear honey all over you and then roll you in feathers, and take you on a leash to fairs, to say to all: He was announcing the truth to you and telling you that the truth has the taste of death, and you believed, not in his words, but in his grimness. (477)

And in his last conversation with Adso, after the destruction of the library:

> The Antichrist can be born from piety itself, from excessive love of God or of the truth, as the heretic is born from the saint and the possessed from

the seer.... Jorge feared the second book of Aristotle because it perhaps really did teach how to distort the face of every truth, so that we would not become slaves of our ghosts. Perhaps the mission of those who love mankind is to make people laugh at the truth, *to make truth laugh,* because the only truth lies in learning to free ourselves from insane passion for the truth. (491)[5]

Never mind, then, how the issue is decided. Since the argument questions the integrity of truth, the question of the truth of the argument may well be out of the question. Be that as it may, my proposition is complete. The argument of this text rehearses and reaffirms the argument of Aristotle's text. What *The Name of the Rose contains,* in essence and in excerpt, it *also is,* in fact and in fiction. As Aristotle himself might have put it, subjecting logic to comedic, the book of laughter is both present in and predicated of the book of Adso. And the name of this book, improperly called *The Name of the Rose,* is—really and in truth—: Aristotle's *Poetics,* Book II.

Really and in truth. But if we turn from the name of the book to the book itself, we find only a gathering of names. Not in the (perhaps) nugatory sense that any book is made of words, but in the deeper (or is it more superficial?) sense that this book is nothing but words. Not signs that direct us, perhaps along a trajectory of other signs, to some thing (be it fact or meaning) of which they *are* the signs; but rather, signs that traverse an endless detour of signs and return again and again to nothing but themselves.

The prefatory note should have prepared us for this. The text we have in hand is the fifth in a line of transcriptions, editions, and translations, of which the original and two subsequent generations are lost: a representation without a represented and several times removed at that. "A tale of books" (5), most of them non-existent. Adso's text (edited by..., etc., etc.) more than once anxiously recollects its own disconnection from origin. It begins with "incontrovertible truth"—"In the beginning was the Word and the Word was with God, and the Word was God"—but straightway recalls the apostolic reservation—"we see now through a glass darkly." Of the truth we long to know *in toto* and with the clarity of vision we garner only illegible fragments. Faithfully spelling out its signals, however obscure they are and however malign they sometimes seem to be, Adso records not the truth itself but only "signs of signs" to be interpreted by prayer. (11) Thus the confident beginning-with-the-Word trails off in a scattering of words.

At his first appearance, William of Baskerville deduces the abbot's lost horse—name, description, and location—from a combination of natural signs and conventional characters. The monks firmly believe the horse they find is the Brunellus described by Isidore and John Buridan (22-25), and William instructs his novice that "signs and signs of signs are used...when we are lacking things." (28) A lesson finally conned by Adso in mid-narrative:

> "True," I said, amazed. Until then I had thought each book spoke of the human things, or divine, that lie outside books. Now I realized that not infrequently books speak of books: it is as if they spoke among themselves. (286)

When Adso despairs of winding his way through the labyrinth of signs to the truth of things—"the individual unicorn"—William reassures him—"Don't worry: one of these days you will encounter it"—and immediately adds: "however black and ugly it may be." (317)[6] A timely admonition. For, contrary to what we might like to believe, *nomina non sunt consequentia rerum* but *ad placitum data.* (353) What Adso eventually finds at the heart of the labyrinth—his unicorn turned minotaur—is the terrible Jorge de Burgos eating his and everyone's words, and—is it his Ariadne's thread?—the ultimacy of material supposition, the realization that the critical discourse which opens the maze, penetrates the mystery, and brings him face to face with the thing itself is presumed only *de dictu* and not *de re.* (457)

The critical discourse. Including (it goes without saying) this one. The name of the book is only a name, and the book of the name is a book of names. A clutter of material suppositions in a matter suppositious in the extreme. Here as everywhere the story describes itself as it enacts itself. And finally consumes itself. As he approaches the end of his manuscript—that manuscript which is now lost forever—Adso-become-reader suspects what his readers have guessed all along:

> I have almost had the impression that what I have written on these pages, which you will now read, unknown reader, is only a cento, a figured hymn, an immense acrostic that says and repeats nothing but what those fragments have suggested to me, nor do I know whether thus far I have been speaking of them or they have spoken through my mouth.... And it is a hard thing for this old monk, on the threshold of death, not to know whether the letter he has written contains some hidden meaning, or more than one, or many, or none at all. (501)

The Name of the Rose is a pastiche of quotations and allusions gathered by its author from the ruins of the greatest library in Christendom: a conversation of books. An annotated edition would require margins much larger than those provided by Mr. Harcourt Brace Jovanovich, and they would be black with names: Bernard of Cluny, Hugh of St. Victor, the false Areopagite, Brother Tommaso of Aquino, Hildegard of Bingen, Alain de Lille, Bernard of Clairvaux, the bishop of Hippo, a caravan of Arabs, William Ockham, Roger Bacon, a smiling Stagirite, Meister Eckhart, the Poverello, Isidore of Seville, an assortment of popes and emperors and heretics, not to mention Conan Doyle...is there anyone we may safely presume is *not* there adding his penny's worth to the clamor of voices?

Amplifying the polyglot speech of Salvatore, *The Name of the Rose* is a cacophony of mutually interfering and reciprocally frustrating sign systems. The principal line of signification—the tale of detection—is blocked and misdirected by the tangle of semiotic coordinates—ecclesiological, philosophical, theological, and political—on which it is fatefully mapped. Normally a hermeneutic of truth that tracks the *signa* to their originating *res*, here the detective story turns on itself and proves to be—like the other plots with which it colludes—a multiple feedback circuit of overdetermined and indeterminable signifiers. Wherefore William's contradictorily coherent confession: "There was no plot..., and I discovered it by mistake." (491) As a former inquisitor (former for this reason), William has come to distrust his own or anyone's power to link the signs of guilt securely to their unequivocal cause. And indeed, at the center of the maze, opened by the most fortuitous Ockhamite recollection, there is no solid substantial malicious intent. Nothing but fatal accidents of reading. Like the catastrophic debate between papists and Franciscans, this criminal proceeding is undecidable save by fire.

The Name of the Rose achieves something approaching total intertextuality; it is "a library made up of fragments, quotations, unfinished sentences, amputated stumps of books." (500) Like the greater library of which it is the symbol, this lesser collocation is a labyrinth of signifiers from which the signified is missing—absent from the first or presently removed by violence. Which finally, violently, removes itself.

"Itself." Adso's manuscript (along with its editions and translations), *The Name of the Book* (*id est* Aristotle's *Poetics*, Book II): both (or all) of them go up in flames. They are all there in the *finis Africae*, and they are all lost. Like the girl, who is *within* the book a parable *of* the book. When Adso, early in the story, recollects Alan of Lille's celebrated *rhythmus*, he ever so slightly misquotes, reading *scriptura* where Alan has *pictura*. (106) Later, thinking of the girl and glossing Alan's poem—perhaps recalling the passage from Bernard's *De Contemptu Mundi* that furnishes his own *explicit*—, he is reminded that "the humblest rose becomes a gloss of our terrestrial progress." (279) The girl, who is Adso's solitary deviation from the grim face of truth, his one moment of laughter, the Rose whose name he cannot name (407) and of whom nothing remains *but* the name: she too is burned. *Ubi sunt?* Like Aristotle's lost book on comedy and Adso's lost love, both of which it is, *The Name of the Rose* destroys itself when it destroys its eponyms.

Necessarily so. Is it possible that any reader encountering Jorge de Burgos, has failed to think of Jorge Luis Borges? I think not. The allusion is too obvious to be missed. Too obvious, and obviously perverse. For while Señor Borges is indeed blind and somewhiles a librarian, a Spaniard of sorts, a lover of labyrinths and a writer of labyrinthine fictions, though by now escaped from the labyrinth of this world, it is utterly impossible to suppose him an enemy of laughter. The allusion is perverse. But the perversity is precisely the point. For, in spite of his bitter hatred of laughter, it is Jorge de Burgos who has the last laugh. Trapped in his labyrinth, Jorge takes comedy into himself sacramentally, as one receives the body of Christ, and devours it. Whereupon, becoming what is not to be said: "He laughed, he, Jorge. For the first time I heard him laugh." (481) It is Jorge's first laugh and the last laugh in this story. The laughter of a truth that consumes itself. Shortly thereafter, when the destruction of the library is assured, William of Baskerville, the Philosopher's advocate and the prophet of a truth that laughs at itself—William *weeps.* (487)

The Name of the Rose is Aristotle's *Poetics,* Book II. As such, it cannot survive itself. If this book is the lost book on comedy, and if it says what it reports itself to say, then it must self-destruct. So ambitious a transumption was bound to swallow its own metalepsis. If "the only truth lies in learning to free ourselves from the insane passion for truth" (491), then, with a perversity that is wholly appropriate, Jorge is vindicated. As Aristotle's lost work on comedy, *The Name of the Rose* must necessarily be the deconstruction of Aristotle's etc. This book—along with all its ancestors, descendants, and collaterals—is a book necessarily lost, a poisoned book whose "venomous power" (470) turns at last on itself.

But only after it has destroyed its reader. This is a book to read with your gloves on and your mouth shut, for the poison works only if you ingest it. The victim poisons himself when he is alone, and just to the extent that he wants to read. (472) As perhaps this reader, barehanded and big mouthed and only too hot in pursuit of his own grim hermeneutic intent, has done himself in. An invitation to suicide! Ironic that it should have become a best-seller. Jorge laughs again. He tried to warn us. But God created the monsters too, and He wants everything to be spoken of. (478) If I have not (as doubtless I haven't) succeeded in discovering the name of the book but only in displaying my own marginal monstrosity, I have at least the cold comfort of Baskerville, the universal consolation of losers: "It is not necessary for somebody one day to find that manuscript again. The only truths that are useful are instruments to be thrown away." (492) Throw it away therefore (it's disposable) or eat it (it's poisonous), this preterite text, which has no commitment to the present and is guaranteed not to change the world but only to erase itself, was written happily out of the love of writing (5) and, with regard to the text that occasioned it, a pure love of reading. To Umberto Eco, who bears absolutely no responsibility for the monstrosities I have doodled in the margins of his manuscript, my heartfelt thanks.

12

Seeing How Things Aren't:
Science Fiction and the Mainstream

I'm so tired, I'm so damn tired, so weary of seeing how things are, you see
it once, you've seen it for all time.... I mean, even though it's pretty spooky
having things turning into other things all the time, it did have its sweet
side....

—Robert Coover, *Rip Awake*.

Science fiction, long relegated to the underworld of "popular" literature
and more or less benignly neglected, has now begun to make its way
into college curricula. It has even received some critical attention. But it is
still by and large regarded as negligible pulp, and even when critically noticed
is frequently handled with a certain measure of condescension. Many of the
"better" bookstores—even those that sell detective novels, the favored light
reading of intellectuals—will not stock it. In the supermarket racks it usually
appears alongside the westerns and the romances. Only in stores that
specialize in SF—and there are many good ones—is the genre represented
fully, fairly, and without apology.

The disdain of the literary establishment for SF is not difficult to
understand. Much of it *is* little more than pulp. But it may be said in defense
that a lot of mainstream fiction is also spilled ink and soiled paper. Judged
by the strictest standards of "high art" (define them who will), most of SF
and mainstream writing has no literary distinction. The difference is that in
the case of mainstream fiction we have been trained to recognize merit
when we see it: provided with criteria of value, or at least told which books
to read. With SF we are left in the dark, and as a result it all looks uniformly
gray. Add to that an elitist prejudice against "popular" art—another effect
of our literary-critical education—and the deck is pretty well stacked.

Some writers on SF have wanted to legitimize their critical preoccupations by demonstrating that SF is a distinct genre, and much of their work has been an attempt to define this unique literary-critical entity. What they have done is helpful. But every categorization abets, if it does not actually constitute, an evaluation. And the SF genre, once clearly demarcated, all too easily becomes the occasion for further invidious comparisons. I'm wary of any attempt to achieve status-by-classification; and so, rather than assigning it a drawer in the files of the English Department, I prefer to contest the demeaning of SF in the opposite way: by blurring the distinction between SF and the mainstream.

To some extent this blurring has already been done by the writers themselves without the belated permission of philosopher-critics. SF has already contaminated the mainstream. The texts of—among others—Calvino, Borges, DeLillo, Vonnegut, and Pynchon, all certified mainstream (though some of them are suspiciously popular), embed elements of SF and use SF motifs as generative devices. From the other side of the line, many books classified as SF are straightforward mainstream novels with a bizarre premise or a counterfactual setting.

But this phenomenon, important as it is, could be no more than the communication that is bound to take place sooner or later at the boundaries of adjacent literary domains. More significant, it seems to me, is the participation of SF in the larger movement of recent fiction. In the twentieth century we have seen the modernist movement, the last devolution from the premises of Romanticism, climax in the work of Joyce. I say "climax" rather than "collapse" because I think it clear that Joyce (though he is obviously not in thrall to them) does not explicitly question or deliberately violate the classical norms of representation. On the contrary, a book like *Finnegans Wake* aims at something like global representation. It creates—it means to create—the impression that everything has been said and everything shown, so that the ideal reader with an ideal case of insomnia would achieve an ideal omniscience. So powerful is the Joycean illusion that one might define the purpose of a liberal education as preparation for reading *Finnegans Wake*.

But it is an illusion nevertheless. And this perception is enough to explain (even if it is not the actual reason for) the direction taken by mainstream fiction since Joyce. The Joycean climax leads to its appropriate denouement—the "literature of exhaustion"—and (since the story of stories never ends) the "literature of repletion" called "post-modern" fiction.[1] All fiction is conscious that it *is* fiction. The most resolutely realist novel, so long as it calls itself a novel, confesses that it has produced only the semblance of reality. An imitation is not a presentation and only in the most problematic sense a re-presentation. The distinctive mark of post-modern fiction is that it *writes* this self-consciousness, exposing it on the surface of the text rather than suppressing it or allowing it to remain the unacknowledged secret of the text. Informed like all fiction by the specular awareness of its own ficticity, the post-modern novel undoes the illusion as it produces it, using the techniques of representation to question the possibility of representation. For example, the novel about a novelist trying to write a novel (Sorrentino's *Mulligan Stew*, Federman's *Double or Nothing*) or the story about a storyteller who is a character in his own story (Barth's *Lost in the Funhouse*). Post-modern fiction doubles back on itself, doubts itself, and subverts itself.

These are commonplaces of contemporary post-modern mainstream writing. They are also perennial if not peculiar options for SF: possibilities always exploitable and sometimes actually exploited by the authors and the texts that populate this alternate literary universe.

Let me bring this down to earth with a few remarks about a popular novel by Philip K. Dick.[2] In some ways UBIK, published in 1969, is a typical Dickian dystopia. Set in 1992, the novel depicts an America oppressively overcrowded. Although the moon is colonized and the conquest of farther space well under way, most people live in cramped dwellings that combine the worst features of the American small town and the communist cell, their manners and morals subject to constant scrutiny by their neighbors. The mind itself is open to examination by teams of precognitives and telepaths, most of them retained by businesses to oneup the competition. So threatening is this particular invasion of privacy that organizations called "Prudence Societies" will protect you (and your company) from teeps and precogs by employing "inertials"—people who can block psionic snoopery. There is even (it seems) the power, uniquely embodied in a character named Pat Conley, to alter the past.

One other feature of Dick's America needs to be noted. By 1992 the newly dead, if caught in time, can be put in cryonic suspension ("coldpac") and preserved indefinitely in "half-life"—not forever, but well beyond normal life expectancy. During half-life, friends and family of the half-dead can communicate with them (through the miracle of electronics) at their "moratoria" or waiting stations. Physically inert, the half-alive are provided with a full and varied mental life. They literally do not know if they are (being in fact neither) alive or dead.

In UBIK the boundary between self and other is habitually transgressed. Since time can be reversed and history diddled, the distinction between past (necessity), present (opportunity), and future (possibility) no longer holds. And there is no clear line demarcating life from death. There are no mooring points: no facts and no truths, only a continuing anxiety about what (if anything) is reliably real and credibly the case.

You (dear reader) enter this world simply by reading the novel. Dick tells his story from the viewpoints of his characters, mainly that of his "little protagonist" Joe Chip.[3] He does not provide you with an authoritative map of reality, and the reader, in Joe Chip's position, experiences all of his insecurity and disorientation. Equivalently, Joe is in the position of the reader, confronted with a baffling and ever-shifting world/text the meaning of which he cannot confidently decode. UBIK—the world and the novel—is an unreadable text. Joe Chip tries a number of hermeneutic hypotheses. Each of them is contradicted by some of the available data. None of the reader's hunches pan out either.

So what's the story? The Hollis organization employs psionics to spy on people's personal lives and corporate ventures. Glen Runciter's Prudence Society (he's the "big protagonist") uses inertials to thwart the activities of Hollis' psi-agents. His people regard themselves, plausibly, as guardians of human privacy. Runciter runs his organization with the help of his wife Ella, who is in half-life at The Beloved Brethren Moratorium in Geneva. Joe Chip works for Runciter as a tester of psionic fields. He's an electronics wizard, but also a lovable schlemiel who can't manage his personal affairs and is chronically bankrupt. He rarely has the coins he needs to run his coffee-maker, open his refrigerator, or let himself out of his apartment.

The telekinetic and shapely Pat Conley appears, moves into Joe's apartment (she has lots of coins), and though Joe regards her with suspicion she is hired by the Runciter group.

Eleven of Runciter's people, including Joe and Pat, are retained, purportedly by the interplanetary entrepreneur Stanton Mick, to protect his operations from the Hollis organization. Runciter and his agents are summoned to Mick's headquarters on Luna. There a humanoid bomb, designed to look and act like Stanton Mick himself, explodes in their midst and kills Glen Runciter. Suspecting a plot by Hollis, Runciter's people put him in temporary coldpac and rush him to Geneva for half-life preservation. But they are took late, and Runciter dies.

Apparently. As the inertials leave for earth, strange things begin to happen. Joe Chip needs a smoke, but the cigarette he draws from his pack is dry and stale and falls apart in his fingers. His friends feel that they, like the cigarettes, have aged years in just a few moments. Though they attribute this feeling to the shock of Runciter's death, it soon becomes evident that something more sinister is afoot. From now on, things and people start to age swiftly, prematurely, unpredictably. Joe orders coffee in a Geneva restaurant: the coffee is tepid and covered with mold, the cream sour. Joe's money is obsolete. He invites another inertial, Wendy Wright, to spend the night with him. She agrees, but does not appear. He tries to dial the phone and finds it in use: the voice he hears is the voice of Glen Runciter. In the morning he finds the shriveled and dehydrated remains of Wendy in his closet. Messages from Runciter show up everywhere: on matchfolders, on cigarette cartons, and on the vidphone. Another inertial, Al Hammond, dies like Wendy. Before he dies, he and Joe see Runciter's handwriting on the men's room wall:

JUMP IN THE URINAL AND STAND ON YOUR HEAD.
I'M THE ONE THAT'S ALIVE. YOU'RE ALL DEAD. (118)

The truth is the opposite of what Joe and his friends had first thought. The explosion on the moon spared Runciter and killed his inertials, who are now in half-life.

Apparently. However, Runciter's corpse is buried in his Iowa home town, and his employees attend the funeral. During the funeral, the artifacts of Des Moines—houses, cars, and assorted small objects—are replaced by their 1939 precursors. The face of Glen Runciter appears on the TV screen and informs Joe Chip that UBIK, in the handy spray can, is able (when used as directed) to prevent the reversion of matter to earlier forms. Runciter also tells Joe that he (Runciter) is really dead, and that he (Joe) had better find some UBIK before he too dries up and dies. But Joe has no luck buying UBIK, since it keeps regressing to older kinds of "reality support."

So far Joe has tried two hypotheses to explain what happened on Luna. First hypothesis: a bomb, probably planted by Hollis, has killed Runciter and spared his staff. After their lives begin to get weird, the inertials conclude (second hypothesis) that the bomb spared Runciter and left them in half-life. But there are data not covered by this hypothesis: Runciter's funeral, the reversion of objects to earlier forms, and the sudden deaths of several inertials. Joe tries a third hypothesis. Encouraged by hints from Runciter, he concludes that Pat Conley (in Hollis' employ) is causing the regression of objects and the deaths (three so far) of Runciter's employees. While Pat stands by and gloats over his suffering, Joe himself nearly dies—and would have died had Runciter not appeared and sprayed him with UBIK to revivify him.

Runciter, who formerly assured Joe that he (Runciter) was dead, now tells him that he is really alive and consulting with his inertials at the Beloved Brethren Moratorium. Back to hypothesis 2. But Runciter's body has shrunken and mummified in its coffin. Whereupon Joe formulates a fourth hypothesis: there are two forces at work, a preserver and a destroyer. The destroyer is a character named Jory. A half-lifer at the moratorium who is "eating" the other half-lifers in order to prolong his own existence, Jory has produced the entire Des Moines episode as a mass hallucination. The friend and preserver is the half-dead Ella Runciter, who provides Joe with a certificate good for a lifetime supply of UBIK. But Jory and Ella are only symbols, and there is nothing more ultimate than the conflict of good and evil, no single source of the warring powers of creation and entropy.

Three pages before the end of the novel we are told the origin and nature of UBIK. Those who like hard science in their SF will not be encouraged. The explanation of its nature is pseudo-scientific poppycock, and the account of its origin—it was invented by a group of responsible half-lifers—does not inspire confidence. So much for verisimilitude.

With this helpful information under his belt, Joe forms his fifth and final hypothesis, a combination of the second and the fourth. Runciter is alive. His staff are all in half-life, within which demi-monde the Manichaean conflict of life and death continues without end.

And that's that. Well...maybe. Earlier in the novel, the appearance of Runciter's image on coins suggested to Joe the hypothesis (number 2) that Runciter, believed dead, was really alive, and that his inertials, who thought themselves alive, were really half-dead. On the last page of the book Glen Runciter, after consulting his cold-packed employees at the Beloved Brethren Moratorium, digs in his pocket for a coin to tip the attendant. To his surprise he discovers...

> Joe Chip on a fifty-cent piece? It was the first Joe chip money he had ever seen. He had an intuition, chillingly, that if he searched his pockets, and his billfold, he would find more. This was just the beginning. (212)

These are the last words (if not the last word) of the novel. And while it does not reinstate hypothesis 1, this turn of events certainly undercuts hypothesis 5 and throws the whole thing wide open once more. Just when you thought it was safe to close the book and go to bed, you're back to square one. The end is "just the beginning."

The beginning of what? What kind of beginning? At the head of each of the first sixteen chapters of the book stands a commercial for UBIK. It is, successively, an automobile, a beer, instant coffee, salad dressing, a pain reliever, a razor, a permanent plastic coating for all household surfaces, a savings and loan company, hairspray, deodorant, a sleeping pill, an aphrodisiac poptart, an uplift bra, plastic food wrap, a cure for halitosis, and an adult breakfast cereal. All recognizable forms of "reality support." As its name suggests, UBIK (*ubique*) is as omnipresent as advertising. And then, at the head of the concluding chapter, this:

> I AM UBIK. BEFORE THE UNIVERSE WAS, I AM. I MADE THE SUNS. I MADE THE WORLDS. I CREATED THE LIVES AND THE PLACES THEY INHABIT; I MOVE THEM HERE, I PUT THEM THERE. THEY GO AS I SAY, THEY DO AS I TELL THEM. I AM THE WORD AND MY NAME IS NEVER SPOKEN, THE NAME WHICH NO ONE KNOWS. I AM CALLED UBIK, BUT THAT IS NOT MY NAME. I AM. I SHALL ALWAYS BE. (211)

That, with its echoes of *Genesis*, *Exodus*, the *Tao te Ching*, and the Prologue to the *Gospel of St. John,* suggests that we have finally caught a glimpse of reality behind the bewildering flux of appearance, a single stable truth behind the veil of illusion, and the ubiquitous first principle that promises (if it doesn't actually declare) a closure of meaning for this confusing text. But of course this final epigraph is just another commercial. If all those other ads are invested with cosmic and religious portent by this concluding gospel, then it is equally the case that the terminal oracle is trivialized by the crass commercials that precede it. Maybe it's just another word from our Sponsor.

UBIK poses the problem of meaning, and in posing it renders it insoluble. What is real and what is unreal in the world of this novel? What counts as truth and how can you tell? What does this book mean? But there is no omniscient narrator and no privileged point of view, and the text itself discredits every hypothesis it recommends to its characters and its readers. UBIK defeats the hermeneutic it demands. Absolute Reality has laryngitis and will not appear. The definitive edition of Absolute Truth will not be published this year.

Ordinary fiction purports to represent a secondary world structured by laws analogous to those that govern what we take to be the real world. No matter how exotic this world, it has a truth and a reality of its own which the reader can discern and, discerning it, feel that he has understood the meaning of the text and the relation of its world to his own. The comfortable effect of ordinary fiction is to confirm the reader's sense of his own reality by permitting him so perspicuous a view of a world he knows is only imaginary.

UBIK offers us a world we cannot understand and a text we cannot decipher. Reading it disturbs our expectations of fiction and thereby unsettles our confidence in fact.

In this it is not alone. Most interesting SF, like the most interesting mainstream fiction, undermines the assumptions of fictive mimesis and destabilizes the concept of narrative representation. So doing, it deconstructs the conventional opposition between fact and fiction, displacing each in the direction of the other, exposing their mutual supplementarity, and dismantling the hierarchy which by privileging fact over fiction assures the latter its limited legitimacy. When the difference between fact and fiction is (constitutively) confounded in a text that is (constitutively) both fiction and representation (poesis and mimesis), the disorientation is radical, at once compelling and proscribing a redefinition *ab initio* of the fundamental categories of being and knowing. Scrambling our ordinary preconceptions about reality and unsettling our confidence in the standard modes of cognition, the science-fictional text (like the text of mainstream fiction at this spasm in its history) not only raises perplexing ontological and epistemological questions; suspending the very notions of "reality" and "knowledge," it threatens by raising them to leave those questions undecidable. Scare-quotes forever.

It might be argued that SF is uniquely situated to open these questions and insinuate these doubts. After all, nothing has been more disturbing to our conceptual complacency than the rapid development of science and technology in the twentieth century. Extrapolate a bit from state-of-the-art, stipulate a novel condition, actualize a present impossibility, and you quickly achieve escape velocity. Some writers on SF have taken this line.[4] Understandably, since it is the presence of "science" in (what we empirically identify as) SF that enables librarians to get it onto the proper shelf. Darko Suvin has characterized SF as the "literature of cognitive estrangement" which accomplishes its special *Verfremdungseffekt* by the use of science and technology as motives of the text.[5] I like the phrase "literature of cognitive estrangement" because I think it does adumbrate the ontological and epistemological disturbances produced by the science-fictional text. But I doubt that the presence in SF of extrapolations from actual science and technology suffices to define a genre. For one thing, theorists who so define SF (like Lem) are then obliged to forget their definitions in order to include in the genre texts by writers (like Dick) whose use of science is casual, minimal, or half-baked, but whose work is nothing if not SF. And even in the non-marginal cases, the science is normally deviant and the technology aberrant. In a word, fictional.

That's the main thing. Since SF does—importantly—shake up our categories of being and knowing, the presence of science or imaginative projections therefrom in the SF text cannot be definitive but only occasional. One of the things questioned by SF is the ontological and epistemological foundation of science itself: the scientific conception of reality and the scientific method of acquiring reliable knowledge. The discourse of science (not to mention the "founding" discourse of philosophy) is constructed on the basis of invincibly gratuitous decisions about what is "real" and what is "certain." That fiction has become scientific only reveals that science is always already constituted as and by fiction.

Though frequently—perhaps normally—situated within the ambience of science, SF is not generically determined thereby. As *science*-fiction, it often specifies itself by the way it plays within these precincts. As *fiction*, it starts those perturbations in the ontological-epistemological field that are the generic effects of the imagination and the peculiar pertinacity of the post-modern imagination. As *science-fiction* and in the usual case, it exploits science in order to relativize—among others—the scientific construction of knowledge of reality.

The difficulty with every attempt to define fictional genres is that fiction itself is—generically and as such—a trespasser. It will not even respect the boundary between fact and fable, much less the little fences that segregate literary kinds. It doesn't know its place.

SF may not *be*, as Ballard said, the mainstream.[6] Neither is it just a "popular" phenomenon that is safely written off and ignored: if anything deserves that title and that treatment, it may be the kind of fiction that reinforces our prejudices and preconceptions rather than shaking them up. For example, Harlequin romances, Louis L'Amour westerns, and Michener's pot-boilers. But SF *connives with* the mainstream and toward the same end: the construction of a persuasive and impertinent "rhetoric of the unreal."[7] Indeed, since it has never been content with the picture of "things as they are," SF may even have *anticipated* what now appears to be the manifest destiny of the fictional text: to see clearly how they *aren't*. By showing us how things aren't, SF makes us wonder if we know how they are.

IV

13

A Nicer Knowledge of Belief

To say the solar chariot is junk

Is not a variation but an end.
Yet to speak of the whole world as metaphor
Is still to stick to the contents of the mind

And the desire to believe in a metaphor.
It is to stick to the nicer knowledge of
Belief, that what it believes in is not true.

—Wallace Stevens, "The Pure Good of Theory"

In 1978 I attended an interdisciplinary symposium on the nature of narrative held at the University of Chicago. One of the luminaries present was Jacques Derrida. He read an abridged version of a paper later published in full under the title "The Law of Genre" (*La Loi du genre*).[1] The argument of his presentation, difficult to begin with, was made even more difficult by its abridgment, and it was evident that few, if any, of his auditors understood it. Nevertheless, there were the usual polite academic questions from the other symposiasts. After a while, this exchange was interrupted by one of the panelists, who had a not-so-academic and perhaps not-even-so-polite question for the speaker. M. Derrida, he said (or to this effect: I am not quoting), your philosophy bothers me very much. All it seems to do is to put me in a terrible predicament. What good is it anyway?

Derrida smiled and replied (I am still not quoting), As for your predicament, I beg you to remember that it is also my predicament. What good is it? I think it marks a definite progress in the history of our concepts. (That last was almost a quotation.) Derrida's response to his questioner, never (until now) written down and published in the ordinary sense, provides me with an occasion and a text for the ensuing reflections.

The philosophy associated with Derrida is usually called deconstruction. But it is somewhat misleading to call deconstruction a philosophy. Rightly understood, it is anything but a philosophical doctrine. In what follows I shall use "deconstruction" to refer, more accurately, to the metaphilosophical practices, in particular the strategies of reading, introduced and exemplified in Derrida's early writings. To call these ways of reading "metaphilosophy" is itself problematic, for reasons that will become clear later. But it is necessary to begin somewhere, and all starting points, like origin itself, are without authority. So, embracing my own predicament and expanding on the interchange not quite cited above, I shall venture an answer to the troubled symposiast's question, What good is deconstruction? The answer will be: It puts us in a terrible predicament, and it helps us understand the history of our concepts. Each because of the other. It puts us in a terrible predicament because it helps us understand the history of our concepts, and it helps us understand the history of our concepts by putting us in a terrible predicament.

According to Aristotle, what he called "first philosophy" and the philosophical tradition, over-interpreting an editorial catch-all, calls "metaphysics" is the science that studies being itself and all that pertains to it *qua* being. Following Heidegger's reading of Greek philosophy, Derrida says that the root meaning of "being," throughout the entire history of Western thought, is *presence*. Philosophy, as the search for the meaning of being, is fundamentally and foundationally the attempt to locate that which presents itself immediately and ineluctably to the knowing mind. Beyond all illusion and mere appearance, being is that which demands non-negotiably to be acknowledged as irreducibly *there*. Being is the offer you can't refuse and presumably wouldn't want to.

Given these preliminaries, the first principle of deconstructive practice may be formulated in these words: there is no such thing as immediacy. There is no point at which the thing itself is simply given. On the contrary, presence is an effect of representation. As Derrida writes:

> (R)epresentation does not suddenly encroach upon presence; it inhabits it
> as the very condition of experience, of desire, and of enjoyment.[2]

Never simply present, being is always the representation of a presence. The direct confrontation with reality, toward the attainment of which philosophy strives, is no more than the figure of a consummation desired but never enjoyed.

Paradoxical expressions of this sort are not proposed as mystifications, but as means to an end. The end is to force an encounter with the question, What do we get from philosophy? Do we get reality represented in the language of philosophy? Or is it only the language of philosophy represented as reality? When you look into a mirror, do you see yourself reflected in the mirror or a reflection of yourself in the mirror? Is the mirror a means by which you get to know yourself, or is the self you know an effect of the mirror? Are these paradoxes means to an end or preformations of the end they profess to serve?

Put in this way, the question—does the language of philosophy mediate a confrontation with being or dissemble a reality that remains wrapped in its alterity?—is a question that must be decided if the philosophical enterprise is to understand itself. But it is also undecidable, since any decision would be subject to a recursion of the question it presumed to decide. The upshot is that the philosophical undertaking is a project that necessarily deconstructs itself. Philosophy is the deconstruction of philosophy, whether it knows it or not. Deconstruction offers it(self) this disturbing—and disturbed—self-knowledge. What follows is offered in evidence.

I. Misadventures of Ideas: Episodes from the Past

A. The metaphorics of cognition in Plato's dialogues

Plato distinguishes opinion and knowledge in terms of the basic metaphysical difference between appearance and reality. Opinion is unreliable because it represents things as they seem to be, and appearances are famous for deceiving. Knowledge, however, is infallibly certain because it represents things as they really are. An opinion is a judgment solicited by appearances. If I believe that the thing I see before me is a dagger, its handle toward my hand, I am judging an appearance. I judge that this phenomenon, which gives itself out as a dagger and which seems to be a dagger, is in fact a dagger. How do I make this judgment? If I judge responsibly, I do not take the appearance at its word. I compare the appearance-of-dagger with what I already know to be the essential nature of dagger, what Plato would call the Form or Idea of dagger. But how do I know the Form of dagger? Not by an act of judgment. That would postpone the validation of opinion indefinitely, generating an endless regress of judgments but never arriving at knowledge. Plato says in effect that I just know the Form of dagger. In fact, he would insist that I must always already have known it, for I could never have learned it.

What we call learning is actually remembering. Since all learning presupposes a prior knowing, one can not learn anything for the first time. Like opining, learning is judging. It is an act of recognition. But you can only re-cognize what you have already cognized. Therefore opining—or judging or learning—necessarily presumes a recollecting, more or less complete and accurate, of something always already known and always already forgotten.

But if the mode of opinion is judgment, what is the mode of knowledge? Plato's answer is: vision. Opining is judging, but knowing is seeing. All mediate cognition (re-cognition) is rooted in a timeless moment of immediate intellectual vision, in which being is encountered face to face, as it is and not as it seems to be.

It should be clear that seeing and judging, as ways of representing distinct modes of cognition, direct and indirect respectively, are metaphors. Both are radical tropes (catachreses) in which words are turned away from their ordinary uses and made to figure things that lack proper names and cannot be said literally. The kind of judging that is said to occur in the formation of opinion is a figurative derivation and possibly a deviation from the kind of judging that goes on in law courts or in any matter that requires the application of a rule to a case. And the kind of vision that is said to take place when we know the Forms of things is transported from everyday physical seeing to figure a putative purely intellectual seeing or *noesis*. The latter—the direct intellectual vision by which Plato represents immediate cognition—is no less figurative than the judging by which he represents mediate cognition. The immediacy of direct cognition is therefore a figured immediacy. Not immediacy immediately present, but immediacy mediately represented. As one moves from the realm of particulars and the opinions by which they are apprehended to the realm of Forms, direct knowledge of which is the condition of responsible opining, the metaphors change.[3] But they remain metaphors, and the foundation of representation is not presence, but a representation of presence. Not the vis-à-vis encounter of the mind with being, but the metaphor of this epiphanic moment: a figure of truth by which truth itself is brought as close as possible in the absolute proximity of vision, and at the same time kept at the absolute distance of figuration.

It might be objected: granted that Plato's representation of immediate cognition is figurative, it does not follow that the thing itself is so, or that our knowledge of it is necessarily mediated by representation. When you know something, you just know it and you know that you know it, all in one fell swoop. There is no room for mediation. Aristotle thought we could, having made a suitable induction, see the form directly in its singulars.

Why not? Plato takes it for granted that the singular, no matter how vivid our perception of it, is formally defective and requires assessment by reference to a transcendent norm. But if the sensible dagger I perceive prompts me to ask, Is this really a dagger, or does it only appear so? then why may I not, mentally confronting the intelligible Form of dagger, ask, Is this really the Form of dagger or am I fooled again? You might say, though Plato doesn't quite, that at this point the mind is ravished by its object and in this ecstasy from self has neither the will nor the capacity to doubt. But you would then have to acknowledge that words like "rapture" and "ecstasy" are themselves figurative representations of a reality they cannot, as mere words, sacramentally transmit. Plotinus, who meant what Plato said, also made it clear that at this climactic moment, we are beyond both being and knowing, and certainly beyond rational explanations. The neo-Platonist may be right that the logic of Platonism propels us into mysticism. But if the quest for wisdom ends in the ineffable absorption of the alone into the Alone, then the fulfillment of the philosophical project is also its undoing.[4]

In the dialogues of Plato, however, the difference between appearance and reality is a difference between the figures of speech by which we represent the difference between representation and the original. It is, in other words, a rhetorical difference. This is no doubt one reason why Plato was so deeply and inwardly concerned with rhetoric and with the sophists who brazenly opposed their rhetorical logos to philosophy's supposed logos of truth. Like Socrates in the *Phaedrus*, Plato wonders what kind of beast he really is.

This predicament—it is clearly more than a problem—is at the center of the dialogue that attempts to define the sophist. In this dialogue, Plato is not primarily concerned with the relation of image and original, but with the relation between two kinds of images. The question is posed by Parmenides, whose monism rules out all falsehood and negation—it is impossible to say or think the thing that is not—and by the sophists, who traffic professionally in the illusions Parmenides declares non-existent and justify their practice by appealing to Parmenides' denial of the pseudos— whatever anyone thinks is so is so. This paradoxical identity of incompatibles requires Plato to distinguish the deceitful sophist, who says what is not, from the truthful philosopher, who says what is. In other words: to locate the difference between trustworthy *iconic* images (the discourse of the philosopher) and unreliable *fantastic* images (the rhetoric of the sophists).

It is clear what Plato has to say in order to decide the issue: iconic images faithfully represent their originals, whereas fantastic images are misrepresentations. Both icons and phantasms are really images, but neither of them (as image) is the thing it purports to represent. The difference between them can only be recognized if one can compare them with their originals, the ever-present realities that both of them claim to imitate. But, short of that identity which is ruled out by their status as images, who is to say what kind and degree of resemblance constitutes fidelity? And of course no one knows the originals, at least no longer and not yet. Eternally foreknown, the Forms are already forgotten and not yet perfectly recollected. They are representations of the necessary conditions of representation and of the criteria necessary for discriminating faithful and fickle representations. Reality is the represented ground of the possibility of representation, and the truthfulness of the image is founded on the fiction of the original.

It is not surprising that the concept of difference plays such a duplicitous role in the *Sophist*. The difference between true and false representations, not to mention the difference implicit in simple falsehood and negative predication, is the problem of the dialogue. But in the end the Form of difference is offered—i.e., represented—as the solution to the problem. The Form of difference is the imagined reality that is represented as the ground of the actual difference between true and false images, both of which differ from their originals and presumably from difference itself.

Neither is it surprising that Plato finds it impossible to track down the sophist without stumbling over the philosopher. Both of them are said to be elusive. And though the one is lurking in his lair like a hunted animal and the other wrapped in the impenetrable mystery of the divine, neither can be defined and distinguished from his opposite without appealing to a representation of that illusive and elusive difference the dialogue set out to clarify. Presence is always only the representation of presence, and—here's the complication introduced by the *Sophist*—it is not the representation of the self-same but the representation of that which as the different eternally differs from itself as the same. The philosopher and the sophist are not opposites, but dialectical twins. Like dark and light, they define each other. There is no need to puzzle about the fate of Plato's lost dialogue on the philosopher. We have it, and it is called the *Sophist*.[5]

B. Aspects of the Cartesian project

In the letter to the theologians of the Sorbonne that accompanies his *Meditations*, Decartes represents himself as a defender of the faith. One of his objectives was to counter the skepticism that was sweeping across Europe in the wake of the Renaissance and the Protestant Reformation.[6] In troubled times thoughtful people become skeptics because they are persuaded, by the chaos of conflicting doctrines, that all metaphysical positions are merely matters of opinion. Since we have no assured knowledge of reality itself with which to compare our representations of it, we have no criterion by which to measure their truth or falsity. In such situations, a prudent person will suspend judgment and generally keep a low profile. So a Pyrrhonian like Sextus in late antiquity and so, in the Renaissance, the eloquent Montaigne.

Descartes hoped to answer the skeptic by locating an indubitable truth: not another representation, but the reality represented in every representation. The immediate presence of this reality to the mind would forestall all possibility of error and provide us with a truth we can trust. To accomplish his purpose, Decartes proposed to meet the skeptic on his own ground by radicalizing the skeptic's abstention from judgment. Systematically doubting everything dubitable, Descartes is led to the conclusion that every clear and distinct idea is veridical. In particular he is led to the *cogito* as the primary certainty and to the idea of God as the necessarily existent ground of all that is: the former as the *ratio cognoscendi* of the latter and the latter the *ratio essendi* of the former. Both my own existence and the being of God are clearly and distinctly conceived and therefore cannot be shaken by doubt.

Descartes' confidence in these certainties rests on his conviction that all clear and distinct ideas represent their objects not as they seem but as they really are. By Descartes' own definition an idea, in the strictest sense, purports to represent some object.[7] A clear and distinct idea is a representation so perfectly determined by what it represents that it gives us no more and no less than the thing itself. So understood, however, a clear and distinct idea is a representation that is not a representation but a presence or, equivalently, an idea that eludes the definition and the conditions of ideation. In response to critics of his ontological proof, Descartes says, I cannot define God any way I please, just as the geometer is not free to define triangle as it suits his fancy. On the contrary, we are compelled by the thing itself, whether God or triangle, to conceive it as it is.[8] As a representation which is not one, but the represented itself, the idea of God is in no way an effect of ideation but simply God himself present to the attentive mind. Conservative ecclesiastics quite properly anathematized this view, which, in theological terms, confounds the knowledge of wayfaring and the knowledge of the fatherland. But it was for all that a necessary if incoherent consequence of the Cartesian project.

Similar problems beset the *cogito*. "I think, therefore I am" is true only to the extent that the *cogito* is identical with (=) the *sum*. Any discrepancy between the thinking and the being, even the minimal difference suggested by the *ergo*, would open a space for doubt. Therefore, when Descartes asks himself, what is the "I" that "thinks," he is obliged to answer that it is *res cogitans*. But since the *res* is a determination of all things that distinguishes nothing, *res cogitans* simplifies to *cogitans*, a thinking. "I think, therefore I exist" means "I think, therefore I think." Or simply: there is thinking. In his *Discourse on Method* Descartes shuttles back and forth between autobiography and philosophy, usually without warning. As a result, it is difficult to know whether any given instance of the *cogito* refers to René Descartes, or to *res cogitans simpliciter*. It is obvious that M. Descartes, a particular seventeenth-century Frenchman, cannot be the presence that grounds representation. And that which might, *res cogitans*, is a fiction. Not identical with himself, it is René Descartes' representation of the ground of representation. This is even more evident in the *Meditations on First Philosophy*, which rewrites—i.e., rhetorically restages—the experience purportedly reported in the *Discourse*. Even the *Discourse*, as a report of Descartes' experience, is only a representation of the method of doubt, not the thing itself. The *cogito* of the *Meditations*, governed by the literary conventions of the meditation form, is a second-order rhetorical effect: the fiction of the *Discourse* fictionalized to the next higher power.[9]

The rhetoric in this case is the method itself. Cartesian doubt is the figure of hyperbole, personified externally as the evil genius and represented inwardly as the dream problem. Both are imagined conditions under which I could not imaginably be deceived by imaginings. Both vanish immediately once the *cogito* is introduced. Yet the certainty of the *cogito* itself is a product(ion) of the imaginary theater of the mind, both inner and outer, in which Descartes stages his *Meditations*. The indubitable certainty Descartes achieves is an effect of the bizarre rhetorical landscape of the work in which it appears. Not the presence that grounds representation, but the textual representation of that presence, it only iterates the problem it was meant to solve.[10]

C. The critical revolution

The philosophy of Immanuel Kant is a response to the rationalism in which he was nurtured, the empiricism that awakened him from his dogmatic slumbers, and through both to the entire previous history of philosophy. Rationalism—what he calls "dogmatism"—had not produced the certainty it promised, and empiricism—Kant calls it "skepticism"—didn't even promise any.[11] Weary of both, he proposes what he characterizes as a "Copernican revolution" in philosophy: instead of supposing that knowledge revolves around objects, a supposition that has not paid off, let us suppose the contrary, that objects revolve around our knowledge.[12]

It is important not to underestimate the radical nature of this proposal. Knowledge consists of representations. But representations of the object in and for the subject are not formed by the object. Rather, the being of the object is prefigured by the representations of the subject. All we ever know is our own representations or, as Kant most often calls them, appearances. At one stroke the project of all previous philosophy—to locate the presence that grounds representation—is discredited. The thing-in-itself is forever beyond our grasp. There is no moment of noumenal presence, there are only phenomena.

Kant allows that it is necessary to *think* the thing-in-itself. It is evident that we do not create the world *ex nihilo* by knowing it. Something is given to perception, and in any case, Kant says, the logic of "appearance" implies that something appears in the appearances.[13] Kant's readers have sometimes suspected that the "logic" here invoked is strictly verbal, and indeed to argue as Kant does is only to say that the thing-in-itself is a representation: an obligatory representation (a thought) of the unknowable but necessary ground of representation, but a representation nonetheless. As for the conditions of the possibility of experience, the forms of sensibility and the categories of the understanding, they too are but representations *a priori* of the necessary conditions of empirical representation. Even the Cartesian *cogito* is explicitly transformed by Kant into a representation. The synthetic unity of apperception is the representation "I think" that is able to accompany, and must indeed be represented as accompanying, all other representations, binding them together in the unity of the subject.[14] But the unity so achieved is figured unity and the subject a representation of subjectivity.

Looking at the matter in this way may explain why Kant has so much trouble defining the crucial term "transcendental." The ground of representation is a *Bewusstsein überhaupt* that is neither a particular consciousness nor a collection of such nor yet a transcendent metaphysical *nous*, but only the necessary figuration of the subjective ground of the unity of experience. Kant cannot say what he means by "transcendental," except that it has to do with the conditions of the possibility of experience,[15] since in the vocabulary he was constrained to employ there is no word for what he meant. And can be none. For in denying that thoughts conform to objects and proposing that objects conform to thoughts, Kant had deranged the conditions of meaning, and inverted the normative logocentric order of signification.[16] For Kant to define "transcendental" would have been to define definition. But no philosophy, least of all the critical philosophy, can represent the conditions of its own representation or prescribe the limits that determine closure in its own vocabulary.

Perhaps it is for this reason that there is in Kant's philosophy, as in the philosophy of Plato, an abrupt switch at crucial junctures from the metaphoric of judgment to a metaphoric of vision. The switch, however, is proscribed by the Copernican revolution. On Kant's view, our knowledge of appearances is a system (or an approximation to a system) of judgments. Kant invokes the metaphoric of judgment in his second preface and exploits it extravagantly in the transcendental deduction of the categories.[17] As he explains, the latter is not a logical deduction (a syllogistic) but a legal deduction (the determination of a *quaestio quid juris*). For Kant, as for Plato, judgments need to be rooted in immediate cognition or vision. But while there is in Kant's philosophy sensuous intuition (*sinnliche Anschauung*), such intuition provides only the matter of knowledge, not its form. The latter is supplied *a priori*, though not by anything like the Platonic *noesis*. Plato's dream of a vision of the Good that can serve as the immediate ground of all mediate cognition is interdicted at the outset by Kant's claim that there is no *intellectuelle Anschauung*. In order to forestall mystical *Schwärmerei*, it is necessary to insist that the intellect cannot see. The formal grounds of cognitive judgment are not intuited, but derived dialectically as the necessary conditions of the possibility of judgment. The Kantian dialectic does not terminate in vision, so that in Kant's philosophy, even more clearly than in Plato's, the formal conditions of knowledge are never more than figured: represented modes of the unity of representations in the unity of a representation of the subject.

In Kant philosophy becomes fiction, insofar as being is not the foundation of thought but a form and function of thought. Presence is the effect of representation. In Kant's own formulation, transcendental idealism (the view that all the objects of knowledge are appearances) is the condition of empirical realism (the confidence that we can know such objects as they really are, i.e., as appearances). The contrary view—transcendental realism— had led on both sides of the rationalist-empiricist divide to incurable skepticism. By relocating the skepticism at the metaphysical level, we guarantee the certainty of empirical cognition.

Kant's contemporaries were not unaware that the sage of Königsberg had pulled the rug from under the whole philosophical enterprise as traditionally understood. Most of them (the German idealists of the nineteenth century) elaborated ponderous systems designed to save the tradition from Kant's assault on its foundations. Significantly, many of Kant's successors, inspired by the speculations of his third *Critique*, but transgressing its critically imposed boundaries, looked to art for the consummation denied to philosophy.[18] Even a late and most unRomantic post-Kantian like Hans Vaihinger, who recognized the fictional character of philosophical concepts, claimed for his own *Philosophie des 'Als Ob'* the privilege of truth.[19] All of them were inwardly shaken by Kant's demonstration that the mind does not, in its cognitive operations, lay hold of being itself but only alembicates its own apparatus of representation and abstraction.

The example of the German Romantics recommends that we do what mainstream philosophy has never done, or done consistently; namely, to take seriously Kant's claim that the *Critique of Judgment* is the capstone of the critical philosophy. In the third *Critique*, usually handed over, with some condescension, to the aestheticians, Kant locates the creative source of experience in the imagination and redescribes the traditional preoccupation of philosophy with the supersensible as an exercise in "symbolic hypotyposis"—an operation in which reality is not known but figured in the production of what Kant calls "aesthetical ideas" and literary critics call metaphors.[20] Though philosophers by and large have slighted the third *Critique*, the poets, both German and English, did not. The patrimony of Kant passed from the philosophers, obsessed as they were with science and with problems in epistemology, to the entrepreneurs of imagination. As a result Kant's heritage is preserved less faithfully in the subsequent history of philosophy than in the literary movement known as Romanticism and its successor, modernism, whence it has come to troubled rest in these latter days in that peculiar mixture of creative excess and creative self-doubt that we, not knowing what it really is, call the "postmodern."[21]

What I have tried to illustrate by means of these examples is a certain way of reading philosophy. Not the way philosophy is usually read, but a way suggested by Derrida's theory and practice of deconstruction. The suspicion prompted by these readings is that what philosophers call truth is a textual effect; the effect, that is, of certain techniques of representation. Philosophical truth is a figure of discourse, philosophy itself is a kind of writing, and the reality of which philosophy would be the cognitive apprehension is a fiction: the fiction of presence. One must, therefore, read philosophy as one reads literature—as a poetic mimesis that creates the reality it represents and knows better than to credit its own creations.

More of this later. For now, it must be kept in mind that to read a philosophical text the way I have read Plato, Descartes, and Kant is to read the text against itself; that is, against its express intentions. It is to read the text in a way contrary to the conventions of philosophic interpretation and against the generic expectations elicited by the identification of the text as "philosophy." Not to mention the ways in which the text before you asks to be read. Explicitly or implicitly, every text includes as part of its textuality instructions to the reader. To read deconstructively is to refuse to be seduced by these solicitations and to fix your attention on features of the text that the text itself would rather you ignored.

But of course you cannot read the text against itself without first having read it in its own way; that is, by acknowledging the demands of the genre, the conventions of philosophic reading, and the stipulations of the text in hand. Deconstructive reading is not intended to replace ordinary reading. It is not a substitute for but a supplement to "normal" philosophy. "Supplement" is a Derridean term, and to say that deconstructive reading supplements conventional reading is to say two things at once, the apparent incoherence of which marks out the problematic of deconstruction.[22] As a supplement to the usual way of reading, deconstruction is an appendage or addendum to something—philosophy as represented in traditional readings—which is already essentially complete in itself. The supplement in this sense is external to what it supplements. But insofar as the usual reading demands to be supplemented by the deconstructive double-take, to that extent it is not already complete. The supplementary reading makes up an essential deficiency in the ordinary reading. And in this sense the supplementary reading demanded by the philosophical text is internal to it, something it needs in order to be complete. What the deconstructive reading discloses is that the text of philosophy, or any text, is not complete and never can be.

To "do" philosophy—is it significant that we never "write" philosophy?—in the wake of the deconstructive revolution will not produce the certainty sought by philosophers of the past. Deconstruction is an art of disenchantment, and to philosophize deconstructively is to philosophize against the whole philosophical tradition. Philosophical thinking is never consummated in the vision of the Good Plato desired, nor in the Absolute Knowing imagined by Hegel. But neither can the project be abandoned. There is no escape from philosophy into poetry or science or history or some other safe haven. The effects of textuality are everywhere, and the dream of presence that founds philosophy troubles the dogmatic slumbers of the most committed anti-philosopher. To philosophize in this way is to combat the illusions of philosophy and to reinstate them in the very act of disarming them. As philosophical wisdom is always coming but never here, so the dream of presence is a dream from which we are always awakened but never wake.

I remarked at the outset that it would be misleading to think of deconstruction as a form of metaphilosophy. Perhaps it is now clear why this is the case. The deconstructive reading of philosophy is not conducted in nor does it generate a metalanguage by which the first-order language of philosophy is contained and mastered. It does not ascend to a superior vantage point from which the whole philosophical enterprise may be surveyed and evaluated. The deconstructive reading of the history of philosophy is actively engaged with the history it interprets, compromised by that engagement, and itself subjected to the logic of illusion even in its disillusionment. Deconstruction is not anti-philosophy or metaphilosophy, but philosophizing against philosophy. As such, necessarily both philosophy and against itself, deconstruction is obliged to prolong the history it repeatedly undoes.

As an art of disenchantment, deconstruction is a form of sophistication. What deconstruction suspects (it could hardly know this) is not that the loss of innocence is irreversible, but that the innocence lost was never possessed in the first place. Like the paradise inhabited by prelapsarian humanity, it is a nostalgic projection of the postlapsarian consciousness, an imaginary retrofitting of alienated desire. But by the same logic or counter-logic, the disenchantment of philosophy accomplished by deconstruction can never be complete. Deconstruction remains in thrall—by its historicity, by the language it is fated to speak, and by its will to truth—to the enchantments it dispels, and must therefore again and again be submitted, against itself, to its own deconstruction.[23]

That may be why the author of deconstruction could reply, had to reply, to one who complained that deconstruction left him in a terrible predicament: it is also my predicament. It is also our predicament. And, as it is a predicament from which there is, in this life at least, no exit, so there is no end to these reflections. There is no end to these reflections because there is no end to reflection. And no way to prevent it. Our predicament is our destiny. There is an old saying that it is better to travel hopefully than to arrive. That is not always the case. But in the pursuit of wisdom we do not have a choice. By our own powers and apart from supernatural intervention (which deconstruction is in no position to rule out) we never arrive at a final truth in which we may rest. The journey is all we get.

II. The Ever-Presence of Absence:
Deconstruction and the History of Philosophy

Toward the beginning of this discussion I said that philosophy is the deconstruction of philosophy. For similar reasons I might say that deconstruction is the history of philosophy. But to speak in this way could give rise to serious misunderstanding. The misunderstanding—or the danger of it—is twofold. On the one hand, to say that deconstruction is the history of philosophy might seem to situate deconstruction within the familiar and benign territory of philosophical history. On the other hand, such an assertion might seem to corrupt the history of philosophy by associating it with the anarchic subversions of deconstruction. The best way to counter these opposed errors is to indulge them and play them off against each other. In this way, it may be possible to transform the safe but vacuous "and" into the more controversial but also more interesting "is." Deconstruction is neither something well-known and unthreatening, nor is it something scandalous and terminally nihilistic. It is a disruptive event that precipitates a revolution in philosophy. But it is of such crises that the history of philosophy is composed and by which it is moved.

Unlike deconstruction, the history of philosophy appears to be unproblematic. But it is not as easy as it seems to say what it is. The history of philosophy is not a list of the views held by sucessive philosophers and schools of philosophy. Though it has sometimes been treated in this way, the history of philosophy is not a chronicle of opinions. Another closely related view holds that there is a fairly well-defined set of timeless problems that are uniquely the concern of philosophers. The history of philosophy becomes, on this view, the record of attempts by successive generations of philosophers to solve their distinctive disciplinary problems.

Both these ways of conceiving the history of philosophy make it easy to distinguish philosophy proper from the history of philosophy. Philosophy proper consists of working at the solution of philosophical problems. The history of philosophy, of only incidental interest to philosophy proper or proper philosophers, is just the chronological record of these labors. Though it may warn us not to repeat the errors of the past, the history of philosophy is not really philosophy.

This distinction and the views that sponsor it are both wrong. The history of philosophy is really philosophical just as philosophy proper is properly historical; i.e., both history and philosophy are deviations from "reality" and "propriety." The opinions of philosophers, taken out of the historical and dialectical context from which they emerged and to which they responded, are not philsophical. They are little more than antiquarian curiosities. So also the problems of philosophy are so far from timeless that they are continually redefined by the history of which they are part.

When the history of philosophy is written by a philosopher, as it often is, he (as he often is) tends to represent it as a series of brave but failed endeavors to state the truth that has at last found adequate formulation in his own work. The history of philosophy is a steady, if stumbling, progress that culminates in himself. Aristotle, the first philosopher to write a comprehensive account of the development of philosophy from the beginning to his own day, sees the views of previous thinkers as never quite successful or only partially successful attempts to come up with his own theory of causation. His view and others like it—Hegel leaps to mind as the most hybristic of the lot—are much more interesting, both philosophically and historically, than the chronicle view and the laborers-in-the-vineyard view. At least the philosophers who write the history of their discipline in this way see it as a single dramatic narrative with a plot of its own. Usually it's a melodrama, a lot of minor defeats on the way to ultimate victory. But not always. It may be a catastrophe, and the truth that finally triumphs may be the dark truth of skepticism, pessimism, or nihilism. But at least there is a story, and the story has a point whether cheerful or desolate.

Yet it's not quite convincing. Partly because the climactic truth proclaimed by the philosopher who writes the historical narrative sooner or later proves to be just another of those brave but failed attempts he saw in the work of his predecessors. But mainly because the narrative so constructed, even the dialectical divine comedy imagined by Hegel, is too simple, its plot too uniformly directed toward a single end. The history of philosophy is philosophy and vice versa. But both the history and the philosophy are more complicated, and the threads of their development more tangled, than this view would allow.

Thomas Kuhn has pointed out that the history of science is not the smooth and unbroken progress traditionally supposed. On the contrary, the course of "normal" science is periodically interrupted by abrupt changes of direction—agonizing reappraisals of its methods, goals, and problems. Kuhn calls these recurring crises "paradigm shifts," now a household word in the academic menage.[24] Analogously one could argue that philosophy, which is rarely accused of making progress, has had its own paradigm shifts. The course of philosophical history is determined and its progress (if any) defined by philosophers' continual reassessment and revision of their own enterprise.

The history of philosophy would then be the history of these reformulations of the philosophical problematic. Insofar as deconstruction is the latest and to date most radical of these upheavals, it could be said that deconstruction *is* the history of philosophy.

Viewed in this way, the history of philosophy is the process in which philosophy, repeatedly doubling back on itself, again and again reconceives its own history. The history of philosophy is the rewriting of the history of philosophy. As the life of the individual is a series of changes in which he becomes ever more certain of his own direction and ever more acutely conscious of his own mortality, so the history of philosophy is a series of *prises de conscience* by which philosophy becomes ever more certain of its objectives and ever more profoundly aware of the fragility of its project. But while the mortality of the person ends in death, the mortality of philosophy, not tied to the life of the individual, is potentially immortal. Philosophy's obituary would be yet another chapter in its history. And so the story of philosophy is endlessly rewritten. Deconstruction is the newest proposal for rewriting the history of philosophy and—since it too is written—the latest reinscription of that history.

Here again it is necessary to resist the temptation to think that as its history is prolonged, philosophy becomes more and more "metaphilosophical." The truth of deconstructive statements and the truth about them, a truth they themselves insist on, is not a metaphilosophical truth. Just as the self-consciousness of the individual is not a metaconsciousness but only a folding back of consciousness on itself and a rethinking of itself, so deconstruction is not a philosophy of philosophy, it is just philosophy engaged in rewriting its own history. Needless to say, the remarks I here set down, while philosophical, are not a "philosophy of deconstruction," but only one more record of the aftershocks of the deconstructive earthquake.

With these cautions, deconstruction may be identified as the final notch-up or ratcheting-back of self-consciousness in the history of philosophy so far. That history, in turn, is the repeated reinscription of itself from the points of view provided by its repeated *prises de conscience*, each of which is, in its own way and at its own historical moment, a deconstructive event. The history of philosophy is the history of its never-ending attempt to catch up with itself.

Richard Rorty once said, speaking of (and against) Heidegger: if being had anything to tell us, it would have to speak the language of Plato.[25] Long before Rorty, Whitehead remarked that the history of Western philosophy is a series of footnotes to Plato.[26] He had a point. It was after all the Greeks, the greatest of whom was Plato, who invented philosophy, defined rationality, and stipulated for all subsequent Western thinkers the conditions of intelligibility that make up what Derrida calls logocentrism. Being, identified by the pre-Socratics as the object of philosophical inquiry, would therefore have to speak the language of Plato if it wanted to say anything at all. But Whitehead's "footnotes" is too genteel a word. What he calls footnotes were far more subversive than the term suggests. Aristotle, who is Plato's legitimate heir and continuator, is also the subverter of the Platonic wisdom. And the philosophies of Plato and Aristotle alike were reconceived from the bottom up when they were folded into the texts and textures of Judeo-Christian-Islamic religion.

The most devastating revision of ancient, medieval, and early modern philosophy was Kant's Copernican revolution. What Derrida proposes under the name deconstruction is another and yet more disturbing trauma in the ongoing crisis of philosophy. Kant asked us to recognize that the object of knowledge is not being (the thing in itself) but representation (a product of the transcendental imagination). Deconstruction requires us to acknowledge that the very logic by which this distinction of being and representation is sponsored and sustained, not to mention the logic of the deconstructive proposal itself, is an unstable effect of the language in which it is inscribed. Kant asked us to reread the history of philosophy from the critical perspective, for which reality is accessible only as representation. Derrida demands that we rewrite the history of philosophy from the perspective of deconstruction, for which reality is accessible only as textual representation and textuality itself the endless closure of representation. For Kant representation is opposed to presence. The *Ding-an-sich* is still there, on the other side of appearances, albeit inaccessible. For Derrida representation inhabits presence. Being in itself is always only and never more than an effect of representation…so far as we "know."

To philosophize deconstructively is to rethink the history of philosophy in the shadow of the invincible suspicion (it could never become a fact) that philosophy is its history and its history its deconstruction. In that sense deconstruction is the history of philosophy and the history of philosophy is deconstruction. To say this makes it seem as if I had done, after all, one of the things I said I wouldn't do. I may not have domesticated deconstruction, but it does appear that I have demonized philosophy. Yet deconstruction no more demonizes the history of philosophy than the doctrine of original sin— a most deconstructive dogma—demonizes human history. Both of them just make life (and philosophy) infinitely more difficult. The doctrine of original sin puts us in a terrible predicament insofar as it reveals that the history of our race is the history of the fall. Deconstruction puts us in a terrible predicament insofar as it shows that the history of our concepts is the history of their deconstruction. The doctrine of original sin helps us understand our history insofar as it reveals that our history deconstructs itself. Deconstruction helps us understand the history of our concepts insofar as it shows that the history of our concepts is the deconstruction of their history. Would it be perverse to suggest that deconstruction is the philosophical face of original sin, and original sin the existential backside of deconstruction?

Derrida was often asked to say what comes after deconstruction. What happens to philosophy after it has been deconstructed? If what I have suggested is correct, then the answer is: nothing. Nothing comes after deconstruction, since the deconstruction of philosophy is never complete. And nothing comes after philosophy. It continues as its own deconstruction. Nevertheless, in the apocalyptic passages that appear now and then in his early works, Derrida suggests that the other-than-philosophy, its possibility opened up by deconstruction, would be something mute, infant, terrifying, and monstrous. Whatever might lie on the other side of philosophy could not be characterized in the discredited language of logocentrism and, since logocentrism defines the conditions of intelligibility, would not be intelligible at all. But Derrida also says, often in conjunction with these apocalyptic remarks, that you cannot step outside philosophy, go beyond it, turn the page and do something else.[27] Deconstruction announces the closure of philosophy, but both the closure and the announcement are endlessly iterated. More unsettling than any previous critique of the philosophical project, deconstruction is nevertheless not the negation of philosophy. Itself a moment within philosophy, deconstruction is the convulsive continuation of its already convulsive history.

In the United States deconstruction has made more converts among literary critics than it has among philosophers. Whatever one thinks of the practice of those who call themselves deconstructive critics, deconstruction is a way of reading and thereby internally linked to literature and the interpretation of literature. This linkage also has consequences for philosophy. The implications of Kant's philosophy were better understood by Romantic poets and critics than they were by his narrowly philosophical readers. The connections between deconstruction and literature should be taken at least as seriously by philosophers as they are by critics.

The conventional reading of a philosophical text concentrates on the doctrines proposed and the evidence offered in their support. The textual features to which a deconstructive reading calls attention are usually treated as external, perhaps even frivolous accidents of philosophical thought. But insofar as a deconstructive reading discloses that these so-called accidents are necessary to the formulation and defense of any philosophical position, to that extent such accidents are constitutive of the essence of philosophy and therefore conditions of whatever effects it may hope to achieve. The readings offered above recommend this conclusion.

These (as it were) essential accidents of philosophy are the elements of the text ordinarily regarded as literary. And when a philosopher calls them "literary," this is a way of identifying them as mere embellishments. Not part of the argument, they do no philosophical work, but function only as attention-getting or vivid-making devices that may be forgotten once the reader has mastered the argumentative substance. Deconstruction insists that these "literary" features of the text are far from expendable, that indeed the tropics of discourse constitute the object of philosophical thought. The represented is always and to an incalculable degree an effect of the means of representation. The perception of being is aboriginally mediated by its textual figuration.

From all of this it follows that philosophers should study fiction, not as a means of cultural enrichment or intellectual diversification, but as a necessary part of their philosophical formation and practice. For philosophy, while it is not to be confused with literature, is like literature a mode of fiction.

Plato was at pains to clarify the relationship between philosophy and poetry. Partly because their distinction was still contentious in his day. And partly because, himself both philosopher and poet, their ancient quarrel was raging in his own psyche. But most of all because the antagonism and interdependence between philosophy and poetry is staged in his own thinking. For Plato, the goal of philosophy is to arrive by means of dialectic at a vision of eternal and immutable reality, and to express what is thus directly known in clear and unequivocal *logoi*. Yet all our words and all our thoughts are trapped in this world of appearances, never more than imperfect imitations of the eternal and immutable in the realm of time and change. Even if the vision of truth is not altogether beyond our reach, our descriptions of it can never be *verbatim*, but always only figurative. The philosopher, as long as he dwells in the body, is obliged to be a poet, even though the philosophical understanding of truth is inevitably occluded and dissembled in the figures of poetry.

In the philosophy of Kant Plato's problem is declared a destiny. The perception of transcendent truth is denied us, and the only reality of which we have knowledge is an activity of the most august imagination. We may symbolize for ourselves a supersensible ground of appearances, but we only know the world we have made. This implication of Kant's philosophy was eagerly seized upon and inflated to cosmic proportions by his Romantic successors in Germany and beyond, many of whom were poets or poetic philosophers.[28] But there is still, for Kant, a distinction between what we might call the necessary and primary fictions (schemata) produced by the transcendental imagination of the first *Critique* and the secondary fictions elaborated more or less *ad libitum* by the aesthetic imagination of the third *Critique*. The former make up the world of objects available for cognition. The latter give expression to the pre-cognitive disposition of the mind that makes cognition possible and to the ultra-cognitive hope that the mind and its supersensible substrate are somehow in primal and final rapport.[29]

The Kantian distinction between necessary fictions, produced by the imagination under the guidance of the understanding, and the fictions created by the imagination in its freedom, is obliterated by deconstruction. No longer ordered and provided with a referent by the transcendental signified—the object-in-general defined for Kant by the *a priori* conditions of the possibility of experience—the signifiers of discourse now signify only their relations to each other. In the terms of Northrop Frye's distinction, words and structures made of words are no longer signs but motifs, their reference to the signified replaced by the patterns they make among themselves.[30]

Almost. Deconstruction does not substitute for the referentiality of the classical view of language a literary absolute created by the poetic imagination. Language consisting entirely of non-signifying motifs would not be language but only decor. It would certainly not have the quasi-divine potency accorded it by the Romantics. For deconstruction language necessarily incorporates the intention to represent and to refer, though it can no longer know if and when it has succeeded in doing so. Its representationality and its referentiality are therefore indeterminate. It cannot be determined to have terminated at the referent it meant to represent. The conditions of representation cannot be represented, and conditions of closure cannot be stipulated, for and by a language the essence of which is to lack them. Such a language can only, by means of determinate figurations, represent its own indeterminate representationality.

But this is a definition of fiction. Fiction is the determinate (figural) representation of the indeterminate representationality of the means of representation. As such, no piece of language is determined as true or false. Every piece of language is in undecidable potency to both. So understood, fiction is not a deviation from fact, but the ground (*Grund*) and the abyss (*Abgrund*, *abîme*) of the distinction between true and false, real and unreal. Those groups of representations (figures) that we denominate "true" or "real" are selections made, for a variety of reasons ranging from the pragmatic to the profound, out of the whole range of representation (fiction) and invested with the power and value of truth and reality. In this way, fiction is at once the ground of true and false, real and unreal, and their abyssing, since it is the possibility of all such determinations and the sponsor of none.[31]

Their common ficticity is the foundation of the kinship between philosophy and literature and the undoing of their difference. This is not to say that philosophy and literature are identical. It is only to acknowledge that both philosophy and literature, the distinction between them obvious and penultimate, are textual (fictive) and thereby entrusted with all the powers of textuality, engaged with all its problems, and submitted to all its effects. Not the least of these is the way every text both constructs and deconstructs its object in the act of representing it. A philosophy is a system of representations that asserts its truth and in so doing problematizes its veracity. A work of literature is a system of representations that knows itself to be false and by such knowledge betrays its truth. If the literary text has any advantage in this connection, it derives from this specular awareness of its fundamental ficticity. Writers of such works, remembering that they are fabulators and continually reminded of it by philosophers, are by this self-consciousness alerted to the duplicity of the mimetic project: that language creates its object and by creating it perforates its object's purported reality with its own profounder ficticity.

Northrop Frye has remarked that philosophy is not thinking but a verbal imitation of thought.[32] Kierkegaard's anonymous aesthete gives this observation an ironic edge:

> What the philosophers say about reality is often as disappointing as a sign you see in a shop window, which reads: Pressing Done Here. If you brought your clothes to be pressed, you would be fooled; for the sign is only for sale.[33]

Deconstruction adds that neither Frye's thought nor the aesthete's reality is ever directly apprehended. All we get are signs and imitations: simulacra that imply but cannot deliver an original that is therefore not their origin but their effect. Being is a by-product of the means by which we are constrained to think it and to speak it, and in so doing, to misrepresent it as the source and end of our speaking and thinking.

Like all verbal constructs, philosophy is a mode of fiction—in philosophy's case, the fiction of its own truth. This does not mean that it is impossible to tell the truth in philosophy. But it does mean that philosophy must rethink the concept of truth and what it would mean to tell it.

> We have been a little insane about the truth. We have had an obsession. In its ultimate extension the truth about which we have been insane will lead us to look beyond the truth to something in which the imagination will be the dominant component It is not only that the imagination adheres to reality, but, also, that reality adheres to the imagination and that the interdependence is essential.[34]

In philosophy, as in all things, we have to do first, last, and always with representations. But the concept of representation is dialectical. A representation presents again something already given. In that sense imagination depends on reality. At the same time, representation is not presence but mediation, and thus the distancing and deferring (the *différance*) of the represented. In that sense reality depends on the imagination. This dialectical interdependence of the real and the imaginary is essential.

> The final belief is to believe in a fiction, which you know to be a fiction, there being nothing else. The exquisite truth is to know that it is a fiction and that you believe in it willingly.[35]

It is the depth of the complicity of imagination and reality, fiction and belief, that constitutes the relation, and the doubly duplicitous character of the relation, between philosophy and poetry. It is this ambiguous intimacy, to which deconstruction directs our attention, that mandates for philosophers the study of literature. Without a comprehension of the truth of fiction expressed in the text of literature, it is impossible to understand the fiction of truth that drives the text of philosophy. Philosophy, which is born when the rational pursuit of truth declares its independence of myth and fable, is returned by the consideration of its own ficticity to the contemplation of its origin. And the series of deconstructive crises by which the history of philosophy is moved and shaken brings it at last to a total and final confrontation with its never-ending incompletion.

14

Philosophy: To Be Continued

The title of this talk may have led you to conclude that the speaker believes, a propos the theme of this conference, that there is no "last chapter" of philosophy. That conclusion—the only one here tendered—would not be unwarranted. But why did he put it at the beginning? and in the title? "To be continued," the denial of an ending, usually comes at the end of the chapter— every chapter until the last, at the end of which comes, with a sigh of relief, the reassuring words "The End." This is it, this is all there is, there will be no more: THE END. But to put it in the title, after "Philosophy colon," strongly suggests that philosophy is always already incomplete, unfinished from the word Go—and by implication that this conference on the last chapter of philosophy is dedicated to what was a non-entity to begin with. But that might be a misunderstanding. The Call for Papers makes it clear, in the medium-sized print, that the last chapter of philosophy flaunted in the large print really refers to the last *chapters* of philosophy *books*. For example, Book N of *Metaphysics*. Overlooking the fact that the *Metaphysics* is not a book, but an editor's compilation of texts he could not otherwise classify, it is still appropriate to observe that Book N is not the last chapter of that long and difficult (non)book without meter.[1] N and its predecessor M are both collections of, for the most part, assorted criticisms of Plato. If there were a last chapter of the *Metaphysics*, it would have to be the climactic ascent to the Unmoved Mover in L. But even that, as the patchwork character of the text indicates, is not a conclusion but a work still in progress. Maybe there is no last chapter of Aristotle's *Metaphysics*. We have certainly not seen the end of it yet.

St. Augustine is no better when it comes to ending. Book XIII is not the last chapter of the *Confessions*, but rather (along with XI and XII) the first

— CALL FOR PAPERS —

University of Texas at
AUSTIN
Graduate Student
CONFERENCE
April 17-18, 1998

"THE LAST CHAPTER OF PHILOSOPHY"

Republic X   Metaphysics N   Confessions XIII
Meditation VI   Monadology §90
Enquiries XII   The History of Pure Reason
Absolute Knowing   Zarathustra Book 4
Tractatus 7   Being and Time II.VI.§83

Graduate students are invited to submit papers or detailed abstracts dealing with various aspects of the (often under-read or overlooked) final chapters. sections. or moments of philosophical texts. How do these concluding thoughts stand in relation to the remainder of the work? How do they inform or deform the coherence of the philosophical project at hand? How does one properly close a book on philosophy? Papers may focus on a single text or a range of works (the titles above are merely suggestions). and may employ a wide variety of approaches. Panel proposals are welcome. Also. although the conference will focus on this theme. all submitted philosophical papers will be read and considered.

---

installment of an unfinished commentary on *Genesis*. The story of Augustine's life ends with Monica's death and burial in Book IX, after which he interrogates memory—the source from which his narrative is drawn—and memory sends him back to that Beginning from whom heaven and earth are continually proceeding. Origin without end, and no conclusion in sight.

You might expect the moderns to succeed where the ancients failed. No such luck. The "History of Pure Reason" is not the last chapter of the first *Critique*. It is only a title, a project for future workers to carry out. The *Critique* itself ended much earlier in the Dialectic—just where is not perfectly clear—with (you guessed it) a prophecy of things to come. Hume's Essay XII, harking back to Essay I, far from offering a philosophic conclusion, recommends an abstention from philosophizing, except insofar as a certain intellectual discipline may help to curb the excesses of speculation and skepticism alike. *Das absolute Wissen* is not the long-awaited and much-heralded grand finale of the *Phenomenology*, but only a brief promissory note dashed off in haste in order to get a manuscript to the printer before the outbreak of the battle of Jena—concerning which Hegel presumably had advance notice from the *Weltgeist*. And what shall we say of Proposition 7? Whereof the *Tractatus* does not speak, far be it from me to break the silence. The world is everything that is the case, and everything worth saying is ineffable.

So here we are, close to the end of modern philosophy, and still no concluding chapter. Kant went on to write two more *Critiques*, Hegel produced the *Encyclopedia*, and even Wittgenstein started all over again after the resounding finality of Proposition 7. Apparently he never did make the discovery that would enable him to stop philosophizing.

But this might be a misunderstanding. What does it mean, and of what importance is it, that philosophers are not good at reaching conclusions? They *do* write last chapters. The books don't actually go on forever, they only seem to. It's just that these last chapters are not conclusions.

Novelists are much better at conclusions. But that's because they're novelists. They're faking it, writing fictions. Whereas philosophers (permit them this one fiction) are trying to tell the truth. And truth, like the road in Middle Earth, winds ever on beyond zebra.[2] On this inspiriting view of the matter, the philosopher's inability to come to a conclusion, wrap it up and pack it in, is evidence of her election—or at least of her honesty. She will sell no philosophy before its time.[3] It's easy for novelists. They can disregard the truth and make up the facts they need to produce a satisfactory sense of an ending. Much harder to keep the imagination in check and follow the truth wherever it may lead for as long as it takes to get there.

But of course this is nonsense. Life has little to offer in the way of conclusions other than death. And death is not an ending save for (maybe) the deceased. Life goes on without him. But even when it's an end, death is rarely a conclusion. Few indeed are the deaths of which one can say, *consummatum est*. It is much harder to create a convincing and consummatory fictional finale than it is simply to go with the flow until it—and you—peter out.

This is more nonsense. Philosophers don't just quit. It may not do so in the last chapter, but every comprehensive systematic work in philosophy, as opposed to the occasional philosophical essay, at some level and in some respect claims for itself closure and totality. Few philosophers are so crass as to say: what all my predecessors were trying to do I have finally succeeded in doing, what they did poorly I have done well, and what they did wrong I have done right. But every major thinker in the tradition does claim, at least implicitly, to have achieved a perspective from which all the problems of philosophy fall into place and finally admit of solution. Or to have redefined the philosophical enterprise in such a way that it now has at least a chance of success. Or to have found the missing piece of the puzzle, the proper emplacement of which will permit the big picture to be seen clearly for the first time. Or something of what sort. Some variation on the theme: At last! The end is in sight!

Kant modestly confesses that he has not solved all the problems of philosophy. But he candidly admits that he has provided the key to their solution.[4] It is a crude misunderstanding to suppose that Hegel thinks his philosophy the last of which the world shall ever have need. But he did believe that all the wisdom of the past, both East and West, had finally achieved its proper form in his system and that all future philosophy would perpetuate and alembicate his definitive dialectic. Aristotle, it appears, felt that his theory of causation was the truth toward which all his predecessors had been groping.[5] In particular, he thought he had made the adjustments in the Platonic organism—some of them requiring major surgery—necessary to its healthy functioning. Augustine was confidant that the Christian revelation had saved Platonism from the twin perils of skeptical despair and gnostic presumption and granted it access to the truth it had always desired and never possessed.

But there is no point in going on this way, listing to port and starboard. Anyone with even a modest knowledge of the history of philosophy could extend these litanies on his own, *ad tedium* if not *ad infinitum*. The question is not, What happened? We all know what happened. The question is, What does it all mean? What does it mean that philosophers seem to be incapable of writing last chapters that are really final, while at the same time every major philosopher claims to have founded, fulfilled, saved, empowered, or refreshed philosophy in a way that is ... final? Conclusive. Once done, will never have to be done again. What it means perhaps is this. Every philosopher is not only writing her own (small p) philosophical text, every philosopher is also writing (capital P) Philosophy. And the scarcity of really final last chapters in the former means that there is really no finality in the latter. Or maybe the philosopher's claim to have achieved (capital P) Philosophical finality on the whole subsumes, sublates, and *verklärt* the default of convincing conclusions in the parts.

But it is necessary to be serious. And the serious fact of the matter is that every major philosopher both makes large claims to finality and totality and at the same time fails to give us that satisfying sense of an ending we get (though we may think it feigned) from a good novelist or a good playwright. What bodes this strange cohabitation of preposterous promise and paltry performance?

As a way into this question (there is no guarantee that once in we shall find our way out again) we might ask: what would it mean to conclude in philosophy? To conclude Philosophy in general and to conclude philosophies in particular. And, as a corollary to this, why do we desire conclusions in philosophy? Why should things have to end? Why should anything be complete?

Think again about the non-philosophical writer like the novelist or poet. A bit earlier I suggested that the writer of fiction is able to come to a conclusion because, as fabulator or *poietes*, he can fake it—cook up any conclusion that satisfies him. But that's only half the truth, the false half. The whole truth is that the conclusion of a literary work is both a true ending and a false conclusion.

In setting out to produce a novel, the novelist poses a problem for himself—e.g., writing a whole novel without the letter e. If he is sufficiently master of his art, he may well succeed, as Georges Perec did in *La Disparition*.[6] The text he produces will therefore be a true ending: a real solution to a real problem. But a false conclusion, since the vocation of the novelist is not exhausted in the production of one novel or group of novels, no matter how ambitious the project or how successful its prosecution. The novelist's vocation is, in a rough and ready way, to explore and exploit all the problems and possibilities of language. But these, both problems and possibilities, are, it is easy to imagine, infinite, or, if not infinite, so close to infinite as to be indistinguishable therefrom. And no novelist who is well in his wits, assuming that the profession of writing is compatible with sanity, would ever suppose that he had brought literature itself to completion. Nor, for that matter, that he had even produced the unique and definitive solution of the problem he set himself. It is not impossible, even in French, to write two novels without e's. And if two, why not some greater number approaching infinity? The lipogrammatic possibilities are incalculable. In that sense even the writer's solution to his particular literary problem is faked. It is necessarily a finite and therefore a forced closure of a field of possibilities that sprawls out of control in all directions in spite of his best efforts to fence it off.

Happily, the writer's work is never done. I say "happily" because there is no reason to believe that the writer, however pleased he may be to have finished his novel, would want literature itself to be finished thereby and himself immortalized as the the man who brought prose fiction to an end. The history of literature, like the history of science, is propelled on its way by a series of paradigm shifts. Every time it seems that all the problems have been solved and all the fictional possibilities used up, someone redefines the whole project. What appeared to be a literature of exhaustion, or an exhaustion of literature, was only the end of the "normal" novel—whether that be realist, naturalist, modernist, whatever—exhaustion becomes repletion, and we're off and running once more.

I don't know how scientists feel about this. I'm sure that no reputable physicist seriously believes that physics will one day be omniscient, so that physicists can publish the results (a few simple equations accompanied by a slender volume of prose explanation), close the shop, and go home to rest from their labors. What I do not know is whether the scientists would welcome this eventuality as an occasion of rejoicing. I suspect the wiser ones would be suspicious.

Philosophers, however, are more inclined to offer final solutions, or the key to all future final solutions, than scientists are. In one and the same book Kant (a) claims that he has put metaphysics in its proper place once and for all and (b) argues that the labors of the scientist will never end. He was right about science, but the history of philosophy after Kant suggests that his claim to have settled the fortunes of metaphysics may have been just a bit premature. The early analytic philosophers, who were convinced that what are called philosophical problems are really not problems at all but only puzzles generated by an abuse of ordinary language, hoped to expose the illusion and shut down the whole enterprise. Some of them thought it would take about fifty years. But these are the people who eventually became the greatest empire builders in the history of the discipline, so they are not to be taken at their word. My own belief (and I'm not to be taken at my word either) is that the philosopher should take his cue from the novelist. In the remainder of this talk I will try to explain what I mean by this and why I believe it.

I am convinced that, at its deepest level and in its widest extent, philosophy is not concerned with problems but with something that, for want of a better word and in keeping with a suggestion of Gabriel Marcel, can only be called mystery. The difference between problem and mystery I take to be something like this. In the nature of the case, a problem can be solved. The terms in which it is stated define what will count as a solution. Confronted on a math test with a problem that cannot be solved, the student has every right to complain that it "isn't really a problem." Like a problem, a mystery is an indeterminate situation that begs to be made determinate. But its indeterminacy is such that the description of the mystery does not specify conditions of resolution and closure. For that matter, the mystery itself cannot be fully described. Faced with a mystery, you can never be sure what will count as a solution, or even that there is one.

Mysteries are the sort of things that are sometimes called "the big questions:" where did I come from? where am I going? what is the meaning of life? Questions like this are so "big," so crudely formulated, and so underdetermined that the positivistically minded have often dismissed them as "not really questions." And of course they aren't really questions if a question is a problem. But they may be mysteries, sources of puzzlement that demand a response even though they cannot be crisply stated and definitively resolved. Then again, they might be nothing but confusions. That's the difficult thing about mysteries. You never know for sure when you've got a real one on your hands and when you're just confused. With problems you're on surer ground. You know what the question is and how to go about looking for an answer. Herein lies the philosophers' predicament. They never really understand what they're up *against* and what they're up *to*, because they're occupied with mysteries rather than with problems.

Philosophers, I have suggested, are end-of-the-line people even if they aren't very good at final solutions. They're not content to tinker with little mysteries. They want to tackle the big one. And for philosophy the mystery of mysteries—the "puzzle of puzzles"—is the *meaning* and the *fact* of being.

The poet asks, "To be in any form, what is that?"[7] Why should anything exist at all? And what does it mean that something does? No doubt this is a question that cannot, in the usual sense, be answered or even satisfactorily formulated. But it is for all that the founding and persisting question of philosophy.

Philosophy, the ancients tell us, is born in wonder. In this respect Aquinas observes, glossing Aristotle's *philomythos*, the philosopher is akin to the poet, both of them moved by wonder.[8] But you do not wonder at a problem. You gird your intellectual loins and get to work solving it. You wonder at a mystery. And the mystery that inspires the wonder in which philosophy begins, no matter how many problems may have been solved along the way, is still there when philosophy ends. But of course it never really ends at all. The geometer, Aristotle says, wonders at the incommensurability of the diagonal and is satisfied when he has explained why it must be so.[9] But the incommensurability and the mystery of it are not, as the Pythagoreans knew, destroyed by the explanation.

When I say that philosophy originates in and is sustained by mystery, I hope it will be understood that I do not mean to mystify. I certainly do not mean to suggest that philosophy consists in mystification. Far from it. Mystification is no good to anyone who is not up to no good. Philosophy does not consist in gazing, slackjawed and stupefied, into the abyss of its own profundity. Philosophy, as a response to the mystery of being, should be the most rigorous and self-critical kind of thinking. But by "rigorous" I do not intend the exactitude that is properly cultivated in the formal disciplines—an exactitude achieved at the cost of the exclusion or oblivion of substance. Philosophy should not dream the scientistic dream—a dream that no real scientist dreams of dreaming—of distilling the mystery of being down to a set of manageable problems and ticking them off one by one. The rigor proper to philosophy is its fidelity to the mystery of being by which it is first aroused, to the guardianship of which it is perpetually committed—a rigor that prevents both the demotion of mystery to problem and the volatilization of mystery into oracular windbagging. To say that philosophy is a response to mystery is to say that all philosophical problems are formulated and discussed within a context that cannot be saturated or bounded, a context that demands to be articulated in problems, creates problems, but is never exhausted by or reduced to the problems it generates. The kinship between philosophy and poetry (where "poetry" is shorthand for imaginative writing of all sorts), beginning with their common origin in wonder but not ending there, should be evident from the fact that there is in both of them the same conjunction of provisional success at solving problems and ultimate failure to exhaust the mystery that gave them birth.[10] In ancient Greece philosophy created itself by rejecting the poets' mythic accounts of the origin and nature of the cosmos. In creating itself it also created poetry. For neither myth nor poetry were defined as such until philosophers, casting themselves as the custodians of a truth they themselves had defined, classified the authors of the traditional narratives as mendacious fabulists. Quoting with approval what must have been a philosopher's proverb, Aristotle observes that "bards tell many a lie"[11] and points out that the recognition scene in the *Odyssey* is premised on a fallacy of affirming the consequent— though, he adds, its invalidity does not diminish its poetic power.[12] That power is obviously not the power of logic, though poetry may dissemble logic, hoping to appropriate its authority.

The first philosophers of whom we have record, the Milesian physicists, come on as scientists. Their accounts of the nature of things, offered as rational alternatives to myth, are themselves naturalistic in the sense of "materialistic." All things are water, or all things are air. But one of their number, Anaximander, throws a spanner into the works. The *apeiron*, from which he says all things arise and to which they return, is not in any obvious sense material. It certainly is and certainly could have been (I take it this was part of what he meant to say) none of the four elements. The source of the material elements cannot itself be one of them, and if it is matter, it is material only in the ghostly sense that Aristotle's prime matter is material. Even the views of the atomists, so often hailed as prophecies of modern physical science, are embedded in a narrative—the everlasting rain of atoms through the void, the random but fateful *clinamen* that generates infinite worlds, the intermundane abodes of the gods, etc.—that is at least as fantastic as anything Hesiod produced. Though now the fantasy has become something more like science fiction, similar to the alternative creation myths proposed by modern scientists from Darwin to Hawking.

Be that as it may, the philosophers' preoccupation with mystery, a preoccupation they share willy-nilly with the poets, reasserted itself at Ephesus and at Elea. The *logos* or cosmic reason of Heracleitus takes the form of contradiction—war is peace, day is night, strife is justice. Heracleitus' reputation for obscurity, which he no doubt earned by talking in this way, recalls Wallace Stevens' dictum that "poetry must resist the intelligence almost successfully."[13] His conviction of the ultimacy of metaphor and his disdain for the literal-minded medical profession (this much is clear) is revealed in his fatal attempt at self-treatment when the doctors did not understand his meteorological figuration of dropsy. (This we have on the authority of Diogenes Laertius, who hardly ever said anything false.) Meanwhile, at the western end of the Greek world, Parmenides' rigorously logical monism is obliged to express itself in a poem the very existence of which is inexplicable in if not actually proscribed by the terms of his philosophy.

Philosophy is a provisional activity, the provisional character of which can never be fully and finally transcended, just as myth or mythopoeia is an origin that is never original and scientific understanding an end that is not terminal. For myth, the unoriginal original response to mystery, demands rational-critical restatement aimed in the direction of science. And in fact, the sciences did emerge from philosophy. But as philosophy moves from myth to science, translating mystery into problem, so science at its leading edge and outer reaches becomes more and more philosophical and verges at last (for the time being) on myth and the re-encounter with mystery. Scientific cosmogonies of the Big Bang and theological attempts to trace everything that exists to a first cause are not in the end all that different.

The point of all this is that philosophy, like poetry and (yes) like science as well, cannot long ignore its origin in wonder at the mystery of being, an origin to which it returns again and again. Heidegger, remembering Leibniz remembering Aquinas and Avicenna, asks, *Warum ist überhaupt Seindes und nicht vielmehr Nichts?*[14] Why is there anything at all rather than nothing? Lest this be thought just another whiff of the continental gas, it was Wittgenstein, an analytic philosopher in good standing, who said, *"Nicht wie die Welt ist, ist das Mystische, sondern das sie ist."*[15] Not what the world is like, but the fact that it exists—that is the mystical. If a question can be asked, Wittgenstein tells us, it can be answered. Whatever can be said can be said clearly. Yet there are things which, though they make themselves manifest, cannot be put into words. It is of these—the mysteries— that one must be silent. But silence, while it makes an end of question and answer, is not a conclusion. The mystery in which philosophy begins persists and would continue to persist even in the unlikely event that philosophy were to solve all its problems.

For (to return to my theme) philosophers *do* formulate problems, offer solutions, and defend their solutions with arguments. But the formulations, the solutions, and the arguments are all situated within the context of what, following Kuhn, we may call "normal" philosophy. *Some* normal philosophy, for there have been from time to time as many normal philosophies as there have been normal sciences. The philosopher's conception of what philosophy is and does will govern his formulation of the problems he tries to solve. It will tell him what counts as a problem and therewith what will count as a solution. Even the form of his argumentation—what for him counts as an argument—is determined by his conception of philosophy. For there is no logic as such and in general that regulates, or should regulate, all thinking at all times about everything. There are only, but importantly, multiple logics, the "logic" of each determined by the reigning paradigm of philosophy. Within the paradigm of Cartesian rationalism problems suggested by that paradigm can be formulated, discussed, and (occasionally) resolved. Likewise within the paradigm of Lockean empiricism. And since these two are parts of a larger paradigm, early modern philosophy as a whole has a distinctive problematic. That problematic dominated philosophical thought until Kant's Copernican revolution proposed a new paradign, redefined philosophy, and gave birth to a new philosophical norm.

The formulation, discussion, and resolution of philosophical problems is always and irreducibly *situated*. This cannot be recalled too often, so prone are philosophers to forget it. As we are all predisposed to forget that our "universal human" values may be just the values of our culture, so we (philosophers) too easily lose sight of the fact that philosophical problems are located within and defined by a context itself bounded by the reigning philosophical paradigm. But the paradigms themselves, like local and epochal cultures, are situated within larger and ever larger contexts in the history of philosophy. Thus philosophical problems can arise at different levels of generality, and the nature of generality itself repeatedly reconceived. But in the end—which is not and never can be a real end—all problems, all solutions, and all argumentation are located within a context of the whole— which is not and never can be really a whole—the outer limits of which cannot be drawn because it is the philosopher's response to the mystery of being.

That last is what, for example, Platonism is. Not the problems Plato raises or is confronted with, not his solutions to those problems nor the reasons he offers in their support. But rather: Plato's reply to the question— not asked *by* him but asked *of* him—what does it mean to be? What does it mean that there is something and not nothing? If that is not what Platonism is, then Plato is not a philosopher we should remember and to whom we should return again and again, only a professional hack deserving of oblivion. But Plato is in no danger. Northrop Frye has said that the irrefutable philosopher is not the one who cannot be refuted but the one who is still there after he has been refuted.[16] There is only one Plato, who is still alive and well. The number of his refuters—I do not mean revisionists or proponents of new paradigms—is legion, and they are all dead and forgotten.

My title implies that philosophy never ends. Though philosophy books may have (*per accidens*) last chapters, philosophy itself (*simpliciter*) is never finished. Philosophy may have its back pages, but there is no conclusion. I think that is the case, and I have tried to explain why I think so. But there's more to it than that. To say that philosophy is to be continued means that it *will* be continued; there *will be* more, and there will *always* be more. But the expression "to be continued" can also have a gerundive force, so that "philosophy is to be continued" may mean *continuenda est philosophia*: philosophy *should* be, *must* be continued. I believe it does mean that. For if philosophy is the response of wonder to the mystery of existence, and if that mystery is never mastered—turned into a question and answered once and for all—then it is essential that philosophy be the continued and continual renewal of that experience and that response. An articulate response, to be sure, a response that aims at the conceptual clarification of that which it can finally only figure, a response that like science generates problems but always and essentially transgresses its own problematic—in short, a response that explores but never exhausts the mystery that is given it perpetually to ponder. Philosophy in this sense, though akin to poetry in its commitment to figuration, is not like poetry the attempt to adumbrate reality by means of the proliferation of metaphor. Though akin to theology in its response to the gift of existence and its commitment to the ultimacy of mystery, it is not like theology the conceptual restatement of a purported self-revelation of the divine. Philosophy is a sustained meditation, moving ceaselessly and restlessly between figuration and conceptualization, on the fact and the meaning of the fact that there is (*es gibt*) being.[17] The restlessness is essential. Any philosopher who thinks he knows what he's doing, has done, and has yet to do has missed his vocation. Only the philosopher who is dissatisfied is faithful to her calling. "Questioning"—not answering—"is the piety of thought."[18]

Heidegger once proposed that all genuine thinking (*Denken*), as opposed to mere calculation, is a mode of commemoration (*Andenken*), a repeated recollection of its origin in mystery, and by the same token a profound thanksgiving (*Danken*) for the grace of being.[19] A contemporary student of Heidegger, oriented to the future rather than like his teacher, to the past, has remarked the apocalyptic character of philosophy.[20] In which connection we should recall the two marks of every apocalypse: revelation and termination. The full and clear revelation of the meaning of being, by putting an end to mystery, would also terminate philosophy. But this is neither to be feared nor desired. Philosophical thinking is not only the thankful recollection of origin, it is also—and for this too we may be thankful—the annunciation of an apocalypse that will never arrive.[21]

To conclude this entertainment on a serious note, and in order that you may have something of value to take away from this momentary diversion, here is the moral of the story. Actually there are two morals. First: in this time of shifting philosophical paradigms—that it is perceived as such is suggested by the apocalyptic theme of this conference—the most urgent task of philosophers may be to reflect on the nature and purpose of their enterprise. Among the "big questions" are the ones I have here addressed, however rudely, and herewith recommend as topics for further consideration: what are we doing? and why are we doing it? And here's the second moral. Taking a doctorate in philosophy will not guarantee anyone a job. But if what I have said is anywhere within the vast ballpark of truth, the end that is ever announced will never come, and anyone who is a real philosopher will always have something to do.

Notes

Chapter 1

1. The character is called "the Fox" ("Aphrodite" in Greek), and her exact words are "a very long, hard book (without metre) which begins *All men by nature desire knowledge.*" C. S. Lewis, *Till We Have Faces* (London: Geoffrey Bles, 1956), p. 241.
2. Aristotle, *Metaphysics* XII 8 107a1-14.
3. Aristotle, *Poetics* 9 1351a36-b9.
4. Walter Pater, *Plato and Platonism* (New York: Macmillan, 1893), pp 2-4.
5. Aristotle, *Metaphysics* I 2 983a3-4
6. For the father of lies, see John 8: 44 KJV; for an unflattering view of philosophy, see Colossians 2: 8
7. The references in this paragraph are to Oscar Wilde's Preface to *The Picture of Dorian Gray* and to Percy B. Shelley's *A Defense of Poetry, ad finem.*
8. There is a comparable requirement levied against undergraduate majors, to which everything here said applies *mutatis mutandis.*
9. St. Augustine, *De libero arbitrio voluntatis*, Bk. II, XII, 133-136.
10. I Corinthians 10: 11.
11. In *An Apology for Poetry*, Sir Philip Sidney says that the poet "nothing affirms, and therefore never lieth.... And therefore, though he recount things not true, yet because he telleth them not for true, he lieth not." Richard Rorty's essay, "Is There a Problem about Fictional Discourse?", is instructive in this connection. The essay is found in his *Consequences of Pragmatism* (Minneapolis: University of Minnesota Press, 1982), pp.110-138.
12. St. Anselm, *Proslogion, Prooemium*, II-III. Cf. Louis Mackey, *Peregrinations of the Word: Essays in Medieval Philosophy* (Ann Arbor: University of Michigan Press, 1997), ch. 3.
13. Ursula K. LeGuin, unpaginated Introduction to *The Left Hand of Darkness* (New York: Ace Books, 1976).

Chapter 2

1. I quote the Kemp Smith translation, but the original does not suffer by comparison. Parenthetical page references are to *Immanuel Kant's Critique of Pure Reason*, translated by Norman Kemp Smith (London: Macmillan, 1929). I cite both the pages of this edition and of the German text it renders.
2. Vaihinger is not clear about science. Sometimes he speaks as if the sciences, just like philosophy, depend on the use of fictions for their success. But his devotion to the idea of *Wissenschaft* occasionally causes him to claim that in the natural sciences and in history fictions have no place, only verifiable hypotheses. Hans Vaihinger, *The Philosophy of 'As if'*, translated by C. K. Ogden (London: Routledge & Kegan Paul, 1935), p. 79n. Parenthetical page references in the text cite this edition
3. Vaihinger's view, which grew by fits and starts over a period of several years, is set out in a way that only too faithfully mirrors its genesis. The form in which I here present it, for the sake of clarity and brevity, is over-simplified but I hope not distorted.
4. Kant himself seems to have been aware of this. He writes in the first edition deduction, "Psychologists have hitherto failed to realise that imagination is a necessary ingredient of perception itself." (CPR 144/KrV A121a) And of course the imagination is instructed by the forms of intuition and the categories.
5. *The Collected Poems of Wallace Stevens* (New York: Alfred A. Knopf, 1954), p. 332.
6. Peirce made this observation in a 1909 letter to William James. For his exact words, see Nicholas Rescher, *Many-valued Logic* (New York: McGraw-Hill, 1969), p. 5.

Chapter 3

1. Owen Barfield, *Saving the Appearances: A Study in Idolatry* (London: Faber and Faber, 1957), p. 13.
2. Aristotle, *Poetics* 9, 1451a-b7.
3. Hayden White, *Metahistory: The Historical Imagination in Nineteenth-Century Europe* (Baltimore: Johns Hopkins University Press, 1973), especially Part One, but also *passim*. Elements of the argument of *Metahistory* are restated in some of the essays in Hayden White, *Tropics of Discourse. Essays in Cultural Criticism* (Baltimore: Johns Hopkins University Press, 1978).
4. Northrop Frye, *Anatomy of Criticism* (Princeton: Princeton University Press, 1957), First Essay. For Frye's explanation of displacement, see *Anatomy of Criticism*, pp.136-137, 365. See also Northrop Frye, *Fables of Identity: Studies in Poetic Mythology* (New York: Harcourt, Brace and World, 1963), pp.21-38.
5. See Kenneth Burke, *A Grammar of Motives* (Berkeley: University of California Press, 1969), pp. 503-517, for a major theoretical discussion of irony. But

irony is not only a topic discussed in Burke's corpus; it is also the dominant trope of his own texts.

6.   I invoke Frye and Burke partly to suggest a congruence between what Hayden White does with historiography and what I like to do with philosophy; partly because it was White, among others, who gave me the idea of approaching philosophy in this way; and partly because I believe it works.

7.   David Hume, *An Enquiry Concerning Human Understanding* (Indianapolis: Hackett Publishing Co., 1993), second edition, pp. 89-90. Søren Kierkegaard, *Training in Christianity*, translated by Walter Lowrie (Princeton: Princeton University Press, 1947), pp. 132-133.

8.   Frye, *Anatomy of Criticism*, p. 83. For other asides of this sort, see pp. 326-337, 352-353, 12.

9.   Friedrich Nietzsche, *Beyond Good and Evil*, translated by Walter Kaufmann (New York: Random House, 1966), pp. 2, 148-149; and Friedrich Nietzsche, "Truth and Falsity in an Ultramoral Sense," translated by Oscar Levy, in Geoffrey Clive, ed., *The Philosophy of Nietzsche* (New York: New American Library, 1965), pp. 503-515.

10. Josiah Royce, *The Philosophy of Loyalty* (New York: Macmillan, 1924), pp. 101-146.

11. Søren Kierkegaard, *Concluding Unscientific Postscript*, translated by David F. Swenson and Walter Lowrie (Princeton: Princeton University Press, 1941), pp. 169-244.

12. Frye, *Anatomy of Criticism*, p. 337.

13. St. Hilary of Poitiers, *De Trinitate*, Bk. V, nos. 3, 5, 14, and *passim*; cited at, *inter alia*, St. Thomas Aquinas, *Summa Theologica*, Ia, q. 16, a. 1, *corpus*.

14. Frye, *Anatomy of Criticism*, pp. 63-65. On the fallacy involved in arguing that philosophy is nothing but poetry, see also p. 353.

15. Anselm of Canterbury, *On Truth*, in Jasper Hopkins and Herbert Richardson, ed. and trans., *Anselm of Canterbury* (Toronto: Edwin Mellen, 1976), vol. II, pp. 75-102.

16. St. Augustine, *Contra Academicos*, Bk. II; *Soliloquia*, Bk. II; *De Vera Religione*, xxix, 73; and many other places.

17. St. Thomas Aquinas, *Summa Theologica*, Ia, q. 16, esp. a. 2.

18. Kenneth Burke, *A Rhetoric of Motives* (Berkeley: University of California Press, 1969), esp. pp. 174-189, 267-294.

19. Jacques Derrida, "Structure, Sign, and Play in the Discourse of the Human Sciences," in Richard Macksey and Eugenio Donato, eds., *The Structuralist Controversy* (Baltimore: Johns Hopkins University Press, 1970), p. 262.

20. Jacques Derrida, *Of Grammatology*, translated by Gayatri C. Spivak (Baltimore: Johns Hopkins University Press, 1977), p. 10.

21. For a different but related critique of the idea of displacement, to which I am indebted, see Geoffrey H. Hartman, "Ghostlier Demarcations: The Sweet Science of Northrop Frye," in Hartman's *Beyond Formalism* (New Haven: Yale University Press, 1970), esp. p. 37.

22. James Branch Cabell, *Figures of Earth* (New York: Ballantine Books, 1969), p. 126.
23. Derrida, "Structure, Sign, and Play in the Discourse of the Human Sciences."

Chapter 4

1.   All parenthetical page references are to Northrop Frye, *Anatomy of Criticism* (Princeton: Princeton University Press, 1957). Several writers have taken note of the implication of fiction in the title, *Anatomy of Criticism*, but none of them have done anything very extensive or helpful with this clue. For example, the following. Robert D. Denham, *Northrop Frye and Critical Method* (University Park: The Pennsylvania State University Press, 1978), p. 225. Frank Kermode, review of *Anatomy of Criticism*, in *Review of English Studies*, n.s., v. 10, n. 39, 1959, pp. 317-323. Kermode, however, calls the book "a work of sixth-phase Symbolism." (p.323) He means "mythos," not "Symbolism." According to Frye's Third Essay, the sixth phase of every mythos is negative, marked by images of fragmentation, sterility, and death. Graham Hough, *An Essay on Criticism* (New York: W. W. Norton, 1966), p. 154, says that the *Anatomy* is poetry of a fine sort, but not a useful critical tool. Harry Levin, *Why Literary Criticism is Not an Exact Science* (Cambridge: Harvard University Press, 1967), remarks that Frye's work is an anatomy in the medical sense (p. 22) and also that it belongs to the genre Frye calls anatomy. (p. 24) René Wellek, *Discriminations* (New Haven: Yale University Press, 1970), p. 257, says that the *Anatomy* is indeed a fiction. But he intends this pejoratively: it is *not* science. While rummaging in the library for these references, I also came across the following coincidence: Henry Hazlitt, *The Anatomy of Criticism: A Trialogue* (New York: Simon and Schuster, 1933). Apart from the title, Hazlitt's work seems to have no relationship to Frye's book.
2.   Northrop Frye, *The Educated Imagination* (Bloomington: Indiana University Press, 1964), p. 152. My emphasis.
3.   Northrop Frye, *A Study of English Romanticism* (New York: Random House, 1968), pp. 121-122.
4.   Wallace Stevens, *Opus Posthumous* (New York: Alfred A. Knopf, 1989), p. 183.
5.   Wallace Stevens, *The Necessary Angel* (New York: Vintage Books, 1951), p. 173.
6.   *Ibid.*, p.33.
7.   *Ibid.*, p. 175.
8.   On Burton and in this connection, see Stanley E. Fish, *Self-Consuming Artifacts* (Berkeley: University of California Press, 1972), ch. VI, "Thou Thyself Art the Subject of My Discourse: Democritus Jr. to the Reader," pp. 303-352.
9.   Robert Burton, *The Anatomy of Melancholy* (New York: Vintage Books, 1977), pp.19-20.

10. On this point see Jacques Derrida, "Structure, Sign, and Play in the Discourse of the Human Sciences," in R. Macksey and E. Donato, eds., *The Structuralist Controversy* (Baltimore: Johns Hopkins University Press, 1972), pp. 247-272.
11. For a collection of such formulas, see St. Thomas Aquinas, *Summa Theologica* Ia, q. 16, a. 1, *corpus*.
12. Northrop Frye, *Fables of Identity* (New York: Harcourt, Brace, and World, 1963), p. 27.
13. *Ibid.*, p. 35
14. *Ibid.*, p. 36. Elsewhere Frye suggests that "life" itself is largely a matter of the conventions we are used to, and that the function of literary conventions is to make literature non-lifelike. See *The Educated Imagination*, ch. 4.
15. *Fables of Identity*, p. 38.
16. Geoffrey Hartman, *Beyond Formalism* (New Haven: Yale University Press, 1970), "Ghostlier Demarcations: The Sweet Science of Northrop Frye," p. 37. I owe a lot to Hartman's essay, even though I have here torn his sentences out of context and yoked them to my own purposes.
17. See Ernst Cassirer, *The Philosophy of Symbolic Forms* (New Haven: Yale University Press, 1955), vol. II, part IV, "The Dialectic of the Mythic Consciousness," pp. 235-261. See also Cassirer, *Language and Myth* (New York: Harper and Bros., 1946), esp. ch. 6, "The Power of Metaphor," pp. 83-99. And Jacques Derrida, *op. cit.*, pp. 257ff.
18. See Jacques Derrida, "White Mythology: Metaphor in the Text of Philosophy," in Derrida, *Margins of Philosophy* (Chicago: University of Chicago Press, 1982), pp.207-271. Also Derrida, *Of Grammatology* (Baltimore: Johns Hopkins University Press, 1976), esp. pp. 89, 270ff.
19. See also Kenneth Burke, *A Rhetoric of Motives* (Berkeley: University of California Press, 1969), pp. 84-90.
20. For the most elaborate instance, see Denham, *op. cit.*, pp. 4, 12, 35, 61, 67, 68, 77, 81, 82, 90, 92, 102-104, 107, 123, 127.

Chapter 5

1. Søren Kierkegaard, The *Concept of Dread*, Second Edition (Princeton: Princeton University Press, 1957), pp. vi, viii.
2. Walter Lowrie, *A Short Life of Kierkegaard* (Princeton: Princeton University Press, 1955), p. 261.
3. Søren Kierkegaard, *On Authority and Revelation* (Princeton: Princeton University Press, 1955), pp. xiii-xiv.
4. Søren Kierkegaard, *Concluding Unscientific Postscript* (Princeton: Princeton University Press, 1941), p. 214.
5. *The Wind and the Rain*, v. 6, n. 1, Summer 1949, p. 18. Ignoring Lowrie's animadversions, Prof. Stephen D. Crites did produce an elegant translation of *The Crisis and a Crisis in the Life of an Actress*, accompanied by an insightful

introduction explaining the important role this essay plays in Kierkegaard's corpus (New York: Harper & Row, 1967).

6. Søren Kierkegaard, *Prefaces* (Tallahassee: The Florida State University Press, 1989), p. 26. Hereafter all references to this work will be given in parentheses in the text as (P + page number).

7. Walter Lowrie, *Kierkegaard* (New York: Harper & Bros., 1962), v. I, p. 281.

8. This paper was read at a session of the Søren Kierkegaard Society held in conjunction with the annual meeting of the Eastern Division of the American Philosophical Association in 1994. Prof. Crites, who was the previous speaker, had noted that Nicholaus Notabene, alone among Kierkegaard's pseudonyms, does not consistently speak in character but frequently falls out of his pseudonymous identity. As my remarks here indicate, his lapses are no more than one might expect, since "N.N." is both everyone in general and no one in particular. For the same reason, "N. N." is an identity from which one *cannot* lapse.

9. Lowrie, *Kierkegaard*, loc. cit.

10. We have his own word for it: "I always stand in an altogether poetic relation to my works, and I am, therefore, a pseudonym." *Søren Kierkegaards Papirer*, V A 34. What credence shall we give, and to whom, when the pseudonym itself assures us that it is (only?) a pseudonym? The implied identity of "poet" and "pseudonym" suggests that every authorial *persona* is (as such) pseudonymous. But if he (?) himself tells us this...?

11. The phrase here translated "revert" is *skubbet tilbage*, a passive participle that literally says "pushed back." It could mean revert, but it could just as well be rendered "suppressed" or "repressed." Or for that matter, why not "returns" or "is pushed back (one degree)" and so iterated? I prefer the literal rendering, but the relation—and the question of the relation—between preface and book may be too slippery to be caught in a single word.

12. Wallace Stevens, "The Motive for Metaphor," in *Collected Poems* (New York Alfred A. Knopf, 1954), p. 288.

Chapter 6

1. For the information in this paragraph, and for much else that I know about Richards, I am indebted to John Paul Russo's *I. A. Richards: His Life and Work* (Baltimore: Johns Hopkins University Press, 1989). Needless to say, Professor Russo is not responsible for my reading of Richards.

2. I. A. Richards, *The Philosophy of Rhetoric* (New York: Oxford University Press, 1965). Hereafter, numbers in parentheses in the text refer to the pages of this edition.

3. Jacques Derrida, "Structure, Sign, and Play in the Discourse of the Human Sciences," in Richard Macksey and Eugenio Donato, eds., *The Structuralist Controversy* (Baltimore: Johns Hopkins University Press, 1972), p. 272.

4. Wallace Stevens, *Collected Poems* (New York: Alfred A. Knopf, 1954), p. 93.
5. Jacques Derrida, *Of Grammatology* (Baltimore: Johns Hopkins University Press, 1976), p. 312.
6. Kenneth Burke, *A Grammar of Motives* (Berkeley: University of California Press, 1969), pp. 35, 38. It has been suggested that in the works of Kenneth Burke, especially in his "motives" books, we have a home-grown American deconstructionist *avant la lettre*. I believe this suggestion could be extensively documented and persuasively defended. But that would be another essay.
7. I. A. Richards, ed., *The Portable Coleridge* (New York: The Viking Press, 1950), p. 398.
8. *Ibid.*, p. 388.
9. Wallace Stevens, *The Necessary Angel* (New York: Vintage Books, 1951), p. 87.
10. Jacques Derrida, *Margins of Philosophy* (Chicago: University of Chicago Press, 1982), pp. 207-271.
11. In this connection, see Geoffrey Hartman, "I. A. Richards and the Dream of Communication," in his *The Fate of Reading* (Chicago: University of Chicago Press, 1975), pp. 20-40.
12. Richards' skill as a practicing critic is abundantly illustrated by his readings of, e.g., Plato, Dante, and the Book of Job (see especially his *Beyond* (New York: Harcourt Brace Jovanovich, 1974)), as well as the mini-readings found in his *Practical Criticism* (Harcourt, Brace and World, 1929) and other places. His critical pragmatism, his fascination with Platonism, and his conviction that we cannot presume to have discovered the intentions of the author are clearly expressed in his *How to Read a Page* (Boston: Beacon Press, 1942.)
13. I am thinking, e.g., of the essays collected in W. J. Mitchell, ed., *Against Theory: Literary Studies and the New Pragmatism* (Chicago: University of Chicago Press, 1985). In this connection one should not fail to consult the title essay in Paul de Man, *The Resistance to Theory* (Minneapolis: University of Minnesota Press, 1986), pp. 3-20.

Chapter 7

1. Leonard B. Meyer, *Emotion and Meaning in Music* (Chicago: University of Chicago Press, 1956), esp. Chapter I.
2. Susanne K. Langer, *Feeling and Form* (London: Routledge & Kegan Paul, 1953), esp. Chapter 7.
3. For example: Plato, *Republic*, III, 398c-399e, and Boethius, *De Institutione Musica*, Book I, Ch. 1.
4. *Julius Caesar*, Act I, Scene II. Caesar is warning Antony against Cassius.
5. The phrase is Wallace Stevens', from "The Idea of Order at Key West," in *Collected Poems* (New York: Alfred A. Knopf, 1954), p. 130.
6. *De Musica*, Book VI.

7. See Paul Hindemith, *A Composer's World* (Cambridge: Harvard University Press, 1952), Chapter 1, and Igor Stravinsky, *Poetics of Music* (New York: Vintage Books, 1947), esp. Chapters 2, 3, and Epilogue.
8. Eduard Hanslick, *The Beautiful in Music* (New York: The Liberal Arts Press, 1957), Chapter III.
9. Kenneth Burke, *The Philosophy of Literary Form* (Berkeley: University of California Press, 1973), pp. 8-33, 293-304.
10. Oscar Wilde, "The Decay of Lying," esp. *ad finem*, in Richard Ellman, ed., *The Artist as Critic: Critical Writings of Oscar Wilde* (Chicago: University of Chicago Press, 1969), pp. 290-320.
11. Leonard Cohen, *The Favorite Game* (New York: Avon Books, 1963), p. 9.
12. Jacques Maritain, *Art and Scholasticism and The Frontiers of Poetry* (New York: Charles Scribner's Sons, 1962), p. 36. My epigraph is quoted from the first English edition (New York: Charles Scribner's Sons, 1930), p. 29.

Chapter 8

1. For a discussion of Andreas and his work in their historical setting, see the editor's Introduction to John Jay Parry, trans., *The Art of Courtly Love* (New York: W. W. Norton, 1969). Parenthetical page references in my text are to this edition, which reprints the first edition, by Columbia University Press (1941), in its Records of Civilization series.
2. See St. Augustine, *De Libero Arbitrio Voluntatis*, I, IV, 31.
3. Matthew 5: 27-28.
4. Andreas, following Isidore of Seville (*Etymologies* X, i, 5), derives *amor* (love) from *(h)amus* (hook). This may be the origin of the "tender trap."
5. See Kenneth Burke, *A Rhetoric of Motives* (Berkeley: University of California Press, 1969), pp. 174-180, 208-212.
6. As Kenneth Burke might say, they are dancing an attitude. (See *The Philosophy of Literary Form* (Berkeley: University of California Press, 1973), pp. 9-10). The lovers execute a *pas de deux* in the larger ballet of courtly demeanor: a performance compounded of stylized poses, prescribed ripostes, rhetorical thrust and parry, etc.—all carried out in obedience to purely formal demands and in the service of purely formal ends.
7. Is it ever? Desire is always the reflection of desire and its object the representation of its object. In any case, it is tautologous but tragic that no desire survives its own gratification. Eros that is not subsumed into logos is consumed by thanatos.
8. Matthew 22: 37-39, Mark 12: 30-31, Luke 10: 27.
9. And for that matter to some modern minds. The extreme case is D. W. Robertson, Jr., who denies the existence of a courtly love tradition. For Robertson, what is called courtly love is actually an allegory of charity. See his *Preface to Chaucer* (Princeton: Princeton University Press, 1962), esp. pp. 151-165, 202-206, and 257-272. Others, like C.S. Lewis in *The Allegory of Love* (New York: Oxford

University Press, 1936), esp. pp. 1-43, simply acknowledge the conflict between Christianity and courtly love and declare it irreconcilable.

10. See Kenneth Burke, *A Grammar of Motives* (Berkeley: University of California Press, 1969), pp. 402-443.

11. Leonard Cohen, *The Favorite Game* (New York: Avon Books, 1965) p. 9.

Chapter 9

1. Robert Coover, *Pricksongs and Descants* (New York: New American Library, 1969), pp. 76-79. All further references to this work will be given parenthetically in the text. On Coover's *Dedicatoria y Prológo*, see Jackson I. Cope, "Robert Coover's Fictions" (*The Iowa Review*, v. 2, n. 4., 1971), pp. 99-100. Cope's essay, which deals mainly with *The Universal Baseball Association, Inc., J. Henry Waugh, Prop.*, is also, not quite *per accidens*, an illuminating commentary on the Valeryan epigraph Coover chose for *Pricksongs and Descants*: "They therefore set me this problem of the equality of appearance and numbers." Unfortunately Cope's book, *Robert Coover's Fictions* (Baltimore: Johns Hopkins University Press, 1986), appeared too late to be taken into consideration in the preparation of this essay. For Coover's perception of his debt to Cervantes, see "Robert Coover: An Interview with Alma Kadragic," *Shantih*, v. 2, n. 2, 1972, pp. 57-60; Frank Gado, *First Person: Conversations on Writers and Writing* (Schenectady: Union College Press, 1973), pp. 142-159; and Robert Coover, "The Last Quixote," *New American Review*, 11, 1971, pp. 132-143. My approach to Coover in this essay is anticipated (so far as I know only) by Monique Armand in "*Les jeux de l'enonciation dans* 'Panel Game'", *Delta*, 8, 1979, pp. 189-203.—One salient fact about Coover's fiction that I have ignored and perhaps obscured is that it is funny. In Leo J. Hertzel, "An Interview with Robert Coover," *Critique*, v. 11, n. 3, p. 28, Coover says: "I tend to think of tragedy as a kind of adolescent response to the universe—the higher truth is a comic response…there is a kind of humor extremity which is even more mature than the tragic response…. Thus some of the great ironic, comic fiction can nevertheless be equal to the same kind of strange emotion you get out of tragedy because your emotions can be mixed." In the novels and in many of the short pieces, though the subject-matter is often grim enough, the overall tone is comic. This is not true of "Seven Exemplary Fictions," for which reason I have been silent about Coover's dark gray humor. But I do not want to give a misleading impression of his work as a whole. He may be a scribe of mournful countenance, but he is never grave.

2. For Coover's interpretation of the title, *Pricksongs and Descants*, see Gado, *op. cit.*, pp. 150-151.

3. Samuel Putnam, trans. and ed., *The Portable Cervantes* (New York: Penguin Books, 1978), p. 707.

4. *Ibid.* My brackets.

5.   *Ibid.* My brackets. Cf. *Pricksongs and Descants*, p. 77. Though Cervantes himself is not explicit about the sense in which his stories are exemplary, Coover provides him with a rationale. *V. infra.*

6.   Elsewhere in *Pricksongs and Descants*, especially in "The Magic Poker," (20-45), Coover explores the problems and possibilities of writing.

7.   On the demands of the law, see Jacques Derrida, "*La Loi du genre*/The Law of Genre," GLYPH 7, pp. 176-229.

8.   For what it's worth, "Klee Dead" speaks directly to its reader. In "Panel Game" the reader is written into the story as one of its characters. In the remaining five stories the reader, though always presupposed, is neither addressed nor inscribed.

9.   Quoted in Robert Scholes, *Fabulation and Metafiction* (Urbana: University of Illinois Press, 1979), p. 76.

10.   Herman Melville, *Moby-Dick* (New York: W. W. Norton, 1967), p. 144.

11.   See David Porter, *Emerson and Literary Change* (Cambridge: Harvard University Press, 1978), ch. 3.

12.   Kadragic, *op. cit.*, p. 60. Coover's experiments in narration have their example in Cervantes. In the *Novelas* and in *Don Quijote* Cervantes tampers more or less irreverently with the conventions of, e.g., romance and the picaresque in order to produce the generically eclectic narrative that eventually becomes the modern novel. It may well be the case that the novel has always been an experimental form, and that the experimentation of post-modern writers, while different in kind and in degree from past experiments, is as such nothing new.

13.   Hertzel, *op. cit.*, p. 27.

14.   On the encounter with "reality" in Coover's fiction, see Hertzel, *idem.*; Kathryn Hume, "Robert Coover's Fiction: The Naked and the Mythic," *Novel*, v. 12, n. 2, 1979, pp. 127-148; Gado, *op. cit.*, pp. 152, 157-158; and the following speech of Coover's talking cunt (*A Theological Position*, New York: E. P. Dutton and Co., 1972, p. 166): "We have to stir the senses, grab you where it hurts! Any penetration, however slight, is a bloody business!" It is difficult to take seriously Joyce Carol Oates' contention that there is no emotion in Coover's stories which she says are not human but magical; and it is equally hard to credit Neil Schmitz's cavalier dismissal of Coover's work and his gratuitously invidious comparison of Coover with other metafictionists. See Joyce Carol Oates, "Realism of Distance, Realism of Immediacy," *The Southern Review*, v. 7, n. 1, 1971, pp. 295-313; Neil Schmitz, "Robert Coover and the Hazards of Metafiction," *Novel*, v. 7, n. 3, 1974, pp. 210-219.

Chapter 10

1.   Thomas Pynchon, *Gravity's Rainbow* (New York: The Viking Press, 1973). I quote, in parentheses, from this edition.

2.   William Pynchon, *The Meritorious Price of Our Redemption*, a facsimile reproduction of the 1650 original, edited by M. W. Vella, L. Schachterle, and L. Mackey (New York: Peter Lang, 1992).

3. See Thomas Hooker, "The Soul's Vocation, Doctrine 7," in P.M. Jones and N.R. Jones, eds., *Salvation in New England* (Austin: University of Texas Press, 1977), pp. 91-99, esp. p. 93. Cf. Pynchon, *Gravity's Rainbow*, pp. 22, 677.

4. George Levine and David Leverenz, eds., *Mindful Pleasures: Essays on Thomas Pynchon* (Boston: Little, Brown, 1976), p. 3. Hereafter abbreviated LL.

5. See note 1 above.

6. I am indebted to Scott Sanders, "Pynchon's Paranoid History," in LL, pp. 139-159. It will be obvious where I depart from his account of the Calvinism in *Gravity's Rainbow*. I have profited even more from John M. Krafft, "' And How Far-Fallen': Puritan Themes in *Gravity's Rainbow*," *Critique*, 18, n. 3 (1977), pp. 55-73.

7. See above, pp. 153-167, and note 2. An account of the Pynchon affair, together with an almost complete text of *The Meritorious Price*, may be found in Henry M. Burt, *The First Century of the History of Springfield* (Springfield: Henry M. Burt, 1898), v. I.

8. The quotation comes from the O.E.D., under the entry "preterite," and is attributed to *Fraser's Magazine*, May 1864, p. 533. The seventeenth-century divine is, according to the same entry, Vilvain, *Theological Treatise*, 1654, ii, 66. The entry also gives references to Burton's *Anatomy of Melancholy*, 1621, Third Partition, Section 4, Member 2, Subsection 3; the *Works* of John Wesley, 1872, *VII*, p. 375; and the journal *Evangelical Christendom* for Oct. 1863, p. 475.

9. Arthur Edward Waite, *The Pictorial Key to the Tarot* (New York: Samuel Weiser, 1973), p. 285. This appears to be the work Pynchon consulted on the Tarot. See the reference to Waite in *Gravity's Rainbow*, p. 738. Although my edition was published in 1973, the book was first published in 1910 and would therefore have been available to Pynchon during the period when he was working on *Gravity's Rainbow*.

10. *Webster's Seventh New Collegiate Dictionary* (Springfield: G. and C. Merriam, 1963), definition 2 under the entry "preterite." The authorities of Springfield still seem to be the arbiters of orthodoxy.

11. David Leverenz, "On Trying to Read *Gravity's Rainbow*," in LL, p. 230

12. Tony Tanner, "V. and V-2," in Edward Mendelson, ed., *Pynchon: A Collection of Critical Essays* (Englewood Cliffs: Prentice-Hall, 1978), p. 50. Hereafter abbreviated EM.

13. F. S. Schwarzbach, "A Matter of Gravity," in EM, p. 66.

14. George Levine, "V-2," in EM, p. 179.

15. See Mark Richard Siegel, *Pynchon: Creative Paranoia in "Gravity's Rainbow"* (Port Washington: Kennikat Press, 1978), p. 63. In his refusal of omniscience the Pynchon-narrator is reminiscent of that other very American, very Puritan, and very paranoid romancer, the Nathaniel Hawthorne of *The Scarlet Letter*. Though he is the *author* of his book, Hawthorne (who claims not to have invented but only to have embellished his story) is not the *authoritative*

interpreter of the Letter. More than a little doubtful of his own election, Hawthorne has remanded his narratorial authority to one who is much of the time tormentingly unforthcoming. On his own (now suspect) authority, the *authority* of/in Hawthorne's text is the inarticulate and secretive Pearl, who is of course the Letter itself in another form.

16. Frank Kermode, "Decoding the Trystero," in EM, p. 166.
17. Mathew Winston, "Appendix: The Quest for Pynchon," in LL, p. 251.
18. My indebtedness throughout the following discussion to Kenneth Burke, *A Rhetoric of Motives* (Berkeley: University of California Press, 1969), is too profound and too extensive to be documented *seriatim*. Any distortion or Procrustean stretching of Burke's view is my responsibility.
19. Kermode, *op. cit.*, p. 163.
20. Thomas Pynchon, *The Crying of Lot 49* (New York: Bantam Books, 1967), p. 95.
21. Pynchon seems to be indebted to Norman Mailer's *The Naked and the Dead* for the parabola. But the symbolic values of their parabolas are quite different: Mailer's parabola is not at all hopeful. See Frank D. McConnell, *Four Postwar American Novelists* (Chicago: The University of Chicago Press, 1977), p. 184.
22. "A Slumber Did My Spirit Seal" ends with the lines:

     Rolled round in earth's diurnal course.
     With rocks. and stones. and trees.

    This lyric has also been found ambiguous: is Lucy dehumanized or has the world been infused with her spirit?
23. On Calvinism in Pynchon, see the references in note 6 above.
24. Some of them are remanded to his journals, where they function as the unconscious of his public pronouncements.
25. Michael Wigglesworth, *The Day of Doom*, stanzas 181 and 219, in Harrison Meserole, ed., *Seventeenth-Century American Poetry* (Garden City: Doubleday, 1968), pp. 102, 112.
26. See Jacques Derrida, *Of Grammatology* (Baltimore: Johns Hopkins University Press, 1976), p. 18.
27. See note 1 above.
28. Happily, they are not tempted to seek an anodyne in any of the varieties of self-mystification exported by the East. The point is not to elude one's heritage (the example of Emerson argues against that), but to confront the West and combat it on its own ground.
29. See St. Augustine, *Confessions*, trans. Rex Warner (New York: Mentor, 1963), I, 6, p. 20 (translation slightly adapted): "I do not know where I came from into this mortal life or (should I say?) into this living death."
30. It may be argued that Pynchon's fiction is sexist, since (with the notable exception of Oedipa Maas) the women in his novels exist mainly to be used (more often abused) by the men. As the hapless creatures complain, "'Tits'n'ass..., tits'n'ass. That's all we are around here.'" (GR 507). Well, after all, it *is* a man's world,

it's still the 60s, and even the remark quoted is ironized by its context. But the message of GR in this connection (if it has one) is that sooner or later *Gravity wins*. And Gravity is a female force. Gravity alone receives *and reverses* the thrust of a self-assertive masculinity. Mother Nature will not be fucked over by homosexual technology. The straight arrow : parabola :: the erect phallus : the climaxing and descending phallus. What comes between and makes the difference is the female: Gravity. Receiving the erect phallus (the straight arrow of flight at G=0), she bends it into the parabola of detumescence. Hers is the power of the passive, the venereal potency that always in the end subsumes and subdues the sword of Mars. That may be another reason to regard the rainbow—Gravity's own—as a sign of hope: if not the reality of the dream, then at least its possibility. Whether this is a feminist gesture or just another turn of the chauvinist screw I will not attempt to decide. I do know that it is a pervasive motif throughout GR.

Chapter 11

1. Umberto Eco, *The Name of the Rose*, trans. William Weaver (New York: Harcourt Brace Jovanovich, 1983), p. 279. All further references to this edition are given parenthetically in the text.
2. Umberto Eco, *A Theory of Semiotics* (Bloomington: Indiana University Press, 1976), p. 7.
3. It is rumored that there are translations of the Italian text into several other languages. But the stew is meaty enough already.
4. Valentin Rose, *Aristotelis qui ferebantur librorum fragmenta* (Stuttgart: B. G. Teubner, 1967), p. 81, has as fragment 77 the following: *to de panton kyntotaton* ("the most shameless thing of all"). W. D. Ross, *The Works of Aristotle Translated into English, Volume XII, Select Fragments* (Oxford: The Clarendon Press, 1952), p. 77, omits Rose's fragment 77 "because it seems to belong...to the lost second book of the *Poetics*."
5. As certain also of our own poets have said. See Wallace Stevens, *The Necessary Angel* (New York: Random House, 1951), p. 33.
6. With this remark compare the ill-fated unicorn hunt in T. H. White, *The Once and Future King* (New York: Dell Publishing Co., 1958), pp. 249-263.

Chapter 12

1. John Barth, "The Literature of Exhaustion," in his *The Friday Book* (New York: G. P. Putnam's Sons, 1984), pp. 62-76. Its sequel, "The Literature of Replenishment," is in the same volume, pp. 193-206.
2. Philip K. Dick, *UBIK* (New York: Bantam Books, 1977; first published by Doubleday in 1969). Parenthetical page references are to the 1977 Bantam edition.

3. For some thoughts on the "character system" of Dick's novels, see Kim Stanley Robinson, *The Novels of Philip K. Dick* (Ann Arbor: UMI Research Press, 1984), pp. 17-18. Robinson himself is both an academic critic and a prolific SF writer.

4. E.g., Stanislaw Lem in his *Microworlds* (New York: Harcourt Brace Jovanovich, 1984). For his views on Dick, see pp. 45-135 of this book.

5. Darko Suvin, *Metamorphoses of Science Fiction* (New Haven: Yale University Press, 1979), esp. ch. 1. For another attempt to find a genre for SF, see Patrick Parrinder, *Science Fiction: Its Criticism and Its Teaching* (London: Methuen, 1980).

6. J. G. Ballard, *Crash* (New York: Vintage Books, 1985), pp. 1-2, writes: "I firmly believe that science fiction, far from being an unimportant minor offshoot, in fact represents the main literary tradition of the 20th century."

7. See Christine Brooke-Rose, *A Rhetoric of the Unreal* (Cambridge: Cambridge University Press, 1981). Brooke-Rose's novel *Xorandor* (Manchester: Carcanet, 1986), may plausibly be classed as SF and was in fact so characterized by Thomas Disch in his *New York Times* review. *Xorandor's* sequel, *Verbivore* (Manchester: Carcanet, 1990), is in the same SF mode.

Chapter 13

1. GLYPH 7, 1980, pp. 176-232.

2. Jacques Derrida, *Of Grammatology* (Baltimore: Johns Hopkins University Press, 1976), p. 312.

3. The change in Plato's metaphorics at this point is a form of what Kenneth Burke has called the "paradox of purity." See his *A Grammar of Motives* (Berkeley: University of California Press, 1969), pp. 35-38. According to Burke, every terminology by its own inner logic generates an absolute or god-term. But the god-term is unintelligible in terms of the logic that produced it and must be explicated otherwise.

4. This would be the extreme case of the paradox of purity.

5. The whole complex of Platonic problems—the relation between opinion and knowledge, image and original—reappears transformed in Augustine's account of the relation beween faith and divine illumination. Augustine's commitment to a supernaturally revealed religion requires of him a deeper-than-Platonic skepticism on the one hand, and on the other the ascription to faith of an importance and a centrality that could never be ascribed to the Platonic *pistis/doxa*.— Kant's philosophy has the structural properties of Platonism and Augustinianism without their metaphysical commitments. He therefore has difficulty distinguishing appearances from the conditions of the possibility of our knowing them. However, his denial of intellectual intuition—i.e., his refusal of the metaphorics of vision—makes it hard for him to explain how we know the conditions of the possibility of empirical knowledge, exempts him from

specifying their ontological status, and requires him to define "transcendental" in a way that begged—and got—misunderstanding. More of this below, pp. 226-229.

6. My understanding of Descartes owes a great deal to Dalia Judovitz's *Subjectivity and Representation in Descartes: The Origins of Modernity* (Cambridge: Cambridge University Press, 1988), though she is not responsible for what I have done with her reading of Descartes.

7. René Descartes, *Meditations on First Philosophy* (Indianapolis: Hackett Publishing Co., 1979), III, pp. 24-25.

8. *Ibid.*, V, p. 42.

9. That Descartes wrote meditations and wrote them as he did may be something he owed to his Jesuit mentors at La Fleche, who must surely have acquainted him with the *Spiritual Exercises* of St. Ignatius Loyola. Consider, e.g., the image of the bit of wax in the Second Meditation, the figure of the evil genius, and Descartes' depiction of the vivid "reality" of dream images. Imaging is a standard technique of Ignatian meditation.

10. Analogous observations might be made concerning Hume's empiricism and the nature of those simple impressions of sense and sentiment from which Hume says all our knowledge originates. Of course Hume, who did not escape skepticism, does not claim for his impressions the ontological and epistemological authority with which Descartes invests clear and distinct ideas. But he does represent them as the immediate source of our mediated (i.e., ideal) cognitions. And he does, when skepticism threatens, take refuge in a doctrine of common sense (that nature which he says is fortunately stronger than principle) which is as patently a fictional construct as any of the extravagances of Descartes.

11. Immanuel Kant, *Prolegomena to Any Future Metaphysics* (Indianapolis: Hackett Publishing Co., 1977), Preamble, p. 19.

12. Kant, *Critique of Pure Reason* (London: Macmillan, 1933), Preface to Second Edition, p. 22 (=Bxvi-xvii).

13. *Ibid.*, pp. 266-270 (=A249-252). This passage disappears from the second edition, and is replaced by the assertion that there are "doubtless" noumena corresponding to the phenomena we experience, though we have only a "negative" conception of them. Possibly Kant himself became suspicious of his earlier "argument."

14. *Ibid.*, pp. 152-155 (=B129-135).

15. *Ibid.*, p. 59. See also Kant, *Prolegomena*, Appendix, p. 113, n. 48.

16. See Kenneth Burke, "What Are the Signs of What?" in his *Language as Symbolic Action* (Berkeley: University of California Press, 1966), pp. 359-379. Burke's contention, that things are the signs of words rather than vice versa, suggests the connection between Platonic metaphysics and Kantian criticism.

17. Kant, *Critique of Pure Reason,* pp. 20, 120-125.

18. See Philippe Lacoue-Labarthe and Jean-Luc Nancy, *The Literary Absolute* (Albany: State University of New York Press, 1988).

19. See above, chapter 2.
20. Immanuel Kant, *The Critique of Judgment* (Oxford: The Clarendon Press, 1952), sec. 49, pp. 175-179. See also John Crowe Ransom, "The Concrete Universal: Observations on the Understanding of Poetry," in his *Poems and Essays* (New York: Vintage Books, 1955), pp. 159-185.
21. In fairness it must be said that continental philosophers have continued to explore the implications of Kant's revolution more faithfully than Anglo-American philosophers, who have either ignored Kant or treated him as an epistemologist. The exceptions to the latter are the great British and American idealists of the nineteenth century. But their days were numbered, and the number was small.
22. See Derrida, *Of Grammatology*, esp. pp. 141-157.
23. *Ibid.*, p. 24.
24. See Thomas S. Kuhn, *The Structure of Scientific Revolutions*, Second Edition (Chicago: University of Chicago Press, 1970), esp. chs. IX, X.
25. Richard Rorty, "Derrida on Language, Being, and Abnormal Philosophy," *The Journal of Philosophy*, v. 74, n. 11, November 1977, p. 678. Rorty writes, "If Being had a message to get across, it would have to use the Platonic jargon when it talked to you. What else would you understand?"
26. Alfred North Whitehead, *Process and Reality* (New York: Macmillan Co., 1929), p. 63. "The safest general characterization of the European philosophical tradition is that it consists of a series of footnotes to Plato."
27. Jacques Derrida, "Structure, Sign and Play in the Discourse of the Human Sciences," in his *Writing and Difference* (Chicago: University of Chicago Press, 1978), p. 288.
28. See Lacoue-Labarthe and Nancy, *The Literary Absolute*, note 18 above. The most important literary proponent of Kantianism and German idealism in England is of course Samuel Taylor Coleridge, especially his *Biographia Literaria* (Princeton: Princeton University Press, 1983). See René Wellek, *Immanuel Kant in England, 1793-1838* (Princeton: Princeton University Press, 1931) and "Emerson and German Philosophy," *New England Quarterly*, 16 (1943), 41-63.
29. Kant, *Critique of Pure Reason*, pp. 180-187 and *The Critique of Judgment*, pp. 146-154, 175-180.
30. Northrop Frye, *Anatomy of Criticism* (Princeton: Princeton Univeristy Press, 1957), pp. 73-82.
31. For a fuller discussion of this conception of fiction, see Louis Mackey, *Fact, Fiction, and Representation: Four Novels by Gilbert Sorrentino* (Columbia, SC: Camden House, 1997), esp. ch. 2.
32. Frye, *Anatomy of Criticism*, p. 83.
33. Søren Kierkegaard, *Either/Or* (Princeton : Princeton University Press, 1987), I, p. 32.
34. Wallace Stevens, *The Necessary Angel* (New York: Vintage Books, 1951), p. 33.

35. Wallace Stevens, *Opus Posthumous* (New York: Alfred A. Knopf, 1989), p. 189.

Chapter 14

1. See note 1 for Chapter 1 above.
2. J. R. R. Tolkien meets Dr. Seuss.
3. She drinks wine with Orson Welles.
4. Immanuel Kant, *Critique of Pure Reason* (London: Macmillan and Co., 1929), Preface to First Edition, p. 10 (=Axiii).
5. Aristotle, *Metaphysics*, I, 3-10.
6. As did his translator. See Georges Perec, *A Void*, translated by Gilbert Adair (London: Harvill, 1994). The French original was published by Editions Denoël of Paris in 1969.
7. Walt Whitman, "Song of Myself" 26-27, in *Leaves of Grass*.
8. St. Thomas Aquinas, *Commentary on the Metaphysics of Aristotle* (Chicago: Henry Regnery, 1961), Vol. I, I.L.3:C 55, p. 24.
9. Aristotle, *Metaphysics*, I, 2, 983a18-21.
10. This may also be true of real science, as opposed to the fantasy of science that many contemporary philosophers seem to take as their professional role model.
11. Aristotle, *Metaphysics*, I, 2, 983a3-4.
12. Aristotle, *Poetics*, 24, 1460a 19-26.
13. Wallace Stevens, *Opus Posthumous* (New York: Alfred A. Knopf, 1989), p. 197.
14. Martin Heidegger, "Was ist Metaphysik?" in his *Wegmarken* (Frankfurt am Main: Vittorio Klostermann, 1967), p. 19.
15. Ludwig Wittgenstein, *Tractatus Logico-Philosophicus* (London: Routledge and Kegan Paul, 1961), 6.44.
16. Northrop Frye, "Letter to the English Institute 1965," in Murray Krieger, ed., *Northrop Frye in Modern Criticism* (New York: Columbia University Press, 1966), p. 29.
17. Throughout his career, Heidegger repeatedly called attention to the usage "*Es gibt Sein*" (for "there is being"). See, e.g., *Sein und Zeit* (Tübingen: Max Niemeyer Verlag, 1953), p. 212; but also "*Brief über den 'Humanismus'*", in *Wegmarken*, p. 167; and *On Time and Being* (New York: Harper and Row, 1972), pp. 5-24.
18. Martin Heidegger, "Die Frage nach der Technik," in his *Vorträge und Aufsätze* (Pfullingen: Verlag Günter Neske, 1954), p. 44.
19. Martin Heidegger, "Nachwort zu: 'Was ist metaphysik'", in *Wegmarken*, pp. 104-106.
20. Jacques Derrida, "On a Newly Arisen Apocalyptic Tone in Philosophy," in Peter Fenves, ed., *Raising the Tone of Philosophy* (Baltimore: Johns Hopkins University Press, 1993), pp. 117-171.

21. Compare Reinhold Niebuhr's comment on the apocalyptic passages in the New Testament: "The Kingdom of God…is in fact always coming but never here." *An Interpretation of Christian Ethics* (New York: The Seabury Press, 1979), p. 36.

Index

Abelard, Peter, 127
absence. *See* presence; Richards, I. A.,
    and absence in language
Adagio (Barber), 108
Adso of Melk, 195, 196, 199, 200,
    201, 202, 203, 204, 205
Aged Clown, 136, 137–38
Africa, end of, 197, 200, 204
Alan of Lille, 204
Alfred, 141–42, 146
amor. See love, erotic
amore, De (Capellanus), 118–31
anagogy, 63, 65, 70
Anatomy of Criticism (Frye), 5, 33,
    35, 49–73
  as failed redemption myth, 72–73
  as moral in purpose, 52–53
  as fantastic in purpose, 53
  as a satirical fiction, 49–54, 62, 67
Anatomy of Melancholy, The (Burton)
    49, 50, 58
Anaximander, 249
Anselm, Saint, 15–16, 40
apocalypse, 252–53
Aquinas, Saint Thomas, 41, 82, 200,
    204, 248, 250
archetypes, 65
Aristotle, 3–5, 30–31, 73, 87, 96, 175,
    204, 220, 222, 235, 244, 249
  on comedy, 197–202
  on myth and philosophy, 3–4, 248

  on history, philosophy and poetry, 4,
    10-11, 30-31, 43-44, 248
Armand, Monique, 263n1
Art of Courtly Love, The. See amore,
    De
arte honeste amandi, De. See amore,
    De
Art of the Fugue, The (Bach), 113
Art and Scholasticism (Maritain), 113
art, self-conciousness of, 113
"as if" philosophy, 22, 27
Audience, 136, 138
Aufhebung, 13
Augustine, Saint, 11, 37, 40, 42, 109,
    119, 120–21, 126, 204, 241–43,
    244, 268n5
authenticity, 112
Authority and Revelation, On
    (Kierkegaard), 76
authorship, 81, 83
Avicenna, 204, 250
Ayer, A. J., 85

Bach, Johann Sebastian, 113, 159
Bacon, Francis, 55, 100
Bacon, Roger, 204
Bad Sport, 136–39, 146
Ballard, J.G., 215, 268n6
Barfield, Owen, 29
Barth, John, 146
Barthelme, Donald, 149

Index